D1515625

THE MODERN LIBRARY

OF THE WORLD'S BEST BOOKS

THE MAKING OF SOCIETY

THE MAKING OF SOCIETY

An Outline of Sociology

REVISED EDITION

Edited by Robert Bierstedt

Professor and Chairman,
Department of Sociology and Anthropology.
The City College of New York

The Modern Library

New York

TO ROBERT MORRISON MacIVER

Who, in this century, has contributed scope, and vision,
and a Scot's common sense, to our knowledge
of the nature of society.

Published in New York
by Random House, Inc., and simultaneously in Toronto, Canada,
by Random House of Canada, Limited.
Library of Congress Catalog Card Number: 59-10910

Random House IS THE PUBLISHER OF *The Modern Library*

Manufactured in the United States of America by H. Wolff

PREFACE

This is a new edition of a book edited by V. F. Calverton and published in The Modern Library in 1937. Of the sixty-one selections that Calverton included in the first edition, however, I have retained only eighteen. To the retained items I have added twenty-seven that did not appear there, making a total of forty-five in the present volume.

Calverton's predilections in the mid-thirties were Marxian. He complained in his Preface that inattention to such social philosophies as liberalism, fascism, socialism, and communism had prevented American sociology from functioning as a "progressive technique." My own predilections in the late fifties belong to a tradition that is both Comtean and orthodox, one that considers sociology "value-free" in general and politically neutral in particular, and one finally that emphasizes, rather than erases, the distinction between sociology on the one hand and social and political philosophy on the other.

Of all the forms of literary production the anthology, of course, is the one most vulnerable to criticism. I have doubtless included here selections that some readers would consign to oblivion, and have left on the cutting-room floor selections they would especially invite to the attention of posterity. I should imagine that some of the authors themselves, none of whom was consulted, would have preferred another excerpt from their work than the one I have chosen. In any event, those who appear here have an opportunity to speak on their own account and it is therefore unnecessary to dwell upon sins of commission.

The criteria of omission, however, may require a brief explanation. Although I may be guilty of a species of provincialism, I have excluded all sociologists outside the Western tradition of intellectual history. If excuse be needed, one may say that sociology has not characteristically been a discipline that has appealed to the Eastern mind and there does not exist, in fact, a corpus of Eastern sociological thought.

Temporal limitations, in contrast to geographic, have demanded judgments of a more difficult kind. It is easy to begin with Plato and Aristotle—and we should not hesitate to claim them as progenitors of a sociological tradition. But where to end? I have decided quite arbitrarily to conclude this book with selections from writers who were born around the turn of the twentieth century and whose careers have now probably passed their peak. I have not included contributions from a younger generation of sociologists, those who are now in early or mid-career, not because they lack insight or penetration but because it is presently hazardous to choose among them and impossible to estimate their permanent significance. Some of the sociologists in this category will indubitably take their places in succeeding editions of this book, but to include them now would be premature.

I have also excluded, however excellent their work, sociologists who have fixed their attention not upon society in general but rather upon special sociological problems. Thus, there are many men of unquestionable competence who have attended to special sectors of sociology—the family, public opinion, urban sociology, the sociology of religion, problems of racial and ethnic minorities, the sociology of industry, and so on. Some of these clearly warranted inclusion on the ground of merit but they were nevertheless excluded because of the character of their sociological interests.

I have, finally, excluded those who for the most part have applied their energies and their talents to methodological rather than to substantive problems in sociology. The use of this criterion does not imply that I demean this kind of endeavor—on the contrary this work is essential if sociology is to prosper—but only that I do not regard the present volume as the proper locus for its exhibition.

What I have tried to do, in short, is to place before the reader in the pages that follow selections from the works of sociologists who, in all ages of Western history including our own, have looked about them and have wondered what kind of a thing society might be, who have seen society itself as a fit and dignified subject of inquiry, and who have made, in my opinion, a superior effort to understand it.

ROBERT BIERSTEDT

CONTENTS

INTRODUCTION

The Story of Sociology

ROBERT BIERSTEDT

The story of sociology is as old as human thought—and as new as the day's newspaper. Behind the reports of domestic troubles and foreign quarrels, of weapons-testing and summit conferences, of elections and cities and wars, there lies the simple and ineluctable fact that, for as long as the human species has inhabited the earth, men have always lived in groups and in societies with others of their kind. The isolated individual does not exist or, if he does, his isolation is never long sustained. As Aristotle noted long ago, man is a social animal, a *zoon politikon,* and only a beast or a god is fit to live alone.

If men have always lived with others, and in societies, it is not surprising that society itself should become an object of inquiry and investigation. What is society? What are the elements that constitute its structure? What are the factors that cause it to change? Are the relations that men have with one another, their social relations, wholly haphazard and unpredictable, or can an order and a regularity be discerned in them? If the latter is the case, what is the fundamental nature of this order, and of this regularity? What characteristics, if any, do all societies have in common, no matter where they may appear on earth, or in the earth's history? These, and many more, are sociological questions.

Questions like these, of course, were asked long before there was such a word as *sociology*. Those who ask them and who try to answer them are therefore sociologists even though they may also be philosophers or historians or even natural scientists. In the earlier centuries of our era the disciplines were undifferentiated. If we go back far enough we find only one—philosophy—and those who indulged in it were afflicted with the itch of curiosity and the love of wisdom. It is easy to surmise that they were curious not only about the earth beneath them and the sky above but also about the human society that surrounded and encompassed them. In any event, curiosity about society and the knowledge that results from it, however difficult the latter may be to acquire, are as admirable as any other. This book contains selections from the writings of those who, in times both past and present, have tried to add their tithe to this kind of knowledge.

The first edition of this book, edited by V. F. Calverton, began with selections from the Bible, the Koran, the Code of Hammurabi, and from the two ancient Chinese philosophers, Confucius and Lao Tse. It is not necessary, however, to "trace the dark footsteps of antiquity" quite so far into the past in order to have a proper beginning for our story. These early admonitions, like the Ten Commandments for example, had a social base, to be sure, and they owe their meaning still today to the fact that men live with other men and have social relations with one another. In intent and emphasis, however, they were ethical rather than sociological, prescriptions for right conduct rather than propositions about any conduct, whether right or wrong, and any behavior, whether impulsive or purposive. Their authors, in short, were law-givers to the race rather than students of society.

To a considerable degree, of course, classical social thought also suffers from inattention to this distinction—a distinction we now largely take for granted—between a moral or a legal command on the one hand and a categorical proposition, principle, or scientific law on the other, between an effort to say what ought to be and an effort to say what is. The former belongs to ethics and to social philosophy; the latter to the positive sciences, and to sociology. In his immortal *Republic,* for example, Plato was interested in describing the good society, or even the best possible society, and not the society he actually lived in and knew. Whatever his motives, however, there are profound sociological insights in his *Dialogues* and one commits no impropriety in saying that Plato was the first sociologist in the great tradition of Western thought. Philosophical he may have been—speculative, imaginative, and even poetic—but he asked exciting questions and his answers gave impetus to sociological inquiry.

There is much warrant indeed for the oft-quoted statement by the late Alfred North Whitehead that the entire history of Western thought is but a series of footnotes to Plato.

Whitehead's preference for Plato, however, should not be permitted to obscure for us the excellence of Aristotle. Here is a thinker who can lay claim to equal and even (to continue a perennial argument) superior rank. The Aristotelians will assert, for example, that Plato's famous doctrine of ideas—an immense contribution to philosophy—is to be found not in the *Dialogues* at all but rather in Book Alpha of Aristotle's *Metaphysics*. However that may be, it was Aristotle who examined the human community, its governments and its constitutions, in an inductive and comparative manner, and who gave us his observations on the sexes, the family, slavery, property, social class, war, and many other subjects that attract the attention of sociologists today. Whatever their relative merit, there is no question that both Plato and Aristotle belong in any history of sociological theory. And they belong at its beginning.

In a brief introduction it is impossible, of course, to do more than offer the most rapid and superficial survey of this history. It will suffice to say, perhaps, that when we turn to Rome we find men of affairs in abundance but not many philosophers, politicians but not many political scientists, and many orators but few sociologists. Cicero raised an interesting question, one concerning the existence of the natural law, and it was Cicero too who seems to have grasped—or at least alluded to—the notion not only of this society or that one but of society in general. But the Roman thinkers, by current consensus, lacked originality and, at least in sociology, gave us few theories that retain any influence or significance today.

The medieval period was also relatively unproductive with respect to the advancement of sociological knowledge. That long and dim tunnel in the history of Western thought that we know as the Middle Ages covers a span of some one thousand years, from roughly the third century to the thirteenth. Once it was fashionable to refer to these centuries as the Dark Ages and to assume that nothing of any importance happened during that enormous period of time. Later a contrary fashion in the writing of history found, in perspective, achievements of moment and merit that contemporary scholars could ignore only at the risk of temporocentrism, which is the temporal analogue of ethnocentrism, the tendency to judge other cultures in terms of standards and criteria taken from one's own. Now, however, it must once again be conceded that, however significant in some respects the achievements of medieval thinkers, it was not a period rich in sociological insights—and this for an important sociological reason. The eye of medieval man was fixed not on this world but rather on the next, on the life to come. For him human society was both a trivial and a temporary phenomenon, hardly worth the energy it would take to improve it, and certainly not worth the industry required to investigate it. The medieval thinkers had a low opinion both of secular society and of secular knowledge, and in such a climate sociology could not prosper. The very expression "medieval sociologist" has an anomalous sound and can hardly survive a challenge.

In any event, the writers of the Middle Ages directed their attention to a heavenly rather than an earthly society, and it was St. Augustine at the beginning of the period who spoke of two cities and who wrote of the wonders of the City of God. Some eight hundred years later, in the thirteenth century, St. Thomas Aquinas, the "Angelic Doctor" of the Church, dressed the pagan Aristotle in Christian vestments, not only in his metaphysical but also in his sociological doctrine, and henceforth there were to be two Aristotles, one the Greek inquirer and the other the Thomistic authority. The poet Dante recapitulates the medieval view of man and of that hierarchical society in which he dwelt, ranging in infinite distance from the lowest circle of hell to the highest summit of heaven; and it is not until we reach such bold thinkers as William of Occam and Marsilius of Padua around the beginning of the fourteenth century that this old social system starts to crack and its weaknesses to become apparent. At least there is a new kind of contention in the world, a new consciousness of contrary interests and of conflict, foreshadowing a time still to come when men would begin again to look at a secular society and inquire into its commotions.

The arrangement of history into periods is a task beset with difficulties, and the difficulties increase perhaps as we move from political to intellectual history. It would not be altogether appropriate, for example, to call Marsilius a medieval man and Machiavelli, two centuries later, a modern man. It is clear, however, that the stirrings of the Renaissance were in Machiavelli and it is even clearer that he was more interested in an effective society than he was in an ethical one. And so with the great Florentine and others of his time we have turned a corner in the history of social thought.

From Machiavelli to Thomas Hobbes and the British empirical tradition is but a step. Where Machiavelli is a political scientist, however, not to say a political strategist, Hobbes is a political philosopher and a sociologist. Hobbes is also one of the leading authors of the social contract theory of government, a theory destined to play an impressive role in Hobbes's own and the succeeding century. Others in what I have labeled The Early Modern Period include "the incomparable Mr. Locke" (so-called by Molyneux after John Locke himself had applied the adjective to Isaac Newton); the skeptical Scot, David Hume; and the father of "the dismal science" of economics, Adam Smith. All of these were members of the empirical and utilitarian school and all were interested in both the practical and the theoretical problems of social and political philosophy. On the continent there was the great Vico in Italy, a representative philosopher of history and an original, almost unique, thinker; and in France Montesquieu, Condorcet, and Jean Jacques Rousseau—another "original"—drawn from a much larger group of savants and philosophers of the Enlightenment.

Two years before the end of the eighteenth century an English clergyman named Thomas Robert Malthus published one of the most influential books ever written in the field of sociology. It was a book on population and it was destined to have percussive consequences in several fields of learning. We are so accustomed to thinking of the biological phase of social thought and of the heavy debt that nineteenth and early twentieth century sociology owes to Darwin that we are apt to forget the debt Darwin, a biologist, owed to Malthus, a sociologist. For, as everyone knows, it was the Malthusian principle of the plenitude—not to say plethora—of reproduction in the human species that gave to the great naturalist the key to nature's selection of the fittest.

Now Malthus, of course, did not know that he was writing

sociology and as a scholar with the usual classical training he might have been uncomfortable with such a word. For *sociology*, as everyone in his day would have known, is a bastard product of two languages, Latin and Greek. About fifty years later Auguste Comte coined the word from the Latin *socius*, meaning friend or companion, and the Greek *logos*, meaning word, thought, discourse, or study of—so that sociology means, literally, talking about companionship or association. John Stuart Mill also talked about a new science, a social science, and used the word *ethology* as a label for some part of it. *Ethology* had the advantage, at least, that it was all Greek, but somehow no one accepted the suggestion and later on, when Herbert Spencer said in the Introduction to his *Principles of Sociology* that the convenience of our symbols is more important than the legitimacy of their derivation, a very old discipline had a very new name.

Here then we have the writers who are often called the founders of sociology—Malthus, Mill, Comte, and Spencer. Henry Thomas Buckle deserves a place here too because it was he who became dissatisfied with the way history was being written in his day and who attempted, in his now classic work, to probe beneath the surface of historical events and to find patterns and repetitions that could be built into sociological principles. Darwin too belongs. The principle of sexual selection, for example, is one that has far-reaching implications for human society. As for the *Communist Manifesto*, a large portion of it is included not because it is one of the most powerful pieces of political propaganda ever written—which of course it is—but because it contains in germ almost all of Marx's sociological views which, in turn, exercised a not inconsiderable influence upon the subsequent course of intellectual history.

With what I have called The Middle Period we have arrived at a narrower and possibly more orthodox sense of the term sociology. Although the lines of demarcation may still be somewhat difficult to draw, sociology is now differentiated from its sister social sciences, there are national and international societies devoted to its development, and the learned journals in the field have made their appearance. Included here are the leading recent figures in the discipline, the writers who accepted for themselves the title of sociologist, the men whose works every young sociologist must master before he may embark upon his own career: the French Durkheim and Tarde; the Italian Pareto; The German Tönnies, Simmel, and Weber; and the American Ward, Ross, Sumner, Cooley, and Giddings.

Finally, in the last section, sociology becomes almost an American science, and the books become too numerous for separate treatment in this introduction. We have here the most recent generation of sociologists, those for the most part whose major achievements are behind them and whose names, so far as one can judge, will go on the permanent roster, along with those of their predecessors in the history of sociology.

These recent contributions suggest something of the pattern that sociology exhibits today, as the twentieth century begins to wane. Certainly contemporary problems differ from those of a generation, a century, a millenium ago. Different climes and cultures produce different questions about society, and the systems of sociology men construct in these different ages have different angles and contours. Few today, for example, would be interested, as Plato was, in the origins of human society, or even, perhaps, as Hobbes and Rousseau were, in the origins of a society's government. Questions of social origin are thought now to be relatively unrewarding. As we move into the "dark backward and abysm of time" the records grow increasingly scanty and finally disappear, leaving only speculation which, however imaginative, must fail ultimately to supply an answer. This is not to say, of course, that such questions may not again arise to agitate the human mind, but only that they are now out of fashion and arouse hardly any contemporary curiosity.

Nor do we argue today, as sociologists used to do, such questions as the "reality" of the group, or of the society, as over against the "reality" of the individual; or whether society is something "more than" the sum of the individuals who comprise it; or whether there is a "group mind" that somehow transcends the minds of its members. On the other hand we are all indebted to Durkheim for his emphasis upon the "exteriority" of social facts, upon "collective representations," and upon the "collective consciousness." We know furthermore that the structure of society, and of its culture, is logically and chronologically antecedent to the structure of personality and, again with Durkheim, that the latter can be understood only with reference to the former. An apparent contradiction here is resolved by the recognition that there is a certain metaphysical extravagance in Durkheim's language, as there was in the language used earlier by the German philosophers of history. The concept of culture, which we use today, enables us fully to exploit Durkheim's insights and at the same time assures that leanness of description which is essential to positive inquiry. We do not have to resort to the mysticism of a collective consciousness to know that we are dependent upon our culture for most of the things we think and have and do as members of society. Thus, the use of a new concept solved an ancient problem.

The methodological controversies that disturbed the sociological scene both a hundred years ago in the problems of the Neo-Kantian philosophers in Germany and twenty-five years ago in the pages of the American journals have now largely subsided. No one argues any more whether or not sociology is or ought to be a science and whether or not the scientific method is applicable to the study of social phenomena. It is now almost universally recognized that all of the empirical instruments invented since the rise of modern science are legitimate, useful, and necessary in sociological research, and almost everyone now concedes that there is a difference between conclusions reached through the use of these powerful methods and conclusions that are the result of speculation, reflection, or the contemplative imagination. Only the former can lead to verifiable and verified knowledge, to "truth" in the ordinary connotation of the word.

On the other hand the scientific method—whatever various writers may mean by it—does not exhaust the resources of scholarship in sociology. It may be that for certain intellectual purposes cogency is more important than truth. That is, the excellence that informs a sustained piece of sociological analysis may be more important, and more useful, in the long run than the conclusions at which the analysis arrives. Thus, to take only one example, Max Weber's thesis on the relationship between the economic ethic of Protestantism and the development of a high capitalism is surely one of the greatest pieces of research ever conducted in sociology and will remain one of the brightest ornaments of our discipline. It contributes immeasurably to our understanding of both of these phenomena and, on a more general level, to the connection between ideologies, especially religious ideologies, on the one hand and the forms of social organization on the other.

In all candor, however, it must be added immediately that no one knows whether or not Weber's thesis is "true." He has marshaled impressive evidence for his hypothesis, but he has not "proved" or "verified" it in a way that would satisfy the canons of scientific research or suffice to establish a scientific law. We judge the thesis not in terms of its truth but rather in terms of its cogency. We pronounce it a distinguished contribution to sociology not because of the verifiability of its conclusions but because of the erudition, the profundity, and the sociological sophistication that the study exhibits. What we are saying, in short, is that unconfirmed conclusions, when they are cogent, can be more significant than verified truths, when they are trivial.

If certain methodological issues have ceased to matter, the same cannot be said about the methods and techniques of empirical research, which have received perhaps an extra share of attention in recent decades. The sociologists of our own time feel a rather keen sense of frustration at the paucity of their positive knowledge about society, especially in comparison with the spectacular advances made in our knowledge of the physical world. They feel as if, by some rude trick of fate, their faith in the scientific method were unrequited. The more they refine this method and render it precise, the more inconsequential are the items of knowledge that result. It is as if they had put together the best butterfly net in the world and were able to catch with it not butterflies and not even an occasional moth, but only a miserable species of gnat.

There is little question in fact that in contemporary sociological research the significance of our conclusions varies inversely with the precision of the methods employed. It is possible, of course, that in the study of human relations we shall never achieve that measure of truth which characterizes a verified proposition in physics or astronomy. This, however, may have to be recorded as one of the accidents of the universe. It just seems to happen, so far as present capacities can disclose, that the physical world can be captured cognitively by mathematical models, tools, and methods, whereas the world of society, in all important respects, evades a similar capture. It may be that this is a situation to which sociologists will have to respond with a Stoic acceptance. It may be one, on the contrary, that they will want continually to challenge and to try to overcome.

No one knows, of course, what the fates will summon up for the future of sociology. There are signs along the horizon that the recent preoccupation with the methods of research, and possibly even with the mechanics of system-building, will recede and that a newer generation of sociologists will once again attend to the substantive problems of sociology and seek the answers that will contribute to our knowledge of the social order. In any event, we may say in conclusion as we did at the beginning that, whatever the difficulties that afflict the enterprise, the nature of society, its structure and change, merits the sustained attention of the very best minds of every age.

I · *Classical and Medieval Statements*

PLATO

Plato (427-347 B.C.) was born of a noble family in Athens and became the most illustrious of the pupils of Socrates. After a period of youthful wanderings he returned to his native city where he founded the Academy and where he taught mathematics and philosophy until his death. Although in his *Dialogues* the state is never adequately distinguished from the community, and although social concerns are seldom treated in separation from ethical ones, it is nevertheless true that sociological problems are never distant from his ranging and restless mind. The *Dialogues* themselves, of course, are among the most searching, subtle, and splendid of all of our works of literary and philosophic art.

The first of the three selections that follow is from the *Protagoras*. It is the famous Prometheus myth in which Plato is discussing the origin of mankind, and of society. He has occasion to touch here on the reason for cities and the beginning of government. Although Plato did not believe in the equality of all men, the concluding paragraph can be construed as a curious argument in favor of democracy.

The second excerpt is from the *Crito* and raises both the sociological question of the relationship between the mores and the laws, and the ethical question of what to do when they are in conflict. On a deeper level it deals with the great problem, larger even than sociology, of the relationship between the individual and his society.

The third selection, which treats of the origin of civil society, of the division of labor, and of war, is from the immortal *Republic*, a dialogue that has been characterized as the greatest sociological treatise every written.

The translation from the Greek is by Benjamin Jowett.

*The Myth of Protagoras**

Once upon a time there were gods only, and no mortal creatures. But when the time came that these also should be created, the gods fashioned them out of earth and fire and various mixtures of both elements in the interior of the earth; and when they were about to bring them into the light of day, they ordered Prometheus and Epimetheus to equip them, and to distribute to them severally their proper qualities. Epimetheus said to Prometheus: "Let me distribute, and do you inspect." This was agreed, and Epimetheus made the distribution. There were some to whom he gave strength without swiftness, while he equipped the weaker with swiftness; some he armed, and others he left unarmed; and devised for the latter some other means of preservation, making some large, and having their size as a protection, and others small, whose nature was to fly in the air or burrow in the ground; this was to be their way of escape. Thus did he compensate them with the view of preventing any race from becoming extinct. And when he had provided against their destruction by one another, he contrived also a means of protecting them against the seasons of heaven; clothing them with close hair and thick skins sufficient to defend them against the winter cold and able to resist the summer heat, so that they might have a natural bed of their own when they wanted to rest; also he furnished them with hoofs and hair and hard and callous skins under their feet. Then he gave them varieties of food—herb of the soil to some, to others fruits of trees, and to others roots, and to some again he gave other animals as food. And some he made to have few young ones, while those who were their prey were very prolific; and in this manner the race was preserved. Thus did Epimetheus, who, not being very wise, forget that he had distributed among the brute animals all the qualities which he had to give—and when he came to man, who was still unprovided, he was terribly perplexed. Now while he was in this

* From the *Protagoras*.

perplexity, Prometheus came to inspect the distribution, and he found that the other animals were suitably furnished, but that man alone was naked and shoeless, and had neither bed nor arms of defense. The appointed hour was approaching when man in his turn was to go forth into the light of day; and Prometheus, not knowing how he could devise his salvation, stole the mechanical arts of Hephaestus and Athene, and fire with them (they could neither have been acquired nor used without fire), and gave them to man. Thus man had the wisdom necessary to the support of life, but political wisdom he had not; for that was in the keeping of Zeus, and the power of Prometheus did not extend to entering into the citadel of heaven, where Zeus dwelt, who moreover had terrible sentinels; but he did enter by stealth into the common workshop of Athene and Hephaestus, in which they used to practice their favorite arts, and carried off Hephaestus' art of working by fire, and also the art of Athene, and gave them to man. And in this way man was supplied with the means of life. But Prometheus is said to have been afterwards prosecuted for theft, owing to the blunder of Epimetheus.

Now man, having a share of the divine attributes, was at first the only one of the animals who had any gods, because he alone was of their kindred; and he would raise altars and images of them. He was not long in inventing articulate speech and names; and he also constructed houses and clothes and shoes and beds, and drew sustenance from the earth. Thus provided, mankind at first lived dispersed, and there were no cities. But the consequence was that they were destroyed by the wild beasts, for they were utterly weak in comparison with them, and their art was only sufficient to provide them with the means of life, and did not enable them to carry on war against the animals; food they had, but not as yet the art of government, of which the art of war is a part. After a while the desire of self-preservation gathered them into cities; but when they were gathered together, having no art of government, they evil intreated one another, and were again in process of dispersion and destruction. Zeus feared that the entire race would be exterminated, and so he sent Hermes to them, bearing reverence and justice to be the ordering principles of cities and the bonds of friendship and conciliation. Hermes asked Zeus how he should impart justice and reverence among men: Should he distribute them as the arts are distributed; that is to say, to a favored few only, one skilled individual having enough of medicine or of any other art for many unskilled ones? "Shall this be the manner in which I am to distribute justice and reverence among men, or shall I give them to all?" "To all," said Zeus, "I should like them all to have a share; for cities cannot exist, if a few only share in the virtues, as in the arts. And further, make a law by my order that he who has no part in reverence and justice shall be put to death, for he is a plague of the state."

And this is the reason, Socrates, why the Athenians and mankind in general, when the question relates to carpentering or any other mechanical art, allow but a few to share in their deliberations; and when any one else interferes, then, as you say, they object if he be not of the favored few, which, as I reply, is very natural. But when they meet to deliberate about political virtue, which proceeds only by way of justice and wisdom, they are patient enough of any man who speaks of them, as is also natural, because they think that every man ought to share in this sort of virtue, and that states could not exist if this were otherwise. I have explained to you, Socrates, the reason of this phenomenon.

*The Address of the Laws**

Socrates. I will go on to the next point, which may be put in the form of a question: Ought a man to do what he admits to be right, or ought he to betray the right?

Crito. He ought to do what he thinks right.

Soc. But if this is true, what is the application? In leaving the prison against the will of the Athenians, do I wrong any? Or rather do I not wrong those whom I ought least to wrong? Do I not desert the principles which were acknowledged by us to be just—what do you say?

Cr. I cannot tell, Socrates; for I do not know.

* From the *Crito*.

Soc. Then consider the matter in this way: Imagine that I am about to play truant (you may call the proceeding by any name which you like) and the laws and the government come and interrogate me: "Tell us, Socrates," they say, "what are you about? Are you not going by an act of yours to overturn us—the laws, and the whole state, as far as in you lies? Do you imagine that a state can subsist and not be overthrown, in which the decisions of law have no power, but are set aside and trampled upon by individuals?" What will be our answer, Crito, to these and the like words? Anyone, and especially a rhetorician, will have a good deal to say on behalf of the law which requires a sentence to be carried out. He will argue that this law should not be set aside; and shall we reply, "Yes; but the state has injured us and given an unjust sentence." Suppose I say that?

Cr. Very good, Socrates.

Soc. "And was that our agreement with you?" the law would answer, "or were you to abide by the sentence of the state?" And if I were to express my astonishment at their words, the law would probably add: "Answer, Socrates, instead of opening your eyes—you are in the habit of asking and answering questions. Tell us—what complaint have you to make against us which justifies you in attempting to destroy us and the state? In the first place did we not bring you into existence? Your father married your mother by our aid and begat you. Say whether you have any objection to urge against those of us who regulate marriage?" None, I should reply. "Or against those of us who after birth regulate the nurture and education of children, in which you also were trained? Were not the laws, which have the charge of education, right in commanding your father to train you in music and gymnastic?" Right, I should reply. "Well then, since you were brought into the world and nurtured and educated by us, can you deny in the first place that you are our child and slave, as your fathers were before you? And if this is true you are not on equal terms with us; nor can you think that you have a right to do to us what we are doing to you. Would you have any right to strike or revile or do any other evil to your father or your master, if you had one, because you have been struck or reviled by him, or received some other evil at his hands?—you would not say this? And because we think right to destroy you, do you think that you have any right to destroy us in return, and your country as far as in you lies? Will you, O professor of true virtue, pretend that you are justified in this? Has a philosopher like you failed to discover that our country is more to be valued and higher and holier far than mother or father or any ancestor, and more to be regarded in the eyes of the gods and of men of understanding? Also to be soothed, and gently and reverently entreated when angry, even more than a father, and either to be persuaded, or if not persuaded, to be obeyed? And when we are punished by her, whether with imprisonment or stripes, the punishment is to be endured in silence; and if she leads us to wounds or death in battle, thither we follow as is right; neither may anyone yield or retreat or leave his rank, but whether in battle or in a court of law, or in any other place, he must do what his city and his country order him; or he must change their view of what is just: and if he may do no violence to his father or mother, much less may he do violence to his country." What answer shall we make to this, Crito? Do the laws speak truly, or do they not?

Cr. I think that they do.

Soc. Then the laws will say, "Consider, Socrates, if we are speaking truly that in your present attempt you are going to do us an injury. For, having brought you into the world, and nurtured and educated you, and given you and every other citizen a share in every good which we had to give, we further proclaim to any Athenian by the liberty which we allow him, that if he does not like us when he has become of age and has seen the ways of the city, and made our acquaintance, he may go where he pleases and take his goods with him. None of us laws will forbid him or interfere with him. Anyone who does not like us and the city, and who wants to emigrate to a colony or to any other city, may go where he likes, retaining his property. But he who has experience of the manner in which we order justice and administer the state, and still remains, has entered into an implied contract that he will do as we command him. And he who disobeys us is, as we maintain, thrice wrong; first, because in disobeying us he is disobeying his parents; secondly, because we are the authors of his education; thirdly, because he has made an agreement with us that he will duly obey our commands; and he neither obeys them nor convinces us that our commands are unjust; and we do not rudely impose them, but give him the alternative of obeying or convincing us;—that is what we offer, and he does neither.

"These are the sort of accusations to which, as we were saying, you, Socrates, will be exposed if you accomplish your intentions; you, above all other Athenians." Suppose now I ask, why I rather than anybody else? They will justly retort upon me that I above all other men have acknowledged the agreement. "There is clear proof," they will say, "Socrates, that we and the city were not displeasing to you. Of all Athenians you have been the most constant resident in the city, which, as you never leave, you may be supposed to love. For you never went out of the city either to see the games, except once when you went to the Isthmus, or to any other place unless when you were on military service; nor did you travel as other men do. Nor had you any curiosity to know other states or their laws: your affections did not go beyond us and our state; we were your special favorites, and you acquiesced in our government of you; and here in this city you begat your children, which is a proof of your satisfaction. Moreover, you might in the course of the trial, if you had liked, have fixed the penalty at banishment; the state which refuses to let you go now would have let you go then. But you pretended that you preferred death to exile, and that you were not unwilling to die. And now you have forgotten these fine sentiments, and pay no respect to us the laws, of whom you are the destroyer; and are doing what only a miserable slave would do, running away and turning your back upon the compacts and agreements which you made as a citizen. And first of all answer this very question: Are we right in saying that you agreed to be governed according to us in deed, and not in word only? Is that true or not?" How shall we answer, Crito? Must we not assent?

Cr. We cannot help it, Socrates.

Soc. Then will they not say: "You, Socrates, are breaking the covenants and agreements which you made with us at your leisure, not in any haste or under any compulsion or deception, but after you have had seventy years to think of them, during which time you were at liberty to leave the city, if we were not to your mind, or if our covenants appeared to you to be unfair.

You had your choice, and might have gone either to Lacedaemon or Crete, both which states are often praised by you for their good government, or to some other Hellenic or foreign state. Whereas you, above all other Athenians, seemed to be so fond of the state, or, in other words, of us her laws (and who would care about a state which has no laws?), that you never stirred out of her; the halt, the blind, the maimed were not more stationary in her than you were. And now you run away and forsake your agreements. Not so, Socrates, if you will take our advice; do not make yourself ridiculous by escaping out of the city.

"For just consider, if you transgress and err in this sort of way, what good will you do either to yourself or to your friends? That your friends will be driven into exile and deprived of citizenship, or will lose their property, is tolerably certain; and you yourself, if you fly to one of the neighboring cities, as, for example, Thebes or Megara, both of which are well governed, will come to them as an enemy, Socrates, and their government will be against you, and all patriotic citizens will cast an evil eye upon you as a subverter of the laws, and you will confirm in the minds of the judges the justice of their own condemnation of you. For he who is a corrupter of the laws is more than likely to be a corrupter of the young and foolish portion of mankind. Will you then flee from well-ordered cities and virtuous men? And is existence worth having on these terms? Or will you go to them without shame, and talk to them, Socrates? And what will you say to them? What you say here about virtue and justice and institutions and laws being the best things among men? Would that be decent of you? Surely not. But if you go away from well-governed states to Crito's friends in Thessaly, where there is great disorder and license, they will be charmed to hear the tale of your escape from prison, set off with ludicrous particulars of the manner in which you were wrapped in a goatskin or some other disguise, and metamorphosed as the manner is of runaways; but will there be no one to remind you that in your old age you were not ashamed to violate the most sacred laws from a miserable desire of a little more life? Perhaps not, if you keep them in a good temper; but if they are out of temper you will hear many degrading things; you will live, but how? As the flatterer of all men, and the servant of all men; and doing what? Eating and drinking in Thessaly, having gone abroad in order that you may get a dinner. And where will be your fine sentiments about justice and virtue? Say that you wish to live for the sake of your children—you want to bring them up and educate them—will you take them into Thessaly and deprive them of Athenian citizenship? Is this the benefit which you will confer upon them? Or are you under the impression that they will be better cared for and educated here if you are still alive, although absent from them; for your friends will take care of them? Do you fancy that if you are an inhabitant of Thessaly they will take care of them, and if you are an inhabitant of the other world that they will not take care of them? Nay; but if they who call themselves friends are good for anything, they will—to be sure they will.

"Listen, then, Socrates, to us who have brought you up. Think not of life and children first, and of justice afterwards, but of justice first, that you may be justified before the princes of the world below. For neither will you nor any that belong to you be happier or holier or juster in this life, or happier in another, if you do as Crito bids. Now you depart in innocence, a sufferer and not a doer of evil; a victim, not of the laws but of men. But if you go forth, returning evil for evil, and injury for injury, breaking the covenants and agreements which you have made with us, and wronging those whom you ought least of all to wrong, that is to say, yourself, your friends, your country, and us, we shall be angry with you while you live, and our brethren, the laws in the world below, will receive you as an enemy; for they will know that you have done your best to destroy us. Listen, then, to us and not to Crito."

This, dear Crito, is the voice which I seem to hear murmuring in my ears, like the sound of the flute in the ears of the mystic; that voice, I say, is humming in my ears, and prevents me from hearing any other. And I know that anything more which you may say will be vain. Yet speak, if you have anything to say.

Cr. I have nothing to say, Socrates.

Soc. Leave me then, Crito, to fulfill the will of God, and to follow whither he leads.

The Origin of the State*

A State, I said, arises, as I conceive, out of the needs of mankind; no one is self-sufficing, but all of us have many wants. Can any other origin of a State be imagined?

There can be no other.

Then, as we have many wants, and many persons are needed to supply them, one takes a helper for one purpose and another for another; and when these partners and helpers are gathered together in one habitation the body of inhabitants is termed a State.

True, he said.

And they exchange with one another, and one gives, and another receives, under the idea that the exchange will be for their good.

Very true.

Then, I said, let us begin and create in idea a State; and yet the true creator is necessity, who is the mother of our invention.

Of course, he replied.

Now the first and greatest of necessities is food, which is the condition of life and existence.

Certainly.

The second is a dwelling, and the third clothing and the like.

True.

And now let us see how our city will be able to supply this great demand: We may suppose that one man is a husbandman, another a builder, some one else a weaver—shall we add to them a shoemaker, or perhaps some other purveyor to our bodily wants?

Quite right.

The barest notion of a State must include four or five men.

Clearly.

And how will they proceed? Will each bring the result of his labors into a common stock? The individual husbandman, for

* From the *Republic*.

example, producing for four, and laboring four times as long and as much as he need in the provision of food with which he supplies others as well as himself; or will he have nothing to do with others and not be at the trouble of producing for them, but provide for himself alone a fourth of the food in a fourth of the time, and in the remaining three-fourths of his time be employed in making a house or a coat or a pair of shoes, having no partnership with others, but supplying himself all his own wants?

Adeimantus thought that he should aim at producing food only and not at producing everything.

Probably, I replied, that would be the better way; and when I hear you say this, I am myself reminded that we are not all alike; there are diversities of natures among us which are adapted to different occupations.

Very true.

And will you have a work better done when the workman has many occupations, or when he has only one?

When he has only one.

Further, there can be no doubt that a work is spoilt when not done at the right time?

No doubt.

For business is not disposed to wait until the doer of the business is at leisure; but the doer must follow up what he is doing, and make the business his first object.

He must.

And if so, we must infer that all things are produced more plentifully and easily and of a better quality when one man does one thing which is natural to him and does it at the right time, and leaves other things.

Undoubtedly.

Then more than four citizens will be required; for the husbandman will not make his own plough or mattock, or other implements of agriculture, if they are to be good for anything. Neither will the builder make his tools—and he too needs many; and in like manner the weaver and shoemaker.

True.

Then carpenters, and smiths, and many other artisans, will be sharers in our little State, which is already beginning to grow?

True.

Yet even if we add neatherds, shepherds, and other herdsmen, in order that our husbandmen may have oxen to plough with, and builders as well as husbandmen may have draught cattle, and curriers and weavers fleeces and hides—still our State will not be very large.

That is true; yet neither will it be a very small State which contains all these.

Then, again, there is the situation of the city—to find a place where nothing need be imported is well-nigh impossible.

Impossible.

Then there must be another class of citizens who will bring the required supply from another city?

There must.

But if the trader goes empty-handed, having nothing which they require who would supply his need, he will come back empty-handed.

That is certain.

And therefore what they produce at home must be not only enough for themselves, but such both in quantity and quality as to accommodate those from whom their wants are supplied.

Very true.

Then more husbandmen and more artisans will be required?

They will.

Not to mention the importers and exporters, who are called merchants?

Yes.

Then we shall want merchants?

We shall.

And if merchandise is to be carried over the sea, skillful sailors will also be needed, and in considerable numbers?

Yes, in considerable numbers.

Then, again, within the city, how will they exchange their productions? To secure such an exchange was, as you will remember, one of our principal objects when we formed them into a society and constituted a State.

Clearly they will buy and sell.

Then they will need a market-place, and a money-token for purposes of exchange.

Certainly.

Suppose now that a husbandman, or an artisan, brings some production to market, and he comes at a time when there is no one to exchange with him—is he to leave his calling and sit idle in the market place?

Not at all; he will find people there who, seeing the want, undertake the office of salesmen. In well-ordered states they are commonly those who are the weakest in bodily strength, and therefore of little use for any other purpose; their duty is to be in the market, and to give money in exchange for goods to those who desire to sell and to take money from those who desire to buy.

This want, then, creates a class of retail traders in our State. Is not "retailer" the term which is applied to those who sit in the market place engaged in buying and selling, while those who wander from one city to another are called merchants?

Yes, he said.

And there is another class of servants, who are intellectually hardly on the level of companionship; still they have plenty of bodily strength for labor, which accordingly they sell, and are called, if I do not mistake, hirelings, hire being the name which is given to the price of their labor.

True.

Then hirelings will help to make up our population?

Yes.

And now, Adeimantus, is our State matured and perfected?

I think so.

Where, then, is justice, and where is injustice, and in what part of the State did they spring up?

Probably in the dealings of these citizens with one another. I cannot imagine that they are more likely to be found any where else.

I dare say that you are right in your suggestion, I said; we had better think the matter out, and not shrink from the enquiry.

Let us then consider, first of all, what will be their way of life, now that we have thus established them. Will they not produce corn, and wine, and clothes, and shoes, and build houses for themselves? And when they are housed, they will work, in summer, commonly, stripped and barefoot, but in winter substantially clothed and shod. They will feed on barley meal and flour of wheat, baking and kneading them, making noble cakes and loaves; these they will serve up on a mat of reeds or on clean leaves, themselves reclining the while upon beds strewn with yew or myrtle. And they and their children will feast, drinking of the wine which they have made, wearing garlands on their heads, and hymning the praises of the gods, in happy converse with one another. And they will take care that their families do not exceed their means; having an eye to poverty or war.

But, said Glaucon, interposing, you have not given them a relish to their meal.

True, I replied, I had forgotten; of course they must have a relish—salt, and olives, and cheese, and they will boil roots and herbs such as country people prepare; for a dessert we shall give them figs, and peas, and beans; and they will roast myrtle berries and acorns at the fire, drinking in moderation. And with such a diet they may be expected to live in peace and health to a good old age, and bequeath a similar life to their children after them.

Yes, Socrates, he said, and if you were providing for a city of pigs, how else would you feed the beasts?

But what would you have, Glaucon? I replied.

Why, he said, you should give them the ordinary conveniences of life. People who are to be comfortable are accustomed to lie on sofas, and dine off tables, and they should have sauces and sweets in the modern style.

Yes, I said, now I understand: the question which you would have me consider is, not only how a State, but how a luxurious State is created; and possibly there is no harm in this, for in such a State we shall be more likely to see how justice and injustice originate. In my opinion the true and healthy constitution of the State is the one which I have described. But if you wish also to see a State at fever heat, I have no objection. For I suspect that many will not be satisfied with the simpler way of life. They will be for adding sofas, and tables, and other furniture; also dainties, and perfumes, and incense, and courtesans, and cakes, all these not of one sort only, but in every variety; we must go beyond the necessaries of which I was at first speaking, such as houses, and clothes, and shoes: the arts of the painter and the embroiderer will have to be set in motion, and gold and ivory and all sorts of materials must be procured.

True, he said.

Then we must enlarge our borders; for the original healthy State is no longer sufficient. Now will the city have to fill and swell with a multitude of callings which are not required by any natural wants; such as the whole tribe of hunters and actors, of whom one large class have to do with forms and colors; another will be the votaries of music—poets and their attendant train of rhapsodists, players, dancers, contractors; also makers of divers kinds of articles, including women's dresses. And we shall want more servants. Will not tutors be also in request, and nurses wet and dry, tirewomen and barbers, as well as confectioners and cooks; and swineherds, too, who were not needed and therefore had no place in the former edition of our State, but are needed now? They must not be forgotten: and there will be animals of many other kinds, if people eat them.

Certainly.

And living in this way we shall have much greater need of physicians than before?

Much greater.

And the country which was enough to support the original inhabitants will be too small now, and not enough?

Quite true.

Then a slice of our neighbors' land will be wanted by us for pasture and tillage, and they will want a slice of ours, if, like ourselves, they exceed the limit of necessity, and give themselves up to the unlimited accumulation of wealth?

That, Socrates, will be inevitable.

And so we shall go to war, Glaucon. Shall we not?

Most certainly, he replied.

Then, without determining as yet whether war does good or harm, this much we may affirm, that now we have discovered war to be derived from causes which are also the causes of almost all the evils in States, private as well as public.

ARISTOTLE

Aristotle (384-322 B.C.) can almost without cavil be called one of the two or three greatest thinkers of all time. Born at Stagira of a physician father named Nicomachus, he studied under Plato at the Academy in Athens, later become the tutor of Alexander the Great, and returned to Athens after the wars in order to conduct a school in the Lyceum.

Aristotle wrote books on almost every known field of human knowledge, books that are still highly influential today. Among these fields are logic, physics, metaphysics, astronomy, biology, psychology, ethics, aesthetics, political science, and sociology. Although his views on matters touching the physical sciences have largely been superseded, his logic endured almost without change until the end of the nineteenth century, his metaphysics became incorporated into Christianity in the thirteenth century, and his ideas on these, as well as other subjects, continue to merit the closest attention.

In his *Politics,* from which the following selection is taken, Aristotle is considering things "in their first growth and origin" in order to obtain the clearest view of them. Civil society arises through an extension and enlargement of two basic social relations, that between husband and wife on the one hand and master and slave on the other. It is here that we learn that man is by nature a political animal or, as we should say today, a social animal, and is destined always to live with others of his kind. Other passages indicate in detail that Aristotle was aware of the significance of social differentiation and of the division of labor in society. The excerpt closes with an historically important condemnation of the collection of interest on money.

From *Politics**

BOOK I

1 Every state is a community of some kind, and every community is established with a view to some good; for mankind always act in order to obtain that which they think good. But, if all communities aim at some good, the state or political community, which is the highest of all, and which embraces all the rest, aims at good in a greater degree than any other, and at the highest good.

Some people think that the qualifications of a statesman, king, householder, and master are the same, and that they differ, not in kind, but only in the number of their subjects. For example, the ruler over a few is called a master; over more, the manager of a household; over a still larger number, a statesman or king, as if there were no difference between a great household and a small state. The distinction which is made between the king and the statesman is as follows: When the government is personal, the ruler is a king; when, according to the rules of the political science, the citizens rule and are ruled in turn, then he is called a statesman.

But all this is a mistake; for governments differ in kind, as will be evident to any one who considers the matter according to the method which has hitherto guided us. As in other departments of science, so in politics, the compound should always be resolved into the simple elements or least parts of the whole. We must therefore look at the elements of which the state is composed, in order that we may see in what the different kinds of rule differ from one another, and whether any scientific result can be attained about each one of them.

2 He who thus considers things in their first growth and origin, whether a state or anything else, will obtain the clearest view of

* Translated by W. D. Ross; reprinted by arrangement with the Oxford University Press.

them. In the first place there must be a union of those who cannot exist without each other; namely, of male and female, that the race may continue (and this is a union which is formed, not of deliberate purpose, but because, in common with other animals and with plants, mankind have a natural desire to leave behind them an image of themselves), and of natural ruler and subject, that both may be preserved. For that which can foresee by the exercise of mind is by nature intended to be lord and master, and that which can with its body give effect to such foresight is a subject, and by nature a slave; distinguished between the female and the slave. For she is not niggardly, like the smith who fashions the Delphian knife for many uses; she makes each thing for a single use, and every instrument is best made when intended for one and not for many uses. But among barbarians no distinction is made between women and slaves, because there is no natural ruler among them: they are a community of slaves, male and female. Wherefore the poets say—

"It is meet that Hellenes should rule over barbarians," as if they thought that the barbarian and the slave were by nature one.

Out of these two relationships between man and woman, master and slave, the first thing to arise is the family, and Hesiod is right when he says—

"First house and wife and an ox for the plow," for the ox is the poor man's slave. The family is the association established by nature for the supply of men's everyday wants, and the members of it are called by Charondas "companions of the cupboard," and by Epimenides the Cretan, "companions of the manger." But when several families are united, and the association aims at something more than the supply of daily needs, the first society to be formed is the village. And the most natural form of the village appears to be that of a colony from the family, composed of the children and grandchildren, who are said to be suckled with the same milk. And this is the reason why Hellenic states were originally governed by kings; because the Hellenes were under royal rule before they came together, as the barbarians still are. Every family is ruled by the eldest, and therefore in the colonies of the family the kingly form of government prevailed because they were of the same blood. As Homer says:

"Each one gives law to his children and to his wives." For they lived dispersedly, as was the manner in ancient times. Wherefore men say that the Gods have a king, because they themselves either are or were in ancient times under the rule of a king. For they imagine, not only the forms of the Gods, but their ways of life to be like their own.

When several villages are united in a single complete community, large enough to be nearly or quite self-sufficing, the state comes into existence, originating in the bare needs of life, and continuing in existence for the sake of a good life. And therefore, if the earlier forms of society are natural, so is the state, for it is the end of them, and the nature of a thing is its end. For what each thing is when fully developed, we call its nature, whether we are speaking of a man, a horse, or a family. Besides, the final cause and end of a thing is the best, and to be self-sufficing is the end and the best.

Hence it is evident that the state is a creation of nature, and that man is by nature a political animal. And he who by nature and not by mere accident is without a state, is either a bad man or above humanity; he is like the

"Tribeless, lawless, hearthless one,"

whom Homer denounces—the natural outcast is forthwith a lover of war; he may be compared to an isolated piece at draughts.

Now, that man is more of a political animal than bees or any other gregarious animals is evident. Nature, as we often say, makes nothing in vain, and man is the only animal whom she has endowed with the gift of speech. And whereas mere voice is but an indication of pleasure or pain, and is therefore found in other animals (for their nature attains to the perception of pleasure and pain and the intimation of them to one another, and no further) the power of speech is intended to set forth the expedient and inexpedient, and therefore likewise the just and the unjust. And it is a characteristic of man that he alone has any sense of good and evil, of just and unjust, and the like, and the association of living beings who have this sense makes a family and a state.

Further, the state is by nature clearly prior to the family and to the individual, since the whole is of necessity prior to the part; for example, if the whole body be destroyed, there will be no foot or hand, except in an equivocal sense, as we might speak of a stone hand; for when destroyed the hand will be no better than that. But things are defined by their working and power; and we ought not to say that they are the same when they no longer have their proper quality, but only that they have the same name. The proof that the state is a creation of nature and prior to the individual is that the individual, when isolated, is not self-sufficing; and therefore he is like a part in relation to the whole. But he who is unable to live in society, or who has no need because he is sufficient for himself, must be either a beast or a god: he is no part of a state. A social instinct is implanted in all men by nature, and yet he who first founded the state was the greatest of benefactors. For man, when perfected, is the best of animals, but, when separated from law and justice, he is the worst of all; since armed injustice is the more dangerous, and he is equipped at birth with arms, meant to be used by intelligence and virtue, which he may use for the worst ends. Wherefore, if he have not virtue, he is the most unholy and the most savage of animals, and the most full of lust and gluttony. But justice is the bond of men in states, for the administration of justice, which is the determination of what is just, is the principle of order in political society.

3 Seeing then that the state is made up of households, before speaking of the state we must speak of the management of the household. The parts of household management correspond to the persons who compose the household, and a complete household consists of slaves and freemen. Now we should begin by examining everything in its fewest possible elements; and the first and fewest possible parts of a family are master and slave, husband and wife, father and children. We have therefore to consider what each of these three relations is and ought to be—I mean the relation of master and servant, the marriage relation (the conjunction of man and wife has no name of its own), and thirdly, the procreative relation (this also has no proper name). And there is another element of a household, the so-called art of getting wealth, which, according to some, is identical with household management, according to others, a principal part of

it; the nature of this art will also have to be considered by us.

Let us first speak of master and slave, looking to the needs of practical life and also seeking to attain some better theory of their relation than exists at present. For some are of opinion that the rule of a master is a science, and that the management of a household, and the mastership of slaves, and the political and royal rule, as I was saying at the outset, are all the same. Others affirm that the rule of a master over slaves is contrary to nature, and that the distinction between slave and freeman exists by law only, and not by nature; and being an interference with nature is therefore unjust.

4 Property is a part of the household, and the art of acquiring property is a part of the art of managing the household; for no man can live well, or indeed live at all, unless he be provided with necessaries. And as in the arts which have a definite sphere the workers must have their own proper instruments for the accomplishment of their work, so it is in the management of a household. Now instruments are of various sorts; some are living, others lifeless; in the rudder, the pilot of a ship has a lifeless, in the lookout man, a living instrument; for in the arts the servant is a kind of instrument. Thus, too, a possession is an instrument for maintaining life. And so, in the arrangement of the family, a slave is a living possession, and property a number of such instruments; and the servant is himself an instrument, an instrument which takes precedence of all other instruments. For if every instrument could accomplish its own work, obeying or anticipating the will of others, like the statues of Daedalus, or the tripods of Hephaestus, which, says the poet,

> "Of their own accord entered the assembly of the Gods,"

if, in like manner, the shuttle would weave and the plectrum touch the lyre without a hand to guide them, chief workmen would not want servants, nor masters slaves. Here, however, another distinction must be drawn; the instruments commonly so called are instruments of production, while a possession is an instrument of action. The shuttle, for example, is not only of use; but something else is made by it, whereas of a garment or of a bed there is only the use. Further, as production and action are different in kind, and both require instruments, the instruments which they employ must likewise differ in kind. But life is action and not production, and therefore the slave is the minister of action. Again, a possession is spoken of as a part is spoken of; for the part is not only a part of something else, but wholly belongs to it; and this is also true of a possession. The master is only the master of the slave; he does not belong to him, whereas the slave is not only the slave of his master, but wholly belongs to him. Hence we see what is the nature and office of a slave; he who is by nature not his own but another's man, is by nature a slave; and he may be said to be another's man who, being a human being, is also a possession. And a possession may be defined as an instrument of action, separable from the possessor.

5 But is there any one thus intended by nature to be a slave, and for whom such a condition is expedient and right, or rather is not all slavery a violation of nature?

There is no difficulty in answering this question, on grounds both of reason and of fact. For that some should rule and others be ruled is a thing not only necessary, but expedient; from the hour of their birth, some are marked out for subjection, others for rule. . . .

8 Let us now inquire into property generally, and into the art of getting wealth, in accordance with our usual method, for a slave has been shown to be a part of property. The first question is whether the art of getting wealth is the same with the art of managing a household or a part of it, or instrumental to it; and if the last, whether in the way that the art of making shuttles is instrumental to the art of weaving, or in the way that the casting of bronze is instrumental to the art of the statuary, for they are not instrumental in the same way, but the one provides tools and the other material; and by material I mean the substratum out of which any work is made; thus wool is the material of the weaver, bronze of the statuary. Now it is easy to see that the art of household management is not identical with the art of getting wealth, for the one uses the material which the other provides. For the art which uses household stores can be no other than the art of household management. There is, however, a doubt whether the art of getting wealth is a part of household management or a distinct art. If the getter of wealth has to consider whence wealth and property can be procured, but there are many sorts of prop-

erty and riches, then are husbandry, and the care and provision of food in general, parts of the wealth-getting art or distinct arts? Again, there are many sorts of food, and therefore there are many kinds of lives both of animals and men; they must all have food, and the differences in their food have made differences in their ways of life. For of beasts, some are gregarious, others are solitary; they live in the way which is best adapted to sustain them, accordingly as they are carnivorous or herbivorous or omnivorous: and their habits are determined for them by nature in such a manner that they may obtain with greater facility the food of their choice. But, as different species have different tastes, the same things are not naturally pleasant to all of them; and therefore the lives of carnivorous or herbivorous animals further differ among themselves. In the lives of men too there is a great difference. The laziest are shepherds, who lead an idle life, and get their subsistence without trouble from tame animals; their flocks having to wander from place to place in search of pasture, they are compelled to follow them, cultivating a sort of living farm. Others support themselves by hunting, which is of different kinds. Some, for example, are brigands, others, who dwell near lakes or marshes or rivers or a sea in which there are fish, are fishermen, and others live by the pursuit of birds or wild beasts. The greater number obtain a living from the cultivated fruits of the soil. Such are the modes of subsistence which prevail among those whose industry springs up of itself, and whose food is not acquired by exchange and retail trade—there is the shepherd, the husbandman, the brigand, the fisherman, the hunter. Some gain a comfortable maintenance out of two employments, eking out the deficiencies of one of them by another: thus the life of a shepherd may be combined with that of a brigand, the life of a farmer with that of a hunter. Other modes of life are similarly combined in any way which the needs of men may require. Property, in the sense of a bare livelihood, seems to be given by nature herself to all, both when they are first born, and when they are grown up.

For some animals bring forth, together with their offspring, so much food as will last until they are able to supply themselves; of this the vermiparous or oviparous animals are an instance; and the viviparous animals have up to a certain time a supply of food for their young in themselves, which is called milk. In like manner we may infer that, after the birth of animals, plants exist for their sake, and that the other animals exist for the sake of man, the tame for use and food, the wild, if not all, at least the greater part of them, for food, and for the provision of clothing and various instruments. Now if nature makes nothing incomplete, and nothing in vain, the inference must be that she has made all animals for the sake of man. And so, in one point of view, the art of war is a natural art of acquisition, for the art of acquisition includes hunting, an art which we ought to practice against wild beasts, and against men who, though intended by nature to be governed, will not submit; for war of such a kind is naturally just.

Of the art of acquisition then there is one kind which by nature is a part of the management of a household, in so far as the art of household management must either find ready to hand, or itself provide, such things necessary to life, and useful for the community of the family or state, as can be stored. They are the elements of true riches; for the amount of property which is needed for a good life is not unlimited, although Solon in one of his poems says that

"No bound to riches has been fixed for man."

But there is a boundary fixed, just as there is in the other arts; for the instruments of any art are never unlimited, either in number or size, and riches may be defined as a number of instruments to be used in a household or in a state. And so we see that there is a natural art of acquisition which is practiced by managers of households and by statesmen, and what is the reason of this. . . .

10 And we have found the answer to our original question, Whether the art of getting wealth is the business of the manager of a household and of the statesman or not their business?—viz. that wealth is presupposed by them. For as political science does not make men, but takes them from nature and uses them, so too nature provides them with earth or sea or the like as a source of food. At this stage begins the duty of the manager of a household, who has to order the things which nature supplies; he may be compared to the weaver who has not to make but to use wool,

and to know, too, what sort of wool is good and serviceable or bad and unserviceable. Were this otherwise, it would be difficult to see why the art of getting wealth is a part of the management of a household and the art of medicine not; for surely the members of a household must have health just as they must have life or any other necessary. The answer is that as from one point of view the master of the house and the ruler of the state have to consider about health, from another point of view not they but the physician; so in one way the art of household management, in another way the subordinate art, has to consider about wealth. But, strictly speaking, as I have already said, the means of life must be provided beforehand by nature; for the business of nature is to furnish food to that which is born, and the food of the offspring is always what remains over of that from which it is produced. Wherefore the art of getting wealth out of fruits and animals is always natural.

There are two sorts of wealth-getting, as I have said; one is a part of household management, the other is retail trade: the former necessary and honorable, while that which consists in exchange is justly censured; for it is unnatural, and a mode by which men gain from one another. The most hated sort, and with the greatest reason, is usury, which makes a gain out of money itself, and not from the natural object of it. For money was intended to be used in exchange, but not to increase at interest. And this term interest, which means the birth of money from money, is applied to the breeding of money because the offspring resembles the parent. Wherefore of all modes of getting wealth this is the most unnatural.

CICERO

Marcus Tullius Cicero (106-43 B.C.), the only Roman in our collection, was at once orator, philosopher, politician, and the greatest prose stylist in the Latin language. His political career, a complicated and controversial one, was punctuated by exile and terminated by assassination. His voluminous writings, expressing in sum the views of the Stoics as against the Epicureans, include *De Amicitia* (On Friendship), *De Officiis* (On Duty), *De Senectute* (On Old Age), *De Finibus* (On Ends), *De Re Publica* (On The Republic), *De Legibus* (On Laws), and—known to every third-year Latin student—the famous Cataline Orations.

The selection that follows is from *The Laws*. The great Greek predecessors of Cicero focussed their attention upon the city-state which was, for them, synonymous with society. Cicero on the contrary extends his vision to society in the large, to "that universal city where gods and men compose one vast association." This society has a universal set of norms, the natural law, which is equivalent to "right reason." The natural law transcends the customs of particular nations and applies to all societies, at all times and places. It thus universalizes morality and confutes both the Epicurean notion of utility and the modern notion of cultural, or ethical, relativity.

From *The Laws**

The subject of our present discussion . . . comprehends the universal principles of equity and law. In such a discussion therefore on the great moral law of nature, the practice of the civil law can occupy but an insignificant and subordinate station. For according to our idea, we shall have to explain the true nature of moral justice, which is congenial and correspondent with the true nature of man. We shall have to examine those principles of legislation by which all political states should be governed. And last of all, shall we have to speak of those laws and customs which are framed for the use and convenience of particular peoples, which regulate the civic and municipal affairs of the citizens, and which are known by the title of civil laws.

It is not so much the science of law that produces litigation, as the ignorance of it (*potius ignoratio juris litigiosa est quam scientia*). But more of this by-and-by.

With respect to the true principle of justice, many learned men have maintained that it springs from Law. I hardly know if their opinion be not correct, at least, according to their own definition; for "Law (say they) is the highest reason, implanted in nature, which prescribes those things which ought to be done, and forbids the contrary." This, they think, is apparent from the converse of the proposition; because this same reason, when it is confirmed and established in men's minds, is the law of all their actions.

They therefore conceive that the voice of conscience is a law, that moral prudence is a law, whose operation is to urge us to good actions, and restrain us from evil ones. They think, too, that the Greek name for law (νομος), which is derived from νέμω, to distribute, implies the very nature of the thing, that is, to give every man his due. For my part, I imagine that the moral essence of law is better expressed by its Latin name (*lex*),

* Translated by Francis Barham.

which conveys the idea of selection or discrimination. According to the Greeks, therefore, the name of law implies an equitable distribution of goods: according to the Romans, an equitable discrimination between good and evil.

The true definition of law should, however, include both these characteristics. And this being granted as an almost self-evident proposition, the origin of justice is to be sought in the divine law of eternal and immutable morality. This indeed is the true energy of nature, the very soul and essence of wisdom, the test of virtue and vice. But since every discussion must relate to some subject, whose terms are of frequent occurrence in the popular language of the citizens, we shall be sometimes obliged to use the same terms as the vulgar, and to conform to that common idiom which signifies by the word law, all the arbitrary regulations which are found in our statute books, either commanding or forbidding certain actions.

We should seek for justice in its native source, which being discovered, we shall afterwards be able to speak with more authority and precision respecting our civil laws, that come home to the affairs of our citizens.

I shall endeavor to describe a system of Laws adapted to that Commonwealth, which Scipio declares to be most desirable in those Six Books which I have written under that title. All our laws, therefore, are to be accommodated to that mixed kind of political government there recommended. We shall also treat of the general principles of morals and manners, which appear most appropriate to such a constitution of society, but without descending to particular details.

Grant me that the entire universe is overruled by the power of God, that by his nature, reason, energy, mind, divinity, or some other word of clearer signification, all things are governed and directed. . . . Since you grant me the existence of God, and the superintendence of Providence, I maintain that he has been especially beneficent to man. This human animal—prescient, sagacious, complex, acute, full of memory, reason and counsel, which we call man—is generated by the supreme God in a more transcendent condition than most of his fellow-creatures. For he is the only creature among the earthly races of animated beings endued with superior reason and thought, in which the rest are deficient. And what is there, I do not say in man alone, but in all heaven and earth, more divine than reason, which, when it becomes ripe and perfect, is justly termed wisdom?

There exists, therefore, since nothing is better than reason, and since this is the common property of God and man, a certain aboriginal rational intercourse between divine and human natures. This reason, which is common to both, therefore, can be none other than right reason; and since this *right reason* is what we call *Law,* God and men are said by Law to be consociated. Between whom, since there is a communion of law, there must be also a communication of Justice.

Law and Justice being thus the common rule of immortals and mortals it follows that they are both the fellow citizens of one city and commonwealth. And if they are obedient to the same rule, the same authority and denomination, they may with still closer propriety be termed fellow citizens, since one celestial regency, one divine mind, one omnipotent Deity then regulates all their thoughts and actions.

This universe, therefore, forms one immeasurable Commonwealth and city, common alike to gods and mortals. And as in earthly states, certain particular laws, which we shall hereafter describe, govern the particular relationships of kindred tribes; so in the nature of things doth an universal law, far more magnificent and resplendent, regulate the affairs of that universal city where gods and men compose one vast association.

When we thus reason on universal nature, we are accustomed to reason after this method. We believe that in the long course of ages and the uninterrupted succession of celestial revolutions, the seed of the human race was sown on our plant, and being scattered over the earth, was animated by the divine gift of souls. Thus men retained from their terrestrial origin, their perishable and mortal bodies, while their immortal spirits were ingenerated by Deity. From which consideration we are bold to say that we possess a certain consanguinity and kindred fellowship with the celestials. And so far as we know, among all the varieties of animals, man alone retains the idea of the Divinity. And among men there is no nation so savage and ferocious as to deny the necessity of worshipping God, however ignorant it may be respecting the nature of his attributes. From whence we conclude that every man must recognize a Deity, who considers the origin of his nature and the progress of his life.

Now the law of virtue is the same in God and man, and cannot possibly be diverse. This virtue is nothing else than a nature perfect in itself, and developed in all its excellence. There exists therefore a similitude between God and man; nor can any knowledge be more appropriate and sterling than what relates to this divine similitude.

Nature, attentive to our wants, offers us her treasures with the most graceful profusion. And it is easy to perceive that the benefits which flow from her are true and veritable gifts, which Providence has provided on purpose for human enjoyment, and not the fortuitous productions of her exuberant fecundity. Her liberality appears, not only in the fruits and vegetables which gush from the bosom of the earth, but likewise in cattle and the beasts of the field. It is clear that some of these are intended for the advantage of mankind, a part for propagation, and a part for food. Innumerable arts have likewise been discovered by the teaching of nature; for her doth reason imitate, and skillfully discover all things necessary to the happiness of life.

With respect to man this same bountiful nature hath not merely allotted him a subtle and active spirit, but moreover favored him with physical senses, like so many guardians and messengers. Thus has she improved our understanding in relation to many obscure principles, and laid the foundation of practical knowledge; and in all respects molded our corporeal faculties to the service of our intellectual genius. For while she has debased the forms of other animals, who live to eat rather than eat to live, she has bestowed on man an erect stature, and an open countenance, and thus prompted him to the contemplation of heaven, the ancient home of his kindred immortals. So exquisitely, too, hath she fashioned the features of the human race, as to make them symbolic of the most recondite thoughts and sentiments. As for our two eloquent eyes (oculi nimis arguti) do they not speak forth every impulse and passion of our souls? And that which we call *expression,* in which we infinitely excel all the inferior animals, how marvellously it delineates all our speculations and feelings! Of this the Greeks well knew the meaning, though they had no word for it.

I will not enlarge on the wonderful faculties and qualities of the rest of the body, the modulation of the voice, and the power of oratory, which is perhaps the greatest instrument of our influence over human society. These matters do not belong to the occasion of our present discourse, and I think that Scipio has already sufficiently explained them in those books of mine which you have read.

As the Deity, therefore, was pleased to create man as the chief and president of all terrestrial creatures, so it is evident, without further argument, that human nature has made the greatest advances by its intrinsic energy; that nature, which without any other instruction than her own, has developed the first rude principles of the understanding, and strengthened and perfected reason to all the appliances of science and art.

You may well describe these topics as grand, which we are now briefly discussing. For of all the questions on which our philosophers argue, there is none which it is more important thoroughly to understand than this, *that man is born for justice, and that law and equity are not a mere establishment of opinion, but an institution of nature*. This truth will become still more apparent if we investigate the nature of human association and society.

There is no one thing more like to another, more homogeneous and analogous, than man is to man. And if the corruption of customs, and the variation of opinions, had not induced an imbecility of minds, and turned them aside from the course of nature, no one would more nearly resemble himself than all men would resemble all men. Therefore whatever definition we give of man, it must include the whole human race. And this is a good argument, that no portion of mankind can be heterogeneous or dissimilar from the rest; because, if this were the case, one definition could not include all men.

In fact, reason, which alone gives us so many advantages over beasts, by means of which we conjecture, argue, refute, discourse, and accomplish and conclude our designs, is assuredly common to all men; for the faculty of acquiring knowledge is similar in all human minds, though the knowledge itself may be endlessly diversified. By the same senses we all perceive the same objects, and that which strikes the sensibilities of the few, cannot be indifferent to those of the many. Those first rude elements of intelligence which, as I before observed, are the earliest developments of thought, are similarly exhibited by all men; and that faculty of speech which is the soul's interpreter, agrees in the ideas it conveys, though it may differ in the syllables that express them. And therefore there exists not a man in any nation, who, adopting his true nature for his true guide, may not improve in virtue.

Nor is this resemblance which all men bear to each other remarkable in those things only which accord to right reason. For it is scarcely less conspicuous in those corrupt practices by which right reason is most cruelly violated. For all men alike are captivated by voluptuousness, which is in reality no better than disgraceful vice, though it may seem to bear some natural relations to goodness; for by its delicious delicacy and luxury it insinuates error into the mind, and leads us to cultivate it as something salutary, forgetful of its poisonous qualities.

An error, scarcely less universal, induces us to shun death, as if it were annihilation; and to cling to life, because it keeps us in our present stage of existence, which is perhaps rather a misfortune than a desideratum. Thus, likewise, we erroneously consider pain as one of the greatest evils, not only on account of its present asperity, but also because it seems the precursor of mortality. Another common delusion obtains, which induces all mankind to associate renown with honesty, as if we are necessarily happy when we are renowned, and miserable when we happen to be inglorious.

In short, our minds are all similarly susceptible of inquietudes, joys, desires and fears; and if opinions are not the same in all men, it does not follow, for example, that the people of Egypt who deify dogs and cats, do not labor under superstition in the same way as other nations, though they may differ from them in the forms of its manifestation.

But in nothing is the uniformity of human nature more conspicuous than in its respect for virtue. What nation is there, in which kindness, benignity, gratitude, and mindfulness of benefits are not recommended? What nation in which arrogance, malice, cruelty, and unthankfulness, are not reprobated and detested! This uniformity of opinions, invincibly demonstrates that mankind was intended to compose one fraternal association. And to affect this, the faculty of reason must be improved till it instructs us in all the arts of well-living. . . .

It follows, then, in the line of our argument, *that nature made us just that we might participate our goods with each other, and supply each other's wants.* You observe in this discussion whenever I speak of nature, I mean *nature in its genuine purity,* and not in the corrupt state which is displayed by the depravity of evil custom, which is so great, that the natural and innate flame of virtue is often almost extinguished and stifled by the antagonist vices, which are accumulated around it.

But if our true nature would assert her rights, and teach men the noble lesson of the poet, who says "I am a man, therefore no human interest can be indifferent to me," then would justice be administered equally by all and to all. For nature hath not merely given us reason, but right reason, and consequently that law, which is nothing else than right reason enjoining what is good, and forbidding what is evil.

Now if nature hath given us law, she hath also given us justice—for as she has bestowed reason on all, she has equally bestowed the sense of justice on all. And therefore did Socrates deservedly execrate the man who first drew a distinction between the law of nature and the law of morals, for he justly conceived that this error is the source of most human vices.

It is to this essential union between the naturally honourable, and the politically expedient, that this sentence of Pythagoras refers: "Love is universal: let its benefits be universal likewise." From whence it appears that when a wise man is attached to a good man by that friendship whose rights are so extensive, that phenomenon takes place which is altogether incredible to worldlings, and yet it is a necessary consequence, that he loves himself not more dearly than he loves his friend. For how can a difference of interests arise when all interests are similar? If there could be such a difference of interests, however minute, it would be no longer a true friendship, which vanishes immediately when, for the sake of our own benefit, we would sacrifice that of our friend. . . .

[I will add a few considerations] in conformity with the method of the philosophers. I do not mean the older sages of philosophy, but those modern philosophers who keep a magazine of arguments in reserve, on every imaginable topic, and who, instead of discussing questions freely and unconstrainedly, will permit us to speak only in accordance with their logical arrangements and dialectical distinctions. These gentlemen will never allow that we have done justice to our subject, unless we demonstrate that nature is just, and justice is natural, in a distinct and scientific disputation. . . .

Was it the fear of punishment, and not the nature of the thing itself that ought to restrain mankind from wickedness, what, I would ask, could give villains the least uneasiness, abstracting from all fears of this kind? And yet none of them was ever so audaciously impudent, but he endeavored to justify what he had done by some law of nature, denied that fact, or else pretended a just sorrow for it. Now if the wicked have the confidence to appeal to these laws, with what profound respect ought good men to treat them?

There is the greater need, therefore, of insisting on the natural and unavoidable penalties of conscience. For if either direct punishment, or the fear of it, was what deterred from a vicious course of life, and not the turpitude of the thing itself, then none could be guilty of injustice, in a moral sense, and the greatest offenders ought rather to be called imprudent than wicked.

On the other hand, if we are determined to the practice of goodness, not by its own intrinsic excellence, but for the sake of some private advantage, we are cunning, rather than good men. What will not that man do in the dark who fears nothing but a witness and a judge? Should he meet a solitary individual in a desert place, with a large sum of money about him, and altogether unable to defend himself from being robbed, how would he behave? In such a case the man who we have represented to be honest from principle, and the nature of the thing itself, would converse with the stranger, assist him, and show him the way. But as to the man who does nothing for the sake of another, and measures everything by the advantage it brings to himself, it is obvious, I suppose, how such a one would act; and should he deny that he would kill the man or rob him of his treasure, his reason for this cannot be that he apprehends there is any moral turpitude in such actions, but only because he is afraid of a discovery, and the bad consequences that would thence ensue. A sentiment this, at which not only learned men, but even clowns must blush.

It is therefore an absurd extravagance in some philosophers to assert that all things are necessarily just, which are established by the civil laws and the institutions of the people. Are then the laws of tyrants just, simply because they are laws? If the thirty tyrants of Athens imposed certain laws on the Athenians, and if these Athenians were delighted with these tyrannical laws, are we therefore bound to consider these laws as just? For my own part, I do not think such laws deserve any greater estimation than that passed during our own interregnum, which ordained, that the dictator should be empowered to put to death with impunity, whatever citizens he pleased, without hearing them in their own defense.

There can be but one essential justice, which cements society, and one law which establishes this justice. This law is right reason, which is the true rule of all commandments and prohibitions. Whoever neglects this law, whether written or unwritten, is necessarily unjust and wicked.

But if justice consists in submission to written laws and national customs, and if, as the Epicureans persist in affirming, everything must be measured by utility alone, he who wishes to find an occasion of breaking such laws and customs, will be sure to discover it. So that real justice remains powerless if not supported by nature, and this pretended justice is overturned by that very utility which they call its foundation.

But this is not all. If nature does not ratify law, all the virtues lose their sway. What becomes of generosity, patriotism, or friendship? Where should we find the desire of benefitting our neighbors, or the gratitude that acknowledges kindness? For all these virtues proceed from our natural inclination to love and cherish our associates. This is the true basis of justice, and without this, not only the mutual charities of men, but the religious services of the gods, would become obsolete; for these are preserved, as I imagine, rather by the natural sympathy which subsists between divine and human beings, than by mere fear and timidity.

If the will of the people, the decrees of the senate, the adjudications of magistrates, were sufficient to establish justice, the only question would be how to gain suffrages, and to win over the votes of the majority, in order that corruption and spoliation, and the falsification of wills, should become lawful. But if the opinions and suffrages of foolish men had sufficient weight to outbalance the nature of things, might they not determine among them, that what is essentially bad and pernicious should henceforth pass for good and beneficial? Or why should not a law able to enforce injustice, take the place of equity? Would not this same law be able to change evil into good, and good into evil?

As far as we are concerned, we have no other rule capable of distinguishing between a good or a bad law, than our natural conscience and reason. These, however, enable us to separate justice from injustice, and to discriminate between the honest and the scandalous. For common sense has impressed in our minds the first principles of things, and has given us a general acquaintance with them, by which we connect with virtue every honorable and excellent quality, and with vice all that is abominable and disgraceful.

Now we must entirely take leave of our senses, ere we can suppose that law and justice have no foundation in nature, and rely merely on the transient opinions of men. We should not venture to praise the virtue of a tree or a horse, in which expression there is an abuse of terms, were we not convinced that this virtue was in their nature, rather than in our opinion. For a stronger reason, it is mainly with respect to the moral nature of things, that we ought to speak of honor and shame among men.

If opinion could determine respecting the character of universal virtue, it might also decide respecting particular or partial virtues. But who will dare to determine that a man is prudent and cautious in his moral disposition, from any external appearances? For virtue evidently lies in perfect rationality, and this resides in the inmost depths of our nature. The same remark applies to all honor and honesty, for we judge of true and false, creditable and discreditable, rather by their essential qualities than their external relations. Thus we judge according to their intrinsic nature, that rationality of life, which is virtue, must be ever constant and perpetual, and that inconstancy must necessarily be vicious.

We form an estimate of the opinions of youths, but not by their opinions. Those virtues and vices which reside in their moral natures, must not be measured by opinions. And so of all moral qualities, we must discriminate between honorable and dishonorable by reference to the essential nature of the things themselves.

The good we commend, must needs contain in itself something commendable. For as I before stated, goodness is not a mode of opinion: it is what it is, by the force of its very essence. If it were otherwise, opinion alone might constitute virtue and happiness, which is the most absurd of suppositions. And since we judge of good and evil by their nature, and since good and evil are the true constituents of honor and shame, we should judge in the same manner all honorable and shameful qualities, testing them by the law of nature, without prejudice or passion. But our steady attention to this moral law of nature is often too much disturbed by the dissension of men and the variation of opinions. We might perhaps obey this law of nature more exactly, if we attended more accurately to the evidence of our senses, which being absolutely natural, are less likely to be deceived by artificial objects. Those objects, indeed, which sometimes present to us one appearance, sometimes another, we term fictions of the senses; but it is far otherwise. For neither parent, nor nurse, nor master, nor poet, nor drama, deceive our senses; nor do popular prejudices seduce them. But our delusions are connected with corruption of our mental opinions. And this corruption is either superinduced by those causes of error I have enumerated, which, taking possession of the young and uneducated, betray them into a thousand perversities, or by that voluptuousness which is the mimic of goodness, implicated and interfused through all our senses—the prolific mother of all human disasters. For she so corrupts us by her bewitching blandishments that we no longer perceive that things may be essentially excellent, though they have none of this deliciousness and pruriency.

From what I have said on this subject, it may then easily be concluded, that justice and equity are desirable for their own sake. For all virtuous men love justice and equity, for what they are in themselves; and we cannot believe that such virtuous men should delude themselves by loving something which does not deserve their affection. Justice and right are therefore desirable and amiable in themselves; and if this is true of right, it must be true of all the moral virtues with which it is connected.

ST. AUGUSTINE

On the surface it may seem curious to include in a book containing representative selections from Western social thought a selection from St. Augustine, an early philosopher whose thought has more affiliations with theology than with sociology, with theodicy than with history. It illustrates nevertheless one of the reasons why a secular sociology could not flourish during the long centuries that followed upon the fall of Rome and, in addition, what sociology would have to be like today if it were an inquiry based upon Augustinian premises. It is also illustrative, of course, of the writings of the Fathers of the Christian Church, a corpus that comprises an important chapter in intellectual history.

Born in Numidia, in North Africa, Augustine (354-430) did not embrace the Christian faith until his thirty-third year. Although his mother was a Christian and his father a later convert, his education, intended originally for a career in the law, exposed him to such influences as Neo-Platonism, Manichaeism, skepticism, and finally Christianity. He became Bishop of Hippo in the year 396, at the age of forty-two, and devoted the remainder of his life to the problems, both theoretical and administrative, of the Church. The details of his life and career are recorded in his *Confessions.*

In *The City of God,* from which the following excerpts are taken, Augustine argues that the fall of Rome, far from being the fault of the Christians, as the adherents of the older religions contended, merely illustrated the fact that Rome was not the Eternal City but only one of a number of cities of this world, destined to enjoy its moment of glory and then to pass forever into history. The Eternal City was not of this earth, but was the City of God, a City where glory was permanent and salvation assured.

From *The City of God*

Now God, our good Master, teaching us in the two great commandments the love of Him, and the love of our neighbor, to love three things, God, our neighbor, and ourselves, and seeing he that loves God, offends not in loving himself; it follows that he ought to counsel his neighbor to love God, and to provide for him in the love of God, sure he is commanded to love him, as his own self. So must he do for his wife, children, family, and all men besides: and wish likewise that his neighbor would do as much for him, in his need: thus shall he be settled in peace and orderly concord with all the world. The order whereof is, first, to do no man hurt, and secondly, to help all that he can. So that his own have the first place in his care, and those, his place and order in human society affords him more conveniency to benefit. Whereupon St. Paul says, "He that provideth not for his own, and, namely, for them that be of his household, denieth the faith, and is worse than an infidel." For this is the foundation of domestic peace, which is, an orderly rule, and subjection in the parts of the family, wherein the provisors are the commanders, as the husband over his wife, parents over their children, and masters over their servants: and they that are provided for, obey, as the wives do their husbands, children their parents, and servants their masters. But in the family of the faithful man, the heavenly pilgrim, there the commanders are indeed the servants of those they seem to command, ruling not in ambition, but being bound by careful duty, not in proud sovereignty, but in nourishing pity.

NATURE'S FREEDOM, AND BONDAGE, CAUSED BY SIN: IN WHICH MAN IS A SLAVE TO HIS OWN PASSIONS, THOUGH HE BE NOT BONDSMAN TO ANY ONE BESIDES

Thus has nature's order prescribed, and man by God was thus created. "Let them rule," saith He, "over the fishes of the sea, and the fowls of the air, and over every thing that creepeth upon the earth." He made him reasonable, and lord only over the unreasonable, not over man, but over beasts. Whereupon the first holy men were rather shepherds than kings, God shewing herein what both the order of the creation desired, and what the merit of sin exacted. For justly was the burden of servitude laid upon the back of transgression. And therefore in all the Scriptures we never read the word servant, until such time as that just man Noah laid it as a curse upon his offending son. So that it was guilt, and not nature that gave original unto that name. The Latin word *servus,* had the first derivation from hence: those that were taken in the wars, being in the hands of the conquerors to massacre or to preserve, if they saved them, then were they called *servi,* or *servo,* "to save." Nor was this effected beyond the desert of sin. For in the justest war, the sin upon one side causes it; and if the victory fall to the wicked (as sometimes it may) it is God's decree to humble the conquered, either reforming their sins herein, or punishing them. Witness that holy man of God, Daniel, who, being in captivity, confessed upon his Creator that his sins, and the sins of the people were the real causes of that captivity.

Sin therefore is the mother of servitude, and first cause of man's subjection to man, which notwithstanding comes not to pass but by the direction of the highest, in whom is no injustice, and who alone knows best how to proportionate his punishment unto man's offenses, and he himself says: "Whosoever committeth sin is the servant of sin," and therefore many religious Christians are servants unto wicked masters, yet not unto freemen, for that which a man is addicted unto, the same is he slave unto. And it is a happier servitude to serve man than lust; for lust (to omit all the other passions) practices extreme tyranny upon the hearts of those that serve it, be it lust after sovereignty or fleshly lust. But in the peaceful orders of states, wherein one man is under another, as humility does benefit the servant, so does pride endamage the superior. But take a man as God created him at first, and so he is neither slave to man nor to sin. But penal servitude had the institution from that law which commands the conservation, and forbids the disturbance of nature's order: for if that law had not first been transgressed, penal servitude had never been enjoined.

Therefore the apostle warns servants to obey their masters and to serve them with cheerfulness, and good will: to the end that if they cannot be made free by their masters, they make their servitude a freedom to themselves, by serving them, not in deceitful fear, but in faithful love, until iniquity be overpassed, and all man's power and principality disannulled, and God only be all in all.

OF THE JUST LAW OF SOVEREIGNTY

Wherefore although our righteous forefathers had servants in their families, and according to their temporal estates, made a distinction between their servants and their children, yet in matter of religion (the fountain whence all eternal good flows), they provided for all their household with an equal respect unto each member thereof. This, nature's order prescribed, and hence came the name of, "The father of the family," a name which even the worst masters love to be called by. But such as merit that name truly, do care that all their families should continue in the service of God, as if they were all their own children, desiring that they should all be placed in the household of heaven, where command is wholly unnecessary, because then they are past their charge, having attained immortality, which until they be installed in, the masters are to endure more labor in their government, than the servants in their service. If any be disobedient, and offend this just peace, he is forthwith to be corrected, with strokes, or some other convenient punishment, whereby he may be reingraffed into the peaceful stock from whence his disobedience has torn him. For as it is no good turn to help a man unto a smaller good by the loss of a greater: no more is it the part of innocence by pardoning a small offense, to let it grow unto a fouler. It is the duty of an innocent to hurt no man, but, withal, to curb sin in all he can, and to correct sin in whom he can, that the sinner's correction may be profitable to himself, and his example a terror unto others. Every family then being part of the city, every beginning having relation unto some end, and every part tending to the integrity of the whole, it follows apparently, that the family's peace adheres unto the city's, that is, the orderly command, and obedience in the family, has real reference to the orderly rule and subjection in the city. So that "the father of the family" may fetch his instructions from the city's government, whereby he may proportionate the peace of his private estate, by that of the common.

THE GROUNDS OF THE CONCORD AND DISCORD BETWEEN THE CITIES OF HEAVEN AND EARTH

But they that live not according to faith, angle for all their peace in the sea of temporal profits, whereas the righteous live in full expectation of the glories to come, using the occurrences of this world, but as pilgrims, not to abandon their course towards God for mortal respects, but thereby to assist the infirmity of the corruptible flesh, and make it more able to encounter with toil and trouble. Wherefore the necessaries of this life are common, both to the faithful and the infidel, and to both their families, but the ends of their two usages thereof are far different.

The faithless, "worldly city" aims at earthly peace, and settles the self therein, only to have an uniformity of the citizens' wills in matters only pertaining to mortality. And the "Heavenly City," or rather that part thereof, which is as yet a pilgrim on earth and lives by faith, uses this peace also: as it should, it leaves this mortal life, wherein such a peace is requisite, and therefore lives (while it is here on earth) as if it were in captivity, and having received the promise of redemption and divers spiritual gifts as seals thereof, it willingly obeys such laws of the "temporal city" as order the things pertaining to the sustenance of this mortal life, to the end that both the cities might observe a peace in such things as are pertinent hereunto. But because that the "earthly city" has some members whom the Holy Scriptures utterly disallow, and who standing either too well affected to the devils, or being deluded by them, believed that each thing had a peculiar deity over it, and belonged to the charge of a several god: as the body to one, the soul to another, and in the body itself the head to one, the neck to another, and so of every member, as likewise of the soul, one had the wit, another the learning, a third the wrath, a fourth the desire, as also in other necessaries or accidents belonging to man's life, the cattle, the corn, the wine, the oil, the woods, the monies, the navigation, the wars, the marriages, the generations, each being a several charge unto a particular power, whereas the citizens of the "Heavenly State" acknowledged but one only God, to whom that worship, which is called λατρεία was peculiarly and solely due; hence came it that the "two hierarchies" could not be combined in one religion, but must needs dissent herein, so that the good part was fain to bear the pride and persecution of the bad, had not their own multitude sometimes, and the providence of God continually stood for their protection.

This "celestial society" while it is here on earth, increases itself out of all languages, never respecting the temporal laws that are made against so good and religious a practice: yet not breaking, but observing their diversity in divers nations, all which do tend unto the preservation of earthly peace, if they oppose not the adoration of one only God. So that you see, the "Heavenly City" observes and respects this temporal peace here on earth, and the coherence of men's wills in honest morality, as far as it may with a safe conscience; yea, and so far desires it, making use of it for the attainment of the peace eternal, which is so truly worthy of that name, as that the orderly and uniform combination of men in the fruition of God, and of one another in God, is to be accounted the reasonable creature's only peace, which being once attained, mortality is banished, and life then is the true life-indeed, nor is the carnal body any more an encumbrance to the soul, by corruptibility, but is now become spiritual, perfected and entirely subject unto the sovereignty of the will.

This peace is that unto which the pilgrim in faith refers the other which he has here in his pilgrimage, and then lives he according to faith, when all that he does for the obtaining hereof is by himself referred unto God, and his neighbor withal, because being a citizen, he must not be all for himself, but sociable in his life and actions.

ST. THOMAS AQUINAS

It was the great achievement of St. Thomas Aquinas (1225-1274) to reconcile the philosophy of the pagan Aristotle with the theological doctrines of the Christian Church. Introduced into Western Europe through Arabic and Jewish sources, Aristotle's works were banned at first both at Oxford and at Paris. So thorough was the task that Thomas accomplished, however, that in less than a century the Thomistic Aristotle had become the orthodox and indeed the only authority on all questions, except those answered in the Bible itself. St. Thomas became, many centuries later, by edict of Pope Leo XIII in 1879, the official philosopher of the Roman Catholic Church.

Born of an aristocratic family in Naples, Thomas entered the Dominican Order and studied at Cologne and Paris under the encyclopedic Schoolman, Albertus Magnus, and taught afterward at Naples, Cologne, Rome, and Paris. His most fruitful career was terminated by an early death, but so monumental is his work that he is today regarded by Catholics and non-Catholics alike as one of the greatest philosophers of all time.

His sociological theory, like the rest of his work, exhibits a harmony between Christianity and Aristotelianism. He agreed with Aristotle that man is a social animal and that human society arises through a natural community of interests. Society is ruled, however, by four kinds of law—eternal, natural, divine, and human—of which the first, implicit in the divine order of the universe, is the most basic. It is natural that men living in society be ruled by somebody and it is better that they be ruled by one than by many. These last two points are argued in the selections that follow from St. Thomas's little book, *On the Governance of Rulers,* written about 1259 for the King of Cyprus.

From *On the Governance of Rulers**

Men Living Together Must Be Diligently Ruled By Somebody

The first step in our undertaking must be to set forth what is to be understood by the term "king." In all things which are ordered towards some end, wherein this or that course may be adopted, some directive principle is needed through which the due end may be reached by the most direct route. A ship, for example, which moves in different directions, according to the impulse of the changing winds, would never reach its destination were it not brought to port by the skill of the pilot.

Now, man has an end to which his whole life and all his actions are ordered; for man is an intelligent agent, and it is clearly the part of an intelligent agent to act in view of an end. Men, however, adopt different methods in proceeding towards their proposed end, as the diversity of men's pursuits and actions clearly indicates. Consequently man needs some directive principle to guid him towards his end.

But, the light of reason is placed by nature in every man, to guide him in his acts towards his end. Were men intended to live alone, as many animals do, he would require no other guide to his end. Then would each man be a king unto himself, under God, the highest King, inasmuch as he would direct himself in his acts by the light of reason given him from on high.

However, it is natural for man to be a social and political animal, to live in a group, even more so than all other animals, as the very needs of his nature indicate. For all other animals nature has prepared food, hair as a covering, teeth, horns, claws as means of defense, or at least speed in flight. Man, on the other hand, was created without any natural provision for these things. But, instead of them all he was endowed with reason, by the use of which he could procure all these things for himself by the work of his hands. But one man alone is not able to procure

* Translated by Gerald B. Phelan. Reprinted by permission of the Pontifical Institute of Mediaeval Studies, Toronto.

them all for himself; for one man could not sufficiently provide for life, unassisted. It is, therefore, natural that man should live in company with his fellows.

Moreover, all other animals are able to discern by inborn skill what is useful and what is injurious; just as the sheep naturally regards the wolf as his enemy. Some animals even recognize by natural instinct certain medicinal herbs and other things necessary for their life. Man, however, has a natural knowledge of the things which are essential for his life only in a general fashion, inasmuch as he has power of attaining knowledge of the particular things necessary for human life by reasoning from universal principles. But it is not possible for one man to arrive at a knowledge of all these things by his own individual reason. It is, therefore, necessary for man to live in a group so that each one may assist his fellows, and different men may be occupied in seeking by their reason to make different discoveries, one, for example, in medicine, one in this and another in that.

This point is, further, most plainly evidenced by the fact that the use of speech is a prerogative proper to man. By this means one man is able fully to express his conceptions to others. Other animals, it is true, express their feelings to one another in a general way, as a dog may express anger by barking and other animals may give vent to their feelings in various manners. So man communicates with his kind more completely than any other animal known to be gregarious, such as the crane, the ant, and the bee. With this in mind, therefore, Solomon says, in Ecclesiastes iv:9—"It is better that two should be together than one: for they have the advantage of their company."

If, therefore, it is natural for man to live in the society of many, it is necessary that there exist among men some means by which the group may be governed. For where there are many men together, and each one is looking after his own interest, the group would be broken up and scattered unless there were also someone to take care of what appertains to the common weal. In like manner the body of a man, or any other animal, would disintegrate unless there were a general regulating force within the body which watches over the common good of all the members. With this in mind Solomon says (Prov. xi:14—"Where there is no governor, the people shall fall."

Indeed it is reasonable that this happen, for what is proper and what is common are not identical. Things differ by what is proper to each: they are united by what they have in common, For, diversity of effects is due to diversity of causes. Consequently, there must exist something which impels towards the common good of the many, over and above that which impels towards the private good of each individual. Wherefore, also in all things that are ordained towards a single end there is something to be found which rules the rest. Thus in the corporeal universe, other bodies are regulated, according to a certain order of divine providence, by the first body, namely, the celestial body, and all bodies are controlled by a rational creature. So, too, in the individual man, the soul rules the body, and among the parts of the soul, the irascible and the concupiscible parts are ruled by the reason. Likewise, among the members of a body, one is the principal and moves all the others, as the heart or the head. Therefore, in every group there must be some governing power.

It happens, however, in certain things which are ordained towards an end, that one may proceed in a right way and also in a wrong way. And so, too, in the government of a group there is a right way and a wrong way. Now, anything whatsoever is rightly directed when it is guided towards its proper (*convenientem*) end, wrongly when it is guided towards an improper (*non convenientem*) end. The proper (*conveniens*) end of a group of free men is different from that of a group of serfs; for the free man is one who is for his own sake (*causa sui*), the serf is one whose whole being belongs to another, If, therefore, a group of free men is governed by their ruler for the common good of the group, that government will be right and just, as is suitable to free men. If, however, the government is organized, not for the common good of the group but for the private interest of the ruler, it will be an unjust and perverted government. The Lord, therefore, threatens such rulers, saying (Ezech. xxxiv:2—"Woe to the shepherds that feed themselves [because they seek their own interests]: should not the flocks be fed by the shepherds?" For shepherds indeed should seek the good of their flocks and every ruler, the good of the multitude subject to him. Now, if an unjust government is carried on by one man alone who seeks his own benefit from his rule, and not the good of the multitude subject to him, such a ruler is called a tyrant—a word derived from strength—because he oppresses by might instead of ruling by justice. Thus among the ancients, all powerful men were called tyrants. But if the unjust government is carried on, not by one, but by several, especially if they be few, it is called an oligarchy, that is, the rule of a few. This occurs when a few, who differ from the tyrant only by the fact that they are more than one, oppress the people by means of their wealth. If, however, the bad government is carried on by the multitude it is called a democracy, that is, control by the populace. This comes about when the plebeian populace by force of numbers oppress the wealthy. In this way the whole people will be as one tyrant.

In like manner we must divide just governments. If the government is administered by a multitude, it is given the name of a polity: as, for instance, when a body of warriors exercises dominion over a city or a province. But, if it is administered by a few, but virtuous, men, this kind of government is called an aristocracy, that is, the best governance or governance by the best men, who for this reason are called the nobility (*optimates*). But, if a just government is in the hands of one man alone, he is properly called a king. Wherefore the Lord says by the mouth of Ezechiel (xxvii:24—"My servant, David, shall be king over them and all of them shall have one Shepherd." From this it is clearly shown that the idea of king implies that he be one man who is chief and that he be a shepherd who seeks the common good of the multitude and not his own advantage.

Now, since men must live in a group, because they are not sufficient unto themselves to procure the necessities of life were they to remain solitary, it follows that a society will be the more perfect the more it is sufficient unto itself to procure the necessities of life. There is, indeed, to some extent sufficiency for life in one family of one household, namely in so far as pertains to the natural acts of nourishment and the begetting of offspring and other things of this kind; it exists, furthermore, in one village with regard to those things which belong to one trade, but it exists in a city, which is a perfect community, with regard to all the necessities of life; but still more in a province because of the need of fighting together and of mutual help against enemies.

So, the man who rules a perfect community, that is, a city or a province, is called a king *par excellence:* he who rules a home is called a father of the family, not a king. Still, he bears a certain resemblance to a king, on account of which, kings are sometimes called the fathers of peoples.

It is plain, therefore, from what has been said, that a king is one who rules the people of one city or province and rules them for the public good. Wherefore Solomon says (Eccles. v:8)—"The King ruleth over all the land subject to him."

It Is More Expedient That a Multitude of Men Living Together Be Ruled by One Man Rather Than by Many

Having set forth these preliminary points we must now inquire what is better for a province or a city; whether to be ruled by one man or by many. Now this may be considered from the very purpose of government. For the aim of any ruler should be directed towards securing the welfare of whatever he undertakes to rule. The duty of the pilot, for instance, is to preserve his ship amidst the perils of the sea and to bring it unharmed to the port of safety. Now, the welfare and safety of a multitude formed into a society is the preservation of its unity, which is called peace, and which, if taken away, the benefit of social life is lost and moreover the multitude in its disagreement becomes a burden to itself. The chief concern of the ruler of a multitude, therefore, should be to procure the unity of peace, and it is not legitimate for him to deliberate whether he shall establish peace in the multitude subject to him, just as a physician does not deliberate whether he shall heal the sick man encharged to him. For no one should deliberate about an end which he is obliged to seek, but only about the means to attain that end. Wherefore, the Apostle, having commended the unity of the faithful people, says (Eph. iv:3)—"Be ye careful to keep the unity of the spirit in the bond of peace." The more efficacious, therefore, a government is in keeping the unity of peace, the more useful it will be. For we call that more useful which leads the better to the end. Now it is manifest that what is itself one can more efficaciously bring about unity than several: just as the most efficacious cause of heat is that which is by its nature hot. Therefore the rule of one man is more useful than the rule of many.

Furthermore, it is evident that several persons could by no means keep a multitude from harm (*conservant*) if they totally disagreed. For a certain union is necessary among them if they are to rule at all: several men, for instance, could not pull a ship in one direction unless joined together in some fashion. Now several are said to be united according as they come closer to being one. So one man rules better than several who come near being one.

Again, whatever is in accord with nature is best: for in all things nature does what is best. Now, every natural governance is governance by one. In the multitude of bodily members there is one which moves them all, namely, the heart; and among the powers of the soul one power presides as chief, namely, the reason. Even among bees there is one queen (*rex*) and in the whole universe there is One God, Maker and Ruler of all things. And this is reasonable. For every multitude is derived from unity. Wherefore, artificial things imitate natural things, and since a work of art is better according as it attains a closer likeness to what is in nature, it necessarily follows that it is best, in the case of a human multitude, that it be ruled by one person.

This is also evident from experience; for provinces or cities which are not ruled by one person are torn with dissensions and are tossed about without peace so that the complaint seems to be fulfilled which the Lord uttered through the Prophet (Jerm. xii:10)—"Many pastors have destroyed my vineyard." But, on the contrary, provinces and cities which are ruled under one king enjoy peace, flourish in justice and delight in prosperity. Hence, the Lord by His prophets promises to His people as a great reward that He will give them one head and that one Prince will be in the midst of them.

DANTE

Tired of the strife that afflicted his native Florence, from which he was exiled for nineteen years, Dante Alighieri (1265-1321), the great Italian poet, sought a formula that would lead to peace and tranquillity. For Dante was not only a poet; he was as well a scholar, statesman, and political philosopher. His contribution to political philosophy was the *De Monarchia,* a work called by Lord Bryce an epitaph for a world that was past rather than a prophecy of a new world to come.

The old world, the medieval world, was a unitary one in almost every respect. It had one language, the Latin; one law, the Roman; one religion, Christianity; one Church, the Holy Universal Catholic Church; one art form, the Gothic; and one polity, feudalism. But it had two governments or "two swords," church and state, *sacerdotium* and *imperium,* and the conflict that raged between them for temporal power. In an effort to solve or at least to soften this conflict Dante wrote his *De Monarchia.*

In this book, selections from which are reprinted in the following pages, Dante exhibited a clear nostalgia for the Roman Empire and the *Pax Romana.* Believing with Aristotle that man is by nature a social animal who nevertheless requires government for the regulation of group life, he addressed himself to the question of what kind of government this ought to be. For him the answer was a world monarchy, an empire holding sway over all communities and deriving its authority not through the Church but directly from God. It is an answer, as can be seen, that looks backward rather than forward, to imperial Rome rather than to the new national states that were even then beginning to develop.

From *De Monarchia*

BOOK I

CHAPTER II

The temporal monarchy, then, which is called empire is "a unique princedom extending over all persons in time," or, "in and over those things which are measured by time"; and there rise three main enquiries concerning the same: for in the first place we may inquire and examine whether it is needful for the well-being of the world; in the second, whether the Roman people rightfully assumed to itself the function of monarchy; and in the third, whether the authority of the monarchy depends immediately upon God, or upon some other minister or vicar of God.

But inasmuch as every truth which is not a first principle is demonstrated by reference to one that is, it behooves us in every inquiry to be clear as to the first principle to which we are to return by analysis, in order to establish the certainty of all such propositions as may afterwards be laid down. . . .

That thing, then, if there is any, which is the goal of the entire civilization of the human race, will give us this first principle, a reduction to which will be held a sufficient explanation of everything to be proved hereafter. But it would be folly to suppose that there is a goal of this civilization and a goal of that, but no one goal of all civilizations.

CHAPTER III

So now we must consider what is the goal of human civilization as a whole, which, when we see, more than half our work will be done, according to the Philosopher *Ad Nicomachum*. And to understand the point in question we must note that like as there is an end for which nature produces the thumb, and another than this for which she produces the whole hand, and again another than either for which the arm, and another than all of these for which the whole man, so there is one end for which she produces the individual man, another for which the domestic group, another for which the district, another for which the city-state, and another for which the kingdom; and lastly, there is an ultimate goal for which the eternal God, by his art, which is nature, brings into being the human race in its universality. And it is this last for which we are now seeking as the first principle to direct our inquiry.

Wherefore be it known in the first place that God and nature makes naught superfluous, but all that comes into being is for some function. For no created being is a final goal in the intention of the Creator, as Creator; but rather is the proper function of that being the goal. Wherefore it comes to pass that the proper function does not come into existence for the sake of the being, but the latter for the sake of the former.

There is, then, some function proper to humanity as a whole for which that same totality of men is ordained in so great multitude, to which function neither one man nor one family, nor one district nor one city-state, nor any individual kingdom may attain. And what this function is will be obvious if the specific potentiality of mankind generally be made clear. I say, then, that no capacity which is shared by many beings, differing in species, is the specific capacity of any one of them. For since that which is specific constitutes a species, it would follow that one essence would be specifically assigned to several species, which is impossible. The specific capacity, then, which differentiates man is not merely *being,* taken without qualification, for this he shares with the elements; neither *compound being,* for this we find in the minerals; nor *animated being,* for this is in plants; nor *apprehension,* for this is shared by the brutes; but *apprehension by means of the potential intellect,* which mode of being is not competent to any other save man, either above him or below. (For although there are other beings which have intellect, as man has, yet theirs is not potential intellect, as is man's; inasmuch as each of these beings is an intellectual species, and naught else; and their being is no other than the act of continuous understanding, else they were not sempiternal.) It is plain, then, that the specific potentiality of humanity as such is a potentiality or capacity of intellect.

And since that same potentiality cannot all be reduced to actuality at the same time by one man, or by any of the limited associations distinguished above, there must needs be multiplicity in the human race, in order for the whole of this potentiality to be actualized thereby. Like as there must be a multiplicity of things generable in order that the whole potentiality of first matter may always be in act; otherwise we should have to grant the existence of sejunct potentiality, which is impossible. And with this Averroes agrees in his commentary on the writings *De Anima*.

Moreover, the intellectual faculty of which I am speaking deals not only with universal forms or species, but also, by a kind of extension, with particular ones. Whence it is commonly said that the speculative intellect by extension becomes the practical intellect, the end of which is *doing* and *making*. And I draw this distinction because there are things to be *done* which are regulated by political wisdom, and things to be *made,* which are regulated by art. But they are all alike handmaids of speculation, as the supreme function for which the Prime Excellence brought the human race into being. And now we have already reached a point at which that saying of the *Politics* begins to be luminous: "The intellectually vigorous have natural sway over others."

CHAPTER IV

It has been sufficiently shown that the work proper to the human race, taken as a whole, is to keep the whole capacity of the potential intellect constantly actualised, primarily for speculation, and secondarily (by extension, and for the sake of the other) for action.

And since it is with the whole as it is with the part, and it is the fact that in sedentary quietness the individual man is perfected in knowledge and in wisdom, it is evident that in the quiet or tranquillity of peace the human race is most freely and favorably disposed towards the work proper to it (which is almost divine, even as it is said "Thou hast made him a little lower than the angels"). Whence it is manifest that universal peace is the best of all those things which are ordained for our blessedness. And that is why there rang out to the shepherds from on high, not riches, not pleasures, not honors, not length of life, not health, not strength, not beauty, but peace. For the celestial soldiery proclaims, "Glory to God in the highest; and, on earth, peace to men of good will." Hence, also, "Peace be with you" was the salutation of him who was the salvation of man. For it was meet that the supreme savior should utter the supreme salutation. And likewise his disciples saw good to preserve this custom, and amongst them Paul, as all may see in his salutations.

Our exposition, then, has made clear what is the better means (or rather the best) whereby the human race attains to its proper work. And thus we perceive the directest means of approach to that whereto as to their ultimate goal all our doings are directed, which directest means is universal peace. Therefore let this underlie the following arguments, as that first principle which we needed (as aforesaid) for a mark, set up in advance; into which, as into the most manifest truth, whatsoever is to be proved must be resolved. . . .

CHAPTER XIII

Having set forth and refuted the errors on which they chiefly rely who say that the authority of the Roman prince depends on the Roman pontiff, we must return to the demonstration of the truth as to this third matter which was laid down for discussion from the beginning. And this truth will be sufficiently unfolded if I show, under the principle of inquiry which we have laid down, that the said authority depends immediately upon the summit of all being, which is God. And this will be shown if we either disprove the church's authority over it (since no other is even alleged) or prove by direct demonstration that it depends immediately on God.

Now that the authority of the church is not the cause of the imperial authority is thus proved. If, while one thing does not exist or is not exercising its virtue, another thing has its full virtue, the first thing is not the cause of that virtue. But when the church did not exist, or was not exercising its virtue, the empire had its full virtue. Therefore the church is not the cause of the virtue of the empire, and not of its authority either, since its virtue and authority are the same. Let the church be A, the empire B, the authority or virtue of the empire C. If when A does not exist, C is in B, it is impossible that A can be the cause of C being in B; since it is impossible for the effect to precede its cause. Further, if, when A is not in action C is in B, then of necessity A is not the cause of C being in B; for it is necessary for the production of an effect that the cause (especially the efficient cause of which we are speaking) should first be in action.

The major proposition of this demonstration is explained by the terms; the second, Christ and the church confirms, Christ by his birth and death as set forth above, the church when Paul in the Acts of the Apostles says to Festus, "I stand at the judgment seat of Caesar where I must be judged"; and also when the angel of God says to Paul a little after, "Fear not, Paul. It behooves thee to stand before Caesar." And below Paul says again to the Jews in Italy, "Now when the Jews opposed I was compelled to appeal to Caesar, not as having aught of which to accuse my nation, but that I might snatch my soul from death." But if Caesar had not already possessed authority to judge temporal things, neither would Christ have supported his claims, nor would the angel have announced those words, nor would he who said, "I desire to be released and to be with Christ" have appealed to a judge who was not competent.

And if Constantine had not possessed authority over the patronage of the Church, what he deputed to her from the empire he could not have deputed of right, and thus the church would be wrongfully enjoying that grant, since God will have offerings without spot, according to that of Leviticus, "every offering which ye shall bring to the Lord shall be without leaven," which precept, though it seems to address those who grant, nevertheless consequentially applies to those who receive. For it were foolish to suppose that God would have that to be received which he forbids to be offered—as indeed in that same book the command is given to the Levites "Pollute not your souls nor touch aught of theirs, lest ye be unclean." But to say that the church thus wrongfully enjoys the patrimony deputed her is most unseemly; therefore that is false from which it follows.

CHAPTER XIV

Further, if the church had power to give the Roman prince his authority, she would either have it from God, or from herself, or from some emperor, or from the universal consent of mortals, or at least the majority of them. There is no other crevice through which this power could have flowed to the church. But she has it not from any of these. Therefore she has not the said power at all.

Now that she has it not from any of these is shown as follows. If she had received it from God, it would have been either by divine or by natural law (for what is received from nature is received from God, though the proposition cannot be converted). But it is not by natural law; for nature imposes laws only on her own effects, since God cannot be insufficient where he produces aught into being without secondary agents. Wherefore since the church is not an effect of nature but of God, who says, "On this rock will I build my church," and elsewhere, "I have finished the work thou gavest me to do," it is manifest that nature did not give laws to her.

But neither is it by divine law, for every divine law is held in the bosom of the two Testaments. In which bosom I cannot find that anxiety or care concerning temporal things was commended to the priesthood, either former or latter. Nay, rather I find that the former priests were expressly excluded therefrom, as is plain from those of God *Ad Moysen,* and the like of the latter priests by those of Christ *Ad Discipulos*. But they could not have been relieved of this care if the authority of the temporal regimen had been derived from the priesthood, since at any rate anxiety would press upon them concerning due provision in granting the authorization, and afterwards in continuous watching lest he whom they had authorized should wander from the path of right.

Now that she did not receive it from herself is easily shown. There is naught that can give what it has not got. Wherefore everything that effects anything must already be in act that which it contemplates effecting, as is seen in what is written *De Simpliciter Ente*. But it is clear that if the church gave herself that virtue she cannot have had it before she gave it; and thus she would have given herself what she had not got, which is impossible.

And that she did not receive it from any emperor is sufficiently plain from what has been set forth above.

And that she had it not from the consent of all, or of the majority of men, who doubts? Since not only all the Asiatics and Africans but the greater part of those dwelling in Europe would repudiate the thought. Nay! It is wearisome to bring proofs of things absolutely manifest.

MARSILIUS OF PADUA

Little is known of the life of Marsilius (or Marsiglio) of Padua (1270-1342) and there is even uncertainty as to the dates of his birth and death. In 1324, however, he published one of the great essays in political philosophy and sociology in the medieval period; namely, his *Defensor Pacis,* or Defender of the Peace. A devastating criticism of the Church's role in secular government and secular affairs, Marsilius' book contains a thoroughgoing and systematic treatment of the origin both of the state and of society. In general he adopted a utilitarian approach, believing that, since the family as one form of social grouping was not adequate to satisfy the needs of men, other and larger groupings came into being through an impulse to cooperation. Unfortunately, men are not only cooperative but also competitive and combative; and thus justice and morality arise to define what actions are to be commended and what are to be restrained. The rules that result make up the natural law.

Natural law, however, needs to be enforced and the state and government are therefore necessary to complete the organization of society. Sentiments like these, heavily based upon utility and rationality, seem entirely sensible to us today. In the period in which Marsilius wrote, however, they represented a radical departure from the accepted scheme of things. In the selection that follows, Marsilius maintains that the establishment of authority and the law belongs not to a single man and not to the few but to the whole body of citizens.

From *Defensor Pacis**

Authority Established by Election

We must next discuss that efficient cause of the laws which is capable of being demonstrated. For I do not intend to deal here with that method of establishing laws which can be effected by the immediate act or oracle of God apart from the human will, or which has been so effected in the past. It was by this method, as we have said, that the Mosaic law was established; but I shall not deal with it here even insofar as it contains commands with regard to civil acts for the status of the present world. I shall discuss the establishment of only those laws and governments which emerge immediately from the decision of the human mind.

Let us say, to begin with, that it can pertain to any citizen to discover the law taken materially and in its third sense, as the science of civil justice and benefit. Such inquiry, however, can be carried on more appropriately and be completed better by those men who are able to have leisure, who are older and experienced in practical affairs, and who are called "prudent men," than by the mechanics who must bend all their efforts to acquiring the necessities of life. But it must be remembered that the true knowledge or discovery of the just and the beneficial, and of their opposites, is not law taken in its last and most proper sense, whereby it is the measure of human civil acts, unless there is given a coercive command as to its observance, or it is made by way of such a command, by someone through whose authority its transgressors must and can be punished. Hence, we must now say who has the authority to make such a command and to punish its transgressors. This, indeed, is to inquire into the legislature or the maker of the law.

Let us say, then, in accordance with the truth and the counsel of Aristotle in the *Politics,* Book III, Chapter 6, that the legis-

* Translated by Alan Gewirth. Reprinted by arrangement with the Columbia University Press.

lator, or the primary and proper efficient cause of the law, is the people or the whole body of citizens, or the weightier part thereof, through its election or will expressed by words in the general assembly of the citizens, commanding or determining that something be done or omitted with regard to civil human acts under threat of temporal punishment. By the *weightier part* I mean to take into consideration the quantity and the quality of the persons in that community over which the law is made. The aforesaid whole body of citizens or the weightier part thereof is the legislator regardless of whether it makes the law directly by itself or entrusts the making of it to some person or persons, who are not and cannot be the legislator in the absolute sense, but only in a relative sense and for a particular time and in accordance with the authority of the primary legislator. And I say further that the laws and anything else established through election must receive their necessary approval by the same primary authority and no other, whatever be the case with regard to certain ceremonies or solemnities, which are required not for the being of the matters elected but for their well-being, since the election would be no less valid even if these ceremonies were not performed. Moreover, by the same authority must the laws and other things established through election undergo addition, subtraction, complete change, interpretation, or suspension, insofar as the exigencies of time or place or other circumstances make any such action opportune for the common benefit. And by the same authority, also, must the laws be promulgated or proclaimed after their enactment, so that no citizen or foreigner who is delinquent in observing them may be excused because of ignorance.

A citizen I define in accordance with Aristotle in the *Politics*, Book III, Chapters 1, 3, and 7, as one who participates in the civil community in the government or the deliberative or judicial function according to his rank. By this definition, children, slaves, foreigners, and women are distinguished from citizens, although in different ways. For the sons of citizens are citizens in proximate potentiality, lacking only in years. The weightier part of the citizens should be viewed in accordance with the honorable custom of politics or else should be determined in accordance with the doctrine of Aristotle in the *Politics*, Book VI, Chapter 2.

Having thus defined the citizen and the weightier part of the citizens, let us return to our proposed objective, namely, to demonstrate that the human authority to make laws belongs only to the whole body of the citizens or to the weightier part thereof. Our first proof is as follows. The absolutely primary human authority to make or establish human laws belongs only to those men from whom alone the best laws can emerge. But these are the whole body of the citizens, or the weightier part thereof, which represents that whole body; since it is difficult or impossible for all persons to agree upon one decision, because some men have a deformed nature, disagreeing with the common decision through singular malice or ignorance. The common benefit should not, however, be impeded or neglected because of the unreasonable protest or opposition of these men. The authority to make or establish laws, therefore, belongs only to the whole body of the citizens or to the weightier part thereof.

The first proposition of this demonstration is very nearly self-evident, although its force and its ultimate certainty can be grasped from what has been said earlier. The second proposition, that is, that the best law is made only through the hearing and command of the entire multitude, I prove by assuming with Aristotle in the *Politics,* Book III, Chapter 7, that the best law is that which is made for the common benefit of the citizens. As Aristotle said: "That is presumably right (i.e., in the laws) which is for the common benefit of the state and the citizens." But that this is best achieved only by the whole body of the citizens or by the weightier part thereof, which is assumed to be the same thing, I show as follows: that at which the entire body of the citizens aims intellectually and emotionally is more certainly judged as to its truth and more diligently considered as to its common utility. For a defect in some proposed law can be better noted by the greater number than by any part thereof, since every whole, or at least every corporeal whole, is greater in mass and in virtue than any part of it taken separately. Moreover, the common utility of law is better considered by the entire multitude, because no one knowingly harms himself. Anyone can look to see whether a proposed law leans toward the benefit of one or a few persons more than of the others or of the community, and can protest against it. Such, however, would not be the case were the law made by one or a few persons, considering their own private benefit rather than that of the community.

Another argument to the principal conclusion is as follows. The authority to make the law belongs only to those men whose making of it will cause the law to be better observed or observed at all. Only the whole body of the citizens are such men. To them, therefore, belongs the authority to make the law. The first proposition of this demonstration is very nearly self-evident, for a law would be useless unless it were observed. Hence Aristotle said in the *Politics,* Book IV, Chapter 6: "Laws are not well ordered when they are well made but not obeyed." He also said in Book VI, Chapter 5: "Nothing is accomplished by forming opinions about justice and not carrying them into effect." The second proposition I prove as follows. That law is better observed by every citizen which each one seems to have imposed upon himself. But such is the law which is made through the hearing and command of the entire multitude of the citizens. The first proposition of this prosyllogism is almost self-evident: "for since the state is a community of free men," as is written in the *Politics,* Book III, Chapter 4, every citizen must be free, and not undergo someone else's despotism, i.e., slavish dominion. But this would not be the case if one or a few of the citizens by their own authority made the law over the whole body of citizens. For those who thus made the law would be despots over the others, and hence such a law, however good it was, would be endured only with reluctance, or not at all, by the rest of the citizens, the more ample part. Having suffered contempt, they would protest against it, and not having been called upon to make it, they would not observe it. On the other hand, a law made by the hearing or consent of the whole multitude, even though it were less useful, would be willingly observed and endured by every one of the citizens, because then each would seem to have set the law upon himself, and hence would have no protest against it, but would rather tolerate it with equanimity. The second proposition of the first syllogism I also prove in this way: the power to cause the law to be observed belongs only to those men to whom belongs coercive force over the transgressors of the law. But these men are the whole body of citizens, or the weightier part thereof. Therefore, to them alone belongs the authority to make the law.

The principal conclusion is also proved in this way. That practical matter whose proper establishment is of greatest importance for the common sufficiency of the citizens in this life, and whose poor establishment threatens harm for the community, must be established by the whole body of the citizens. But such a matter is the law. Therefore, the establishment of the law pertains to the whole body of the citizens. The major proposition of this demonstration is almost self-evident. For men came together to the civil community in order to attain what was beneficial for sufficiency of life, and to avoid the opposite. Those matters, therefore, which can affect the benefit and harm of all ought to be known and heard by all, in order that they may attain the beneficial and repel the opposite. Such matters are the laws, as was assumed in the minor proposition. For in the laws being rightly made consists a large part of the whole common sufficiency of men, whereas under bad laws there arise unbearable slavery, oppression, and misery of the citizens, the final result of which is that the state is destroyed.

Again, and this is an abbreviation and summary of the previous demonstrations: the authority to make laws belongs only to the whole body of the citizens, as we have said, or else it belongs to one or a few men. But it cannot belong to one man alone, for through ignorance or malice or both, this one man could make a bad law, looking more to his own private benefit than to that of the community, so that the law would be tyrannical. For the same reason, the authority to make laws cannot belong to a few; for they too could sin, as before, in making the law for the benefit of a certain few and not for the common benefit, as can be seen in oligarchies. The authority to make the laws belongs, therefore, to the whole body of citizens or to the weightier part thereof, for precisely the opposite reason. For since all the citizens must be measured by the law in due proportion, and no one knowingly harms or wishes injustice to himself, it follows that all or most wish a law conducing to the common benefit of the citizens.

From these same demonstrations it can also be proved, merely by changing the minor term, that the approval, interpretation, and suspension of the laws pertain to the authority of the legislator alone. And the same must be thought of everything else which is established by election. For the authority to approve or disapprove rests with those who have the primary authority to elect, or with those to whom they have granted this authority of election. For otherwise, if the part could dissolve, by its own authority, what had been established by the whole, the part would be greater than the whole, or at least equal to it.

Is the Whole Body Fit to Rule?

Objections will be made to our above statements, to the effect that the authority to make or establish laws does not belong to the whole body of the citizens. The first objection is that those who are vicious and undiscerning in most cases should not make the law. For these two sins, malice and ignorance, must be excluded from the legislator, and it was to avoid them in civil judgments that we upheld the necessity of law. But the people or the whole body of citizens have these sins; for men in most cases seem to be vicious and stupid: "The number of the stupid is infinite," as is said in the first chapter of Ecclesiastes. Another objection is that it is very difficult, or impossible, to harmonize the views of many vicious and unintelligent persons; but such is not the case with the few and virtuous. It is more useful, therefore, that the law be made by the few than by the whole body of the citizens or the overwhelming majority of them. Again, in every civil community the wise and learned are few in comparison with the multitude of the unlearned. Since, therefore, the law is more usefully made by the wise and learned than by the unlearned and uncultivated, it seems that the authority to make laws belongs to the few, not to the many or to all. Furthermore, that which can be done by fewer persons is needlessly done by more. Since, therefore, the law can be made by the wise, who are few, as has been said, the entire multitude or the greater part of it would needlessly be occupied therein. The authority to make laws does not belong, therefore, to the whole body of the citizens or the weightier part thereof.

As for the first objection, that the authority to make laws does not belong to those who in most cases are vicious and undiscerning, this we grant. But when it is added that the whole body of citizens is such, this must be denied. For most of the citizens are neither vicious nor undiscerning most of the time; all or most of them are of sound mind and reason and have a right desire for the polity and for the things necessary for it to endure, like laws and other statutes or customs. For although not every citizen nor the greater number of the citizens be discoverers of the laws, yet every citizen can judge of what has been discovered and proposed to him by someone else, and can discern what must be added, subtracted, or changed. Hence in the major premiss' reference to the *undiscerning,* if what is meant is that those who cannot, in most of their parts or members, discover the law by themselves, ought not to establish the law, this must be denied as manifestly false, as is borne out by sense induction and by Aristotle in the *Politics,* Book III, Chapter 6. By induction we can see that many men judge rightly about the quality of a picture, a house, a ship, and other works of art, even though they would have been unable to discover or produce them. Aristotle also attests to this in the place just cited, answering the proposed objection with these words: "About some things the man who made them is not the only or the best judge." He proves this in many species of arts, and indicates that the same is true for all the others.

Nor is this position invalidated by those who say that *the wise who are few can discern what should be enacted with regard to practical matters better than can the rest of the multitude.* For even if this be true, it still does not follow that the wise can discern what should be enacted better than can the whole multitude, in which the wise are included together with the less learned. For *every whole is greater than its part* both in acting and in discerning.

The second objection carries little weight, for even though it be easier to harmonize the views of fewer persons than of many, it does not follow that the views of the few, or of the part, are superior to those of the whole multitude, of which the few are a part. For the few would not discern or wish the common benefit equally as well as would the entire multitude of the citizens. Indeed, it would be insecure, as we have already shown, to entrust lawmaking to the will of the few. For they would consult therein their own private benefit, as individuals or as a group, rather than the common benefit.

The third objection can be easily refuted from what we have already said: for although the laws can be better made by the wise than by the less learned, it is not therefore to be concluded that they are better made by the wise alone than by the entire multitude of citizens, in which the wise are included. For the assembled multitude of all of these can better discern and desire the common justice and benefit than any part of it taken separately, however prudent that part may be.

Hence those do not speak the truth who hold that the less learned multitude hinders the election and approval of the true or common good; rather, the multitude is of help in this function when it is joined to those who are more learned and more experienced. For although the multitude cannot by itself discover true and useful measures, it can nevertheless discern and judge the measures discovered and proposed to it by others, as to whether they should be added to, or subtracted from, or completely changed, or rejected. For many things which a man would have been unable to initiate or discover by himself, he can comprehend and bring to completion after they have been explained to him by someone else.

It is hence appropriate and highly useful that the whole body of citizens entrust to those who are prudent and experienced the investigation, discovery, and examination of the standards, the future laws or statutes, bearing upon civil justice and benefit, common difficulties or burdens, and other similar matters. Either some of these prudent and experienced men may be elected by each of the primary parts of the state, according to the proportion of each part; or else all these men may be elected by all the citizens assembled together. And this will be an appropriate and useful method whereby to come together to discover the laws without detriment to the rest of the multitude, i.e., the less learned, who would be of little help in the investigation of such standards, and would be disturbed in their performance of the other functions necessary both to themselves and to others, which would be troublesome both to each individual and to the community.

After such standards, the future laws, have been discovered and diligently examined, they must be laid before the assembled whole body of citizens for their approval or disapproval, so that if any citizen thinks that something should be added, subtracted, changed, or completely rejected, he can say so, since in this way the law will be more usefully ordained. For as we have said, the less learned citizens can sometimes perceive something which must be corrected in a proposed law even though they could not have discovered the law itself. Also, the laws thus made by the hearing and consent of the entire multitude will be better observed, nor will anyone have any protest to make against them.

These standards, the future laws, will thus have been made public, and in the general assembly of the citizens those citizens will have been heard who have wanted to make some reasonable statements with regard to them. Then there must again be elected men of the qualities and by the method indicated above, or else the aforesaid men must be confirmed; and they, representing the position and authority of the whole body of the citizens, will approve or disapprove in whole or in part the aforementioned standards which had been investigated and proposed, or else, if it so wishes, the whole body of the citizens or the weightier part thereof will do this same thing. After this approval, the aforesaid standards are laws and deserve to be so called, not before; and after their publication or proclamation, they alone among human commands make transgressors liable to civil guilt and punishment.

We think we have adequately shown, then, that the authority to make or establish laws, and to give a command with regard to their observance, belongs only to the whole body of the citizens or to the weightier part thereof as efficient cause, or else to the person or persons to whom the aforesaid whole body has granted this authority.

II · *The Early Modern Period*

NICCOLÒ MACHIAVELLI

Niccolò Machiavelli (1469-1527) is destined always to be regarded as one of the sinister figures in the history of thought because he addressed himself not to the moral ends of government but to the mechanics of statesmanship—and this in a day in which poison and the sword were prominent among the weapons of politics. Born in Florence, he served his native city in a number of diplomatic missions, some of considerable delicacy, but was forced for a period, like other leaders of his time, to go into exile and to await a more propitious political climate at home. Circumstances made it possible for him to return to Florence in the last year of his life, but he unfortunately failed in his bid for public office.

During the period of his exile he wrote his *Discourses on Livy* and his famous book *The Prince* (1513). In this book Machiavelli offers practical advice on how to seize power and how to retain it once seized. For these purposes proficiency in the art of war is of first importance, and the selection following is devoted to this subject, to which "a prince ought to have no other aim or thought." Although Machiavelli supported a double standard of morality, one for the prince and another for the common citizen, he had as his prime concern the safety of the state and the security of its citizens. He believed, in fact, that morality was futile in the absence of a stable government. One may not agree with Machiavelli in all of his views, but his place in the history of social thought is one of exceedingly high rank.

From *The Prince*

THE ART OF WAR

A prince ought to have no other aim or thought, nor select anything else for his study, than war and its rules and discipline; for this is the sole art that belongs to him who rules, and it is of such force that it not only upholds those who are born princes, but it often enables men to rise from a private station to that rank. And, on the contrary, it is seen that when princes have thought more of ease than of arms they have lost their states. And the first cause of your losing it is to neglect this art; and what enables you to acquire a state is to be master of the art. Francesco Sforza, through being martial, from a private person became Duke of Milan; and the sons, through avoiding the hardships and troubles of arms, from dukes became private persons. For among other evils which being unarmed brings you, it causes you to be despised, and this is one of those ignominies against which a prince ought to guard himself, as is shown later on. Because there is nothing proportionate between the armed and the unarmed; and it is not reasonable that he who is armed should yield obedience willing to him who is unarmed, or that the unarmed man should be secure among armed servants. Because, there being in the one disdain and in the other suspicion, it is not possible for them to work well together. And therefore a prince who does not understand the art of war, over and above the other misfortunes already mentioned cannot be respected by his soldiers, nor can he rely on them. He ought never, therefore, to have out of his thoughts this subject of war, and in peace he should addict himself more to its exercise than in war; this he can do in two ways, the one by action, the other by study.

As regards action, he ought above all things to keep his men well organized and drilled, to follow incessantly the chase, by which he accustoms his body to hardships, and learns something of the nature of localities, and gets to find out how the mountains rise, how the valleys open out, how the plains lie, and to understand the nature of rivers and marshes, and in all this to take the greatest care. Which knowledge is useful in two ways. Firstly, he learns to know his country, and is better able to undertake its defense; afterwards, by means of the knowledge and observation of that locality, he understands with ease any other which it may be necessary for him to study hereafter; because the hills, valleys, and plains, and rivers and marshes that are, for instance, in Tuscany, have a certain resemblance to those of other countries, so that with a knowledge of the aspect of one country one can easily arrive at a knowledge of others. And the prince that lacks this skill lacks the essential which it is desirable that a captain should possess, for it teaches him to surprise his enemy, to select quarters, to lead armies, to array the battle, to besiege towns to advantage.

Philopoemen, Prince of the Acheans, among other praises which writers have bestowed on him, is commended because in time of peace he never had anything in his mind but the rules of war; and when he was in the country with friends, he often stopped and reasoned with them: "If the enemy should be upon that hill, and we should find ourselves here with our army, with whom would be the advantage? How should one best advance to meet him, keeping the ranks? If we should wish to retreat, how ought we to set about it? If they should retreat, how ought we to pursue?" And he would set forth to them, as he went, all the chances that could befall an army; he would listen to their opinion and state his, confirming it with reasons, so that these continual discussions there could never arise, in time of war, or any unexpected circumstances that he could not deal with.

But to exercise the intellect the prince should read histories, and study there the actions of illustrious men, to see how they have borne themselves in war, to examine the causes of their victories and defeat, so as to avoid the latter and imitate the former; and above all do as an illustrious man did, who took as an exemplar one who had been praised and famous before him, and whose achievements and deeds he always kept in his mind, as it is said Alexander the Great imitated Achilles, Caesar Alexander, Scipio Cyrus. And whoever reads the life of Cyrus, written by Xenophon, will recognize afterwards in the life of Scipio how that imitation was his glory, and how in chastity, affability, humanity, and liberality Scipio conformed to those things which have been written of Cyrus by Xenophon. A wise prince ought to observe some such rules, and never in peaceful times stand idle, but increase his resources with industry in such a way that they may be available to him in adversity, so that if fortune changes it may find him prepared to resist her blows.

THE WAY PRINCES KEEP FAITH

Every one admits how praiseworthy it is in a prince to keep faith, and to live with integrity and not with craft. Nevertheless our experience has been that those princes who have done great things have held good faith of little account, and have known how to circumvent the intellect of men by craft, and in the end have overcome those who have relied on their word. You must know there are two ways of contesting, the one by the law, the other by force; the first method is proper to men, the second to beasts; but because the first is frequently not sufficient, it is necessary to have recourse to the second. Therefore it is necessary for a prince to understand how to avail himself of the beast and the man. This has been figuratively taught to princes by ancient writers, who describe how Achilles and many other princes of old were given to the Centaur Chiron to nurse, who brought them up in his discipline; which means solely that, as they had for a teacher one who was half beast and half man, so it is necessary for a prince to know how to make use of both natures, and that one without the other is not durable. A prince, therefore, being compelled knowingly to adopt the beast, ought to choose the fox and the lion; because the lion cannot defend himself against snares and the fox cannot defend himself against wolves. Therefore, it is necessary to be a fox to discover the snares and a lion to terrify the wolves. Those who rely simply on the lion do not understand what they are about. Therefore a wise lord cannot, nor ought he, to keep faith when such observance may be turned against him, and when the reasons that caused him to pledge it exist no longer. If men were entirely good this precept would not hold, but because they are bad, and will not keep faith with you, you too are not bound to observe it with them. Nor will there ever be wanting to a prince legitimate reasons to excuse this nonobservance. Of this endless modern examples could be given, showing how many treaties and engagements have been made void and of no effect through the faithlessness of princes; and he who has known best how to employ the fox has succeeded best.

But it is necessary to know well how to disguise this characteristic, and to be a great pretender and dissembler; and men are so simple, and so subject to present necessities, that he who seeks to deceive will always find some one who will allow himself to be deceived. One recent example I cannot pass over in silence. Alexander the Sixth did nothing else but deceive men, nor ever thought of doing otherwise and he always found victims; for there never was a man who had greater power in asserting, or who with greater oaths would affirm a thing, yet would observe it less; nevertheless his deceits always succeeded according to his wishes, because he well understood this side of mankind.

Therefore it is unnecessary for a prince to have all the good qualities I have enumerated, but it is very necessary to appear to have them. And I shall dare to say this also, that to have them and always to observe them is injurious, and that to appear to have them is useful; to appear merciful, faithful, humane, religious, upright, and to be so, but with a mind so framed that should you require not to be so, you may be able and know how to change to the opposite.

And you have to understand this, that a prince, especially a new one, cannot observe all those things for which men are esteemed, being often forced, in order to maintain the state, to act contrary to fidelity, friendship, humanity, and religion. Therefore it is necessary for him to have a mind ready to turn itself accordingly as the winds and variations of fortune force it, yet, as I have said above, not to diverge from the good if he can avoid doing so, but, if compelled, then to know how to set about it.

For this reason a prince ought to take care that he never lets anything slip from his lips that is not replete with the above named five qualities, that he may appear to him who sees and hears him altogether merciful, faithful, humane, upright, and religious. There is nothing more necessary to appear to have than this last quality, inasmuch as men judge generally more by the eye than by the hand, because it belongs to everybody to see you, to few to come in touch with you. Every one sees what you appear to be, few really know what you are, and those few dare not oppose themselves to the opinion of the many, who have the majesty of the state to defend them; and in the actions of all men, and especially of princes, which it is not prudent to challenge, one judges by the result.

For that reason, let a prince have the credit of conquering and holding his state, the means will always be considered honest, and he will be praised by everybody; because the vulgar are always taken by what a thing seems to be and by what comes of it; and in the world there are only the vulgar, for the few find a place there only when the many have no ground to rest on.

One prince of the present time, whom it is not well to name, never preaches anything else but peace and good faith, and to both he is most hostile, and either, if he had kept it, would have deprived him of reputation and kingdom many a time.

THOMAS HOBBES

"The life of man [is] solitary, poor, nasty, brutish, and short" —so runs one of the most famous sentences in the history of social thought. It is a product of the pen of Thomas Hobbes (1588-1679), "the ruthless logician" and somewhat acerb philosopher. The son of an English vicar, he was educated in church schools and at Oxford, and then became tutor to William Cavendish, afterward the second Earl of Devonshire. In this capacity he had an opportunity to travel abroad, where he met such men as Gassendi and Campanella, and later Descartes and Galileo. He was a prolific writer from the time of his youth, when he translated Homer and Thucydides. In his later years he was accused of atheism for the reason that his views on the relationship between Church and State ran counter to those prevailing in his time. He was protected by the King, however, and during a long old age he enjoyed the visits of many famous Europeans to his home.

Hobbes' most important book, *Leviathan,* from which the following selections are taken, appeared in 1651. In it he declared that man in a state of nature was engaged in a war of all against all (*bellum omnium contra omnes*) and that, in fact, men were so dangerous to one another that they found it necessary to band together for mutual protection. This initial contract accounts for the origin of civil society, a society that, in turn, requires an absolute authority. Civilization can develop only when men in this way give up their natural liberties for an artificial peace. Society is not therefore, as Aristotle maintained, a natural phenomenon, but rather something men find it necessary to construct because of their own ferocity and natural fear.

From *Leviathan*

Nature hath made men so equal, in the faculties of body, and mind; as that though there be found one man sometimes manifestly stronger in body, or of quicker mind than another; yet when all is reckoned together, the difference between man, and man, is not so considerable, as that one man can thereupon claim to himself any benefit, to which another may not pretend, as well as he. For as to the strength of body, the weakest has strength enough to kill the strongest, either by secret machination, or by confederacy with others, that are in the same danger with himself.

And as to the faculties of the mind, (setting aside the arts grounded upon words, and especially that skill of proceeding upon general, and infallible rules, called science; which very few have, and but in few things; as being not a native faculty, born with us; nor attained, as prudence, while we look after somewhat else,) I find yet a greater equality among men, than that of strength. For prudence, is but experience which equal time, equally bestows on all men, in those things they equally apply themselves unto. That which may perhaps make such equality incredible, is but a vain concept of one's own wisdom, which almost all men think they have in a greater degree, than the vulgar; that is, than all men but themselves, and a few others, whom by fame, or for concurring with themselves, they approve. For such is the nature of men, that howsoever they may acknowledge many others to be more witty, or more eloquent, or more learned; yet they will hardly believe there be many so wise as themselves: for they see their own wit at hand, and other men's at a distance. But this proveth rather that men are in that point equal, than unequal. For there is not ordinarily a greater sign of the equal distribution of any thing, than that every man is contented with his share.

From this equality of ability, ariseth equality of hope in the attaining of our ends. And therefore if any two men desire the same thing, which nevertheless they cannot both enjoy, they become enemies; and in the way to their end, (which is principally their own conservation, and sometimes their delectation only,) endeavor to destroy, or subdue one another. And from hence it comes to pass, that where an invader hath more to fear, than an other man's single power; if one plant, sow, build, or possess a convenient seat, others may probably be expected to come prepared with forces united, to dispossess, and deprive him, not only of the fruit of his labor, but also of his life, or liberty. And the invader again is in the like danger of another.

And from this diffidence of one another, there is no way for any man to secure himself, so reasonable, as anticipation; that is, by force, or wiles, to master the persons of all men he can, so long, till he see no other power great enough to endanger him: And this is no more than his own conservation requireth, and is generally allowed. Also because there be some, that taking pleasure in contemplating their own power in the acts of conquest, which they pursue farther than their security requires; if others, that otherwise would be glad to be at ease within modest bounds, should not by invasion increase their power, they would not be able, long time, by standing only on their defences, to subsist. And by consequence, such augmentation of dominion over men, being necessary to a man's conservation, it ought to be allowed him.

Again, men have no pleasure, (but on the contrary a great deal of grief) in keeping company, where there is no power able to overawe them all. For every man looketh that his companion should value him, at the same rate he sets upon himself: And upon all signs of contempt, or undervaluing, naturally endeavors, as far as he dares (which amongst them that have no common power to keep them in quiet, is far enough to make them destroy each other,) to extort a greater value from his contemners, by damage; and from others, by the example.

So that in the nature of man, we find three principal causes of quarrel. First, competition; secondly, diffidence; thirdly, glory.

The first, maketh men invade for gain; the second, for safety; and the third, for reputation. The first use violence, to make themselves masters of other men's persons, wives, children, and cattle; the second, to defend them; the third, for trifles, as a word, a smile, a different opinion, and any other sign of undervalue, either direct in their persons, or by reflexion in their kindred, their friends, their nation, their profession, or their name.

Hereby it is manifest, that during the time men live without a common power to keep them all in awe, they are in that condition which is called war; and such a war, as is of every man, against every man. For War, consisteth not in Battle only, or the act of fighting; but in a tract of time, wherein the will to contend by battle is sufficiently known: and therefore the notion of time, is to be considered in the nature of war as it is in the nature of weather. For as the nature of foul weather, lyeth not in a shower or two of rain; but in an inclination thereto of many days together; so the nature of war, consisteth not in actual fighting; but in the known disposition thereto, during all the time there is no assurance to the contrary. All other time is peace.

Whatsoever therefore is consequent to a time of War, where every man is Enemy to every man; the same is consequent to the time, wherein men live without other security, than what their own strength, and their own invention shall furnish them withal. In such condition, there is no place for industry; because the fruit thereof is uncertain: and consequently no culture of the earth, no navigation, nor use of the commodious building; no instruments of moving, and removing such things as require much force; no knowledge of the face of the earth; no account of time; no arts; no letters; no society; and which is worst of all, continual fear, and danger of violent death; And the life of man, solitary, poor, nasty, brutish, and short.

It may seem strange to some man, that has not well weighed these things; that Nature should thus dissociate, and render men apt to invade, and destroy one another: and he may therefore, not trusting to this inference, made from the passions, desire perhaps to have the same confirmed by experience. Let him therefore consider with himself, when taking a journey, he arms himself, and seeks to go well accompanied; when going to sleep, he locks his doors; when even in his house he locks his chests; and this when he knows there be Laws, and public officers, armed, to revenge all injuries shall be done him; what opinion he has of his fellow subjects, when he rides armed; of his fellow citizens, when he locks his doors; and of his children, and servants, when he locks his chests. Does he not there as much accuse mankind by his actions, as I do my words? But neither of us accuse man's nature in it. The desires, and other passions of man, are in themselves no sin. No more are the actions, that proceed from those passions, till they know a law that forbids them: which till laws be made they cannot know: nor can any law be made, till they have agreed upon the person that shall make it.

It may peradventure be thought, there was never such a time, nor condition of war as this; and I believe it was never generally so, over all the world; but there are many places, where they live so now. For the savage people in many places of America, except the government of small families, the concord whereof dependeth on natural lust, have no government at all; and live this day in that brutish manner, as I said before. Howsoever, it may be perceived what manner of life there would be, where there were no common power to fear; by the manner of life, which men that have formerly lived under a peaceful government, use to degenerate into, in a civil War.

But though there had never been any time, wherein particular men were in a condition of war one against another; yet in all times, kings, and persons of Sovereign authority, because of their independency, are in continual jealousies, and in the state and posture of gladiators; having their weapons pointing, and their eyes fixed on one another; that is, their forts, garrisons, and guns, upon the frontiers of their kingdoms; and continual spies upon their neighbors; which is a posture of war. But because they uphold thereby, the industry of their subjects; there does not follow from it, that misery, which accompanies the liberty of particular men.

To this war of every man against every man, this also is consequent; that nothing can be unjust. The notions of right and wrong, justice and injustice have there no place. Where there is no common power, there is no law: where no law, no injustice. Force, and fraud, are in war the two Cardinal virtues. Justice, and injustice are none of the faculties neither of the body, nor mind. If they were, they might be in a man that were alone in the world, as well as his senses, and passions. They are qualities, that relate to men in society, not in solitude. It is consequent also to the same condition, that there be no propriety, no dominion, no mine and thine distinct; but only that to be every man's, that he can get; and for so long, as he can keep it. And thus much for the ill condition, which man by mere Nature is actually placed in; though with a possibility to come out of it, consisting partly in the passions, partly in his reason.

The passions that incline men to peace, are Fear of death; desire of such things as are necessary to commodious living; and a hope by their industry to obtain them. And reason suggesteth convenient articles of peace, upon which men may be drawn to agreement. These articles, are they, which otherwise are called the Laws of Nature . . .

JOHN LOCKE

John Locke (1632-1704) is the key philosopher in the British empirical tradition, and it is difficult to say whether his importance to the history of thought is greater in the theory of knowledge or in political and social philosophy. Born in Somersetshire, he was educated at Oxford, at first in medicine; later lectured there on philosophy; and then became, in 1667, private secretary to the Earl of Shaftesbury. His political activities forced him at one point to seek exile for three years in France and five in Holland, and he returned to England only with the Glorious Revolution of 1688, after which he held several posts in the government, including membership on the Board of Trade.

Locke's *Essay on Civil Government,* the second of *Two Treatises on Government,* appeared in 1690. It was at once a justification of the Whig revolution, a refutation of Filmer's defense of absolute monarchy, and the most representative work of the social contract school. Locke differed from other writers of this school, however, in viewing the "state of nature" not as a pre-social but rather as a pre-political condition, and this, among other things, is what gives him significance in the history of sociology. The excerpt that follows, in which Locke discourses on these matters, indicates that for him it is part of man's nature to seek society, to enjoy it, and to perpetuate it. In this, of course, he differs from Hobbes, for whom society was an unpleasant necessity.

Locke's ideas on government made an outstanding impression upon the political leaders of the time, including the men who were later to write the Constitution of the United States.

From *Essay on Civil Government*

OF CIVIL GOVERNMENT

. . . I think it may not be amiss to set down what I take to be political power. That the power of a magistrate over a subject may be distinguished from that of a father over his children, a master over his servant, a husband over his wife, and a lord over his slave. All which distinct powers happening sometimes together in the same man, if he be considered under these different relations, it may help us to distinguish these powers one from another, and show the difference betwixt a ruler of a commonwealth, a father of a family, and a captain of a galley.

Political power, then, I take to be a right of making laws, with penalties of death, and consequently all less penalties for the regulating and preserving of property, and of employing the force of the community in the execution of such laws, and in the defense of the commonwealth from foreign injury, and all this only for the public good.

CHAPTER II
OF THE STATE OF NATURE

To understand political power aright, and derive it from its original, we must consider what estate all men are naturally in, and that is, a state of perfect freedom to order their actions, and dispose of their possessions and persons as they think fit, within the bounds of the law of Nature, without asking leave or depending upon the will of any other man.

A state also of equality, wherein all the power and jurisdiction is reciprocal, no one having more than another, there being nothing more evident than that creatures of the same species and rank, promiscuously born to all the same advantages of Nature, and the use of the same faculties, should also be equal one amongst another, without subordination or subjection, unless the lord and master of them all should, by any manifest declaration of his will, set one above another, and confer on him, by an evident and clear appointment, an undoubted right to dominion and sovereignty. . . .

But though this be a state of liberty, yet it is not a state of license; though man in that state have an uncontrollable liberty to dispose of his person or possessions, yet he has not liberty to destroy himself, or so much as any creature in his possession, but where some nobler use than its bare preservation calls for it. The state of Nature has a law of Nature to govern it, which obliges every one, and reason, which is that law, teaches all mankind who will but consult it, that being all equal and independent, no one ought to harm another in his life, health, liberty or possessions; for men being all the workmanship of one omnipotent and infinitely wise Maker; all the servants of one sovereign Master, sent into the world by His order and about His business; they are His property, whose workmanship they are made to last during His, not one another's pleasure. And, being furnished with like faculties, sharing all in one community of Nature, there cannot be supposed any such subordination among us that may authorize us to destroy one another, as if we were made for one another's uses, as the inferior ranks of creatures are for ours. Every one as he is bound to preserve himself, and not to quit his station wilfully, so by the like reason, when his own preservation comes not in competition, ought he as much as he can to preserve the rest of mankind, and not unless it be to do justice on an offender, take away or impair the life, or what tends to the preservation of the life, the liberty, health, limb, or goods of another.

And that all men may be restrained from invading others' rights, and from doing hurt to one another, and the law of Nature be observed, which willeth the peace and preservation of all mankind, the execution of the law of Nature is in that state put into every man's hands, whereby every one has a right to punish the transgressors of that law to such a degree as may hinder its violation. For the law of Nature would, as all other laws that concern men in this world, be in vain if there were nobody that in the state of Nature had a power to execute that law, and thereby preserve the innocent and restrain offenders; and if any one in the state of Nature may punish another for any evil he has done, every one may do so. For in that state of perfect equality, where naturally there is no superiority of jurisdiction of one over another, what any may do in prosecution of that law, every one must needs have a right to do.

And thus, in the state of Nature, one man comes by a power over another, but yet no absolute of arbitrary power to use a criminal, when he has got him in his hands, according to the passionate heats or boundless extravagancy of his own will, but only to retribute to him so far as calm reason and conscience dictate, what is proportionate to his transgression, which is so much as may serve for reparation and restraint. For these two are the only reasons why one man may lawfully do harm to another, which is what we call punishment. In transgressing the law of Nature, the offender declares himself to live by another rule than that of reason and common equity, which is that measure God has set to the actions of men for their mutual security, and so he becomes dangerous to mankind; the tie which is to secure them from injury and violence being slighted and broken by him, which being a trespass against the whole species, and the peace and safety of it, provided for by the law of Nature, every man upon this score, by the right he hath to preserve mankind in general, may restrain, or where it is necessary, destroy things noxious to them, and so may bring such evil on any one who hath transgressed that law, as may make him repent the doing of it, and thereby deter him, and, by his example, others from doing the like mischief. And in this case, and upon this ground, every man hath a right to punish the offender, and be executioner of the law of Nature.

I doubt not but this will seem a very strange doctrine to some men; but before they condemn it, I desire them to resolve me by what right any prince or state can put to death or punish an alien for any crime he commits in their country? It is certain their laws, by virtue of any sanction they receive from the promulgated will of the legislature, reach not a stranger. They speak not to him, nor, if they did, is he bound to hearken to them. The legislative authority by which they are in force over the subjects of that commonwealth hath no power over him. Those who have the supreme power of making laws in England, France, or Holland are, to an Indian, but like the rest of the world—men without authority. And therefore, if by the law of Nature every man hath not a power to punish offenses against it, as he soberly judges the case to require, I see not how the magistrates of any community can punish an alien of another country, since, in reference to him, they can have no more power than what every man naturally may have over another.

Besides the crime which consists in violating the laws, and varying from the right rule of reason, whereby a man so far becomes degenerate, and declares himself to quit the principles of human nature and to be a noxious creature, there is commonly injury done, and some person or other, some other man, receives damage by his transgression; in which case, he who hath received any damage has (besides the right of punishment common to him, with other men) a particular right to seek reparation from him that hath done it. And any other person who finds it just may also join with him that is injured, and assist him in recovering from the offender so much as may make satisfaction for the harm he hath suffered.

From these two distinct rights (the one of punishing the crime, for restraint and preventing the like offense, which right of punishing is in everybody, the other of taking reparation, which belongs only to the injured party) comes it to pass that the magistrate, who by being magistrate hath the common right of punishing put into his hands, can often, where the public good demands not the execution of the law, remit the punishment of criminal offences by his own authority, but yet cannot remit the satisfaction due to any private man for the damage he has received. That he who hath suffered the damage has a right to demand in his own name, and he alone can remit. The damnified person has this power of appropriating to himself the goods or service of the offender by right of self-preservation, as every man has a power to punish the crime to prevent its being committed again, by the right he has of preserving all mankind, and doing all reasonable things he can in order to that end. And thus it is that every man in the state of Nature has a power to kill a murderer, both to deter others from doing the like injury (which no reparation can compensate) by the example of the punishment that attends it from everybody, and also to secure men from the attempts of a criminal who, having renounced reason, the common rule and measure God hath given to mankind, hath, by the unjust violence and slaughter he hath committed upon one, declared war against all mankind, and therefore may be destroyed as a lion or a tiger, one of those wild savage beasts with whom men can have no society nor security. And upon this is grounded that great law of Nature, "Whoso sheddeth man's blood, by man shall his blood be shed." And Cain was so fully convinced that every one had a right to destroy such a criminal, that, after the murder of his brother, he cries out, "Every one that findeth me shall slay me," so plain was it writ in the heart of all mankind.

By the same reason may a man in the state of Nature punish the lesser breaches of that law, it will, perhaps, be demanded, with death? I answer: each transgression may be punished to that degree, and with so much severity, as will suffice to make it an ill bargain to the offender, give him cause to repent, and terrify others from doing the like. Every offense that can be committed in the state of Nature may, in the state of Nature, be also punished equally, and as far forth, as it may, in a commonwealth. For though it would be beside my present purpose to enter here into the particulars of the law of Nature, or its measures of punishment, yet it is certain there is such a law, and that too as intelligible and plain to a rational creature and a studier of that law as the positive laws of commonwealths, nay, possibly plainer; as much as reason is easier to be understood than the fancies and intricate contrivances of men, following contrary and hidden interests put into words; for truly so are a great part of the municipal laws of countries, which are only so far right as they are founded on the law of Nature, by which they are to be regulated and interpreted.

To this strange doctrine—viz., That in the state of Nature every one has the executive power of the law of Nature—I doubt not but it will be objected that it is unreasonable for men to be judges in their own cases, that self-love will make men partial to themselves and their friends; and, on the other side, ill-nature, passion, and revenge will carry them too far in punishing others, and hence nothing but confusion and disorder will follow, and that therefore God hath certainly appointed government to restrain the partiality and violence of men. I easily grant that civil government is the proper remedy for the inconveniences of the state of Nature, which must certainly be great where men may be judges in their own case, since it is easy to be imagined that he who was so unjust as to do his brother an injury will scarce be so just as to condemn himself for it. But I shall desire those who make this objection to remember that absolute monarchs are but men; and if government is to be the remedy of those evils which necessarily follow from men being judges in their own cases, and the state of Nature is therefore not to be endured, I desire to know what kind of government that is, and how much better it is than the state of Nature, where one man commanding a multitude has the liberty to be judge in his own case, and may do to all his subjects whatever he pleases without the least question or control of those who execute his pleasure? and in whatsoever he doth, whether led by reason, mistake, or passion, must be submitted to? which men in the state of Nature are not bound to do one to another. And if he that judges, judges amiss in his own or any other case, he is answerable for it to the rest of mankind.

It is often asked as a mighty objection, where are, or ever were, there any men in such a state of Nature? To which it may suffice as an answer at present, that since all princes and rulers of "independent" governments all though the world are in a state of Nature, it is plain the world never was, nor never will be, without numbers of men in that state. I have named all governors of "independent" communities, whether they are, or are not, in league with others; for it is not every compact that puts an end to the state of Nature between men, but only this one of agreeing together mutually to enter into one community, and make one body politic; other promises and compacts men may make one with another, and yet still be in the state of Nature. The promises and bargains for truck, etc., between the two men in Soldania, in or between a Swiss and an Indian, in the woods of America, are binding to them, though they are perfectly in a state of Nature in reference to one another for truth, and keeping the faith belongs to men as men, and not as members of society.

To those that say there were never any men in the state of Nature, I will not only oppose the authority of the judicious Hooker, where he says, "the laws which have been hitherto mentioned"—

i.e., the laws of Nature—"do bind men absolutely, even as they are men, although they have never any settled fellowship, never any solemn agreement amongst themselves what to do or not to do; but for as much as we are not by ourselves sufficient to furnish ourselves with competent store of things needful for such a life as our Nature doth desire, a life fit for the dignity of man, therefore to supply those defects and imperfections which are in us, as living single and solely by ourselves, we are naturally induced to seek communion and fellowship with others; this was the cause of men uniting themselves as first in politic societies." But I, moreover, affirm that all men are naturally in that state, and remain so till, by their own consents, they make themselves members of some politic society, and I doubt not, in the sequel of this discourse, to make it very clear.

GIOVANNI BATTISTA VICO

An age that is familiar with the works of Spengler, Toynbee, and Sorokin should find interesting also an early eighteenth century representative of their genre. Giovanni Battista Vico (1668-1744) was born in Naples and became a professor of jurisprudence at the University there. In 1725 he published his *Scienza Nuova,* a book that has been called a work of great, and even unique, genius.

The *Scienza Nuova* brought a certain degree of sophistication both to the philosophy of history and to the closely related discipline of sociology. It was Vico's design in this work to inquire into the history of civilization and to discover, if possible, some of the principles that operate in the formation of human societies. Although he is sometimes listed with the geographic determinists, Vico gave at least a comparable emphasis to ideological factors, the mental set and outlook of the successive generations of mankind. He grasped the unitary character of social change, the notion that nations develop in all of their characteristics simultaneously and not one after the other. Although it was not original with him, he developed an idea that Comte was later to refine, namely that societies pass through three stages, the divine, the heroic, and the human, and so all over again in constant cycles or *ricorsi.* The following selections suggest the flavor of his thinking.

From *Scienza Nuova**

I

The human mind, by nature unlimited, when plunged into ignorance, patterns the universe after itself.

This axiom is the cause of two common human habits: one, that renown is magnified as it spreads, the other that presence detracts from fame. Fame has been the perennial source of all the overstatements that have been made concerning the remotest antiquity of the world.

Tacitus, in his life of Agricola, says: "Whatever is unknown is held to be unusually great."

II

Men judge remote and unknown things, of which they cannot form any idea, by the things they see and know.

This axiom bares the inexhaustible source of all the errors committed by entire nations and by all scholars concerning the beginnings of mankind. It is only when nations have reached an enlightened, cultivated, extremely civilized stage of development, that they turn their attention to their origins. It is likewise at this stage that scholars start studying the origins of nations. They judge such origins according to the standards of their own time. But in reality they must have been inconspicuous, uncouth, and very obscure.

This may be blamed on two kinds of conceit: that of nations and that of scholars.

III

There is a golden saying of Diodorus Siculus on the conceit of nations: "Nations, Greek as well as barbarian, showed such

* Translated by Elio Gianturco.

conceit. Each boasted of having preceded the others in inventing the conveniences of human life and of having preserved records of their accomplishments from the beginning of the world."

This destroys the claims of the Chaldeans, Scythians, Egyptians, and Chinese of having founded the civilization of the ancient world.

IV

To this conceit of nations is to be added the conceit of scholars. They claim that their knowledge is coeval with the beginnings of the world.

This axiom destroys all the opinions of scholars concerning the incomparable wisdom of the ancients: it convicts of imposture the oracles of Zoroaster and Chaldean, those of Anacharsis the Scythian, the Pimander of Mercurius Trismegistus, the verses of Orpheus, the *Carmen aureum* of Pythagoras. Moreover it convicts of falsity all the mystical meanings which scholars have read into Egyptian hieroglyphics and the philosophical allegories attributed to Greek fables.

V

Philosophy, in order to be useful to mankind, must raise and support weak and fallen man, not pervert his nature or abandon him to his corruption.

This axiom excludes the Stoics from the system of doctrines set forth in this science, since they advocate the mortification of the senses. It also excludes the Epicureans who make the senses a standard of life. Both deny the existence of Providence. On the other hand this axiom admits political philosophers into this science, especially the Platonists, who are agreed with all legislators on these three points: that Divine Providence exists, that human passions must be moderated and transformed into human virtues, and that human souls are immortal.

VI

Philosophy considers man *such as he must be*. Thus it can be of benefit only to a very few people, those who desire to live in the republic of Plato, not among the scum of Romulus.

VII

Legislation considers man *such as he is,* in order to make good use of him in human society. Legislation transforms three vices, greed, ambition, ferocity, into courtly life, art of war, commerce. Thus wisdom, fortitude, wealth, spring into being; and out of greed, ambition, ferocity, which, if left to themselves, would destroy the human race, legislation compounds the happiness of society.

VIII

Things out of their natural state have neither temporary nor long duration.

IX

Men ignorant of the truth of things stick to certainty. Not being able to satisfy their intelligence with knowledge, they are content to have their will supported by the consciousness of certainty.

X

Philosophy deals with reason, from which the knowledge of truth derives; philology with the authority of the human will whence springs the consciousness of certainty.

I term "philologists" all grammarians, historians, and critics, whose labours are employed in the study of languages and the events of history: events both internal (customs and laws) and external (war, peace, alliances, travel, and trade).

This axiom shows that both philosophers and philologists have accomplished only half their task: the philosophers not having buttressed their reasons with the authority of the philologists, and the philologists not having cared to give truth to their authority by means of philosophical demonstrations.

XII

Common sense is judgment without reflection, held by a whole people, by a whole nation, or by all mankind.

This axiom with the definition following it, gives us a new critical method for judging the traditions which have been handed down concerning the founders of nations. Nations in fact do not show written documents until over a thousand years after their foundation. Critics have been thus far exclusively occupied with these written documents.

XIII

Identical ideas born among nations which have had no contact with each other must have a common basis of truth.

This axiom establishes the fact that the common sense of the human race is a providential criterion wherewith nations arrive at certainty in respect to the dictates of the natural law. Nations form a firm conviction of certainty in respect to the dictates of natural law by grasping the substantial unities of natural law in which they all agree—with some differences. In view of this common agreement of nations, it is possible to compile a mental dictionary, showing the origins of the various languages, and containing an eternal history of ideas, out of which the temporal histories of all nations derive. It is a shocking error to suppose that culture sprang from a single nation which afterwards transmitted it to others. This error was committed by Egyptians and Greeks who boasted of having spread civilization throughout the world. It was because of this error that it was believed that the Law of XII Tables was carried from Athens to Rome. But, if this were so, it would be a civil law communicated to other nations through human agency, *not* a law naturally established by Providence through the instrumentality of human customs.

Each nation evolved its own political and legal institutions separately and in complete ignorance of the others.

XIV

The "nature" of things is nothing but the fact of their being born at certain times and in certain manners. These times and manners being such, things are born such, and not otherwise.

XV

Qualities inseparable from their subjects must be produced by the special manner in which things are born; therefore, they truthfully inform us that such, and no other, is the nature, or *nascence,* of things.

XVI

No tradition is wholly false. Traditions persisting among whole nations for long intervals of time must have had public motives of truth. The goal of this work is the discovery of the elements of truth which, with the passing of the centuries and the changes in language and custom, have come down to us overgrown with falsity.

XVII

Popular languages are the most important testimonies of the customs which were practiced at the time when these languages were formed.

XVIII

A language of an ancient nation, which has been in use up to its point of perfection, must be considered as a great repository of the culture of the early epochs.

This axiom assures us that the philological proofs of the cultural development of nations, drawn from Latin words, have great weight. The same may be said of the words of the German language, which possesses the same quality as the ancient Roman.

XIX

Since the Law of the XII Tables consists of customs of the peoples of Latium, practiced by them as far back as the age of Saturn, always changing elsewhere but fixed in bronze by the Romans and religiously guarded by jurisprudence of Rome, such a law is a great testimony of the ancient natural law of the peoples of Latium.

XX

If the poems of Homer are civil histories containing the ancient customs of the Greeks, they are two great treasures of the natural law of the peoples of Greece.

XXI

Greek philosophers hastened the natural course which their nation had to run. They appeared in Greece when it was still in a state of barbarity, and caused it to pass at once into a state of extreme refinement, while simultaneously the nation preserved its divine and heroic legends intact. On the other hand, the Romans, who, in the development of their national life marched at a moderate pace, completely lost sight of the history of their gods. Therefore the period which the Egyptians called "the age of the gods" Varro terms "the obscure age of the Romans." The Romans preserved in their vulgar language the heroic history which extends from Romulus to the *lex Publilia* and the *lex Poetelia.* I shall show that the heroic history of Rome is a perpetual parallel of the heroic age of Greece.

France ran the same course in the development of her civilization as did Greece. In France, in the midst of the barbarism of the XIIth century, was founded the University of Paris, where the celebrated Pietro Lombardo taught very subtle scholastic philosophy. Like an Homeric poem, the history of Turpin, Bishop of Paris, full of all the legends of the French paladins, which later filled so many novels and poems, was still extant at this time in France. And through this precocious passage from barbarism to the subtlest sciences, the French language acquired an extreme refinement, so that, of all the living languages, it seems to have reproduced in our time the atticism of the Greeks, and like Greek it is superior to all other languages in dealing with scientific matters. And, even as did Greek, French has preserved many diphthongs, which is a characteristic of a barbaric language, still unplastic and experiencing difficulty in combining consonants with vowels.

Romulus founded Rome in the midst of older cities of Latium as a place of refuge. This, Livy defines in general terms as the manner in which cities were founded in ancient times. Violence was still rife, so he naturally founded Rome in the manner in which the primitive cities had their inception. Therefore, after Roman customs had progressed along the lines set down by the establishment of the asylum, in an age in which the vulgar languages of Latium had also made many advances, it must have happened that the events occurring in the Roman community (similar to those which the Greeks expressed in the *heroic* language) were expressed by the Romans in the *vulgar* language. Ancient Roman history is, as it were, a perpetual symbolic mythology of the heroic history of the Greeks. It must have been for this reason that the Romans were the heroes of the world: Rome subjugated the other cities of Latium, then all of Italy, and lastly the world, when heroism was still young among the Romans. Among the other peoples of Latium, instead, from whose subjugation derived the greatness of Rome, heroism must have begun to grow old.

XXII

There is a mental language common to all nations, whereby they uniformly grasp the substance of the actions of associated life, and express this substance with as many different modifications as there are different aspects of such actions.

This mental language is peculiar to this work. Philologists who approach their studies in the light of its principles will be enabled to form a mental vocabulary common to all various articulated languages, past or present. In the first edition of this *Scienza Nuova* I have listed in a great number of dead and living languages the names of the first patriarchal rulers; names referring to the several functions which they exerted in the patriarchal stage, i.e. that stage in which languages were formed.

XXVIII

The Egyptians divided all time preceding their own into three ages: the age of gods, of heroes and of men. In these three ages, three languages were spoken: hieroglyphic or sacred, symbolic or language by similitudes; and "vulgar," consisting of conventional signs, expressing the everyday needs of life.

XXIX

Homer, in five places in both of his poems, mentions a language more ancient than his own, which must undoubtedly have been in the heroic, and calls it "language of the Gods."

XXX

Varro diligently collected no less than twenty thousand names of Gods known to the Greeks. These names indicated the needs of life, natural, moral, economic or civil, from the primeval age onward.

Nations everywhere began with religion.

XXXI

When nations have become savage through warfare, so that human laws no longer command respect among them, the only powerful means of controlling them is religion.

This axiom established the fact that, in the lawless state, Divine Providence made it possible for wild and violent people to take the first steps towards civilization and the founding of nations. It awakened in them a confused idea of deity, so that they, in their ignorance, incongruously attributed divinity to unworthy objects. Thus, through the fear of such an imagined deity, some semblance of order was established.

XXXII

Men, ignorant of the natural causes of things, whenever they cannot explain them by similarities, attribute to things their own nature, as the common people, for example, say that the magnet is *in love* with iron.

XXXIV

A true quality of human nature is noted by Tacitus when he says "mobiles ad superstitiones perculsae semel mentes;" meaning that once haunted by a frightful superstition, men attribute to it whatever they imagine, see, or do.

XXXVII

The sublimity of poetry consists in giving sense and passion to inanimate objects. It is a characteristic of children to take inanimate objects in their hands and, playing with them, talk to them as if they were living persons.

This philologic-philosophic axiom proves that in the beginning of the world, when races were very young, men were by nature sublime poets.

XL

Sacrifices arose out of superstitious religions, which caused cruel, fierce primitive man to make votive offerings and to slay human victims. These victims, as Plautus says, were called by the Latins *Saturni hostiae,* and were the sacrifices to Moloch among the Phoenicians, who flung into the flames babies consecrated to that false god. Some of these consecrations are preserved in the Law of the XII Tables. These things, just as they give the correct meaning to that saying: *"Primus in orbe deos fecit timor,"*—i.e. that false religions were born not out of imposture, but out of credulity—likewise prove that the cruel vow and sacrifice, which Agamemnon made of his pious daughter Iphigenia, impiously commented on by Lucretius when he says that so many ills were caused by religion, was inspired by providence. Nothing less than these cruelties was needed in order that the offspring of primeval man might become human, and that a later civilization might produce such men as Aristides, Socrates, Laelius, and Scipio Africanus.

XLIII

Every heathen nation had its Hercules, who was the son of Jupiter. Varro was able to count forty of them.

This axiom is the principle of the heroism of the first nations, born from a false opinion which they had that heroes stemmed from a divine progenitor.

This axiom also demonstrates that nations could not be founded without religion, nor be enlarged without virtue. Nations were, at the beginning, savage and impenetrable, not knowing, consequently, of each other's existence. The first fables must have contained truths relating to man's life in the social state; they, therefore, must have been the earliest histories of nations.

XLIV

The first sages of the Greek world were the theological poets, who undoubtedly flourished before the heroic ones, just as Jupiter was the father of Hercules.

Heathen nations, since they all had their Jupiters and their Hercules, were, in the beginning, poetic; and among them the first type of poetry to arise was divine, followed by heroic.

XLVII

The human mind tends to take pleasure in uniformity.

This axiom is confirmed by the custom that common people have of devising fables about famous men, placing them in imaginary situations and making them act in conformity with the character attributed to them. These fables are ideal truths corresponding to the type of the men whose deeds they relate. On close inspection, poetic truth is a metaphysical truth. If physical truth is not in conformity with it, then physical truth must be reputed false.

XLIX

Primitive man was a child, incapable of conceiving abstract ideas. He was obliged by his nature to imagine certain *poetic types* which constitute the essence of fables and which are general categories under which all concrete species can be subsumed. Thus the Egyptians attributed to Mercurius Trismegistus, for them the symbolic type of ruler, intent on the welfare of society and anxious to further it by useful discoveries, all the inventions useful or necessary to the human race. They did so because they did not know how to grasp the abstract idea of "the socially minded ruler," and even less the idea of "social wisdom." This shows how little the Egyptians were philosophers.

LI

All pagan civilization had its inception in poetry, from which all other arts derive. The earliest poets were poets not by art but by nature.

LII

All arts pertaining to necessary, useful, convenient and most of the pleasurable human things, were invented in the poetic centuries, before the coming of the philosophers.

LIII

At first men simply feel without consciousness of feeling, then they become conscious of the passionate turmoil of their souls, and finally they reflect with pure intellect.

This axiom is the principle of poetry, which is created from passion and feeling, unlike philosophy which results from reason and reflection. Therefore philosophical truth is best expressed in abstractions and poetic truth in concrete terms.

LIV

Man naturally is influenced in his interpretation of doubtful or obscure things by his nature, passions, and customs.

EMILE DURKHEIM

In choosing a sample of the work of Emile Durkheim (1858-1917) one confronts an embarrassment of riches. For Durkheim, who taught sociology at the Sorbonne, made major contributions to at least four different sectors of the total field of inquiry, as suggested by the titles of his principal works: *The Division of Labor in Society* (1893), *The Rules of Sociological Method* (1895), *Suicide* (1897), and *The Elementary Forms of Religious Life* (1912). He was born in Epinal, Lorraine, was graduated from the *Ecole Normale Supérieure* in Paris, studied economics, folklore, and anthropology in Germany, and taught at the University of Bordeaux before joining the faculty at Paris. He founded the *Année sociologique* in 1896, and served as its editor until 1913. He exerted an imposing influence upon the French sociology of his time and he remains one of the four or five most important figures in the recent history of world sociology.

Durkheim's views represent an extreme of what has been called "sociologism." For him the group was a reality *sui generis,* something that, with its "collective representations," transcended the individual. Society itself was the source both of religion and of the philosophical categories. His position involved a rejection of psychological explanations of social facts; indeed, he went so far as to say that whenever anyone attempts to give a psychological explanation of a social fact one can be sure that the explanation is false. In his empirical work he proved that even such intimate and individual phenomena as decisions to commit suicide exhibit regularities that can be explained only with reference to groups.

In the following excerpt, from *The Rules of Sociological Method,* Durkheim defines a social fact in terms of exteriority and constraint.

*What Is a Social Fact?**

Before inquiring into the method suited to the study of social facts, it is important to know which facts are commonly called "social." This information is all the more necessary since the designation "social" is used with little precision. It is currently employed for practically all phenomena generally diffused within society, however small their social interest. But on that basis, there are, as it were, no human events that may not be called social. Each individual drinks, sleeps, eats, reasons; and it is to society's interest that these functions be exercised in an orderly manner. If, then, all these facts are counted as "social" facts, sociology would have no subject matter exclusively its own, and its domain would be confused with that of biology and psychology.

But in reality there is in every society a certain group of phenomena which may be differentiated from those studied by the other natural sciences. When I fulfil my obligations as brother, husband, or citizen, when I execute my contracts, I perform duties which are defined, externally to myself and my acts, in law and in custom. Even if they conform to my own sentiments and I feel their reality subjectively, such reality is still objective, for I did not create them; I merely inherited them through my education. How many times it happens, moreover, that we are ignorant of the details of the obligations incumbent upon us, and that in order to acquaint ourselves with them we must consult the law and its authorized interpreters! Similarly, the church member finds the beliefs and practices of his religious life ready-made at birth; their existence prior to his own implies their existence outside of himself. The system of signs I use to express my thought, the system of currency I employ to pay my debts, the instruments of credit I utilize in my commercial relations, the

* From *The Rules of Sociological Method* by Emile Durkheim, edited by George E. G. Catlin (Chicago: University of Chicago Press, 1938). Reprinted by permission of the editor.

practices followed in my profession, etc., function independently of my own use of them. And these statements can be repeated for each member of society. Here, then, are ways of acting, thinking, and feeling that present the noteworthy property of existing outside the individual consciousness.

These types of conduct or thought are not only external to the individual but are, moreover, endowed with coercive power, by virtue of which they impose themselves upon him, independent of his individual will. Of course, when I fully consent and conform to them, this constraint is felt only slightly, if at all, and is therefore unnecessary. But it is, nonetheless, an intrinsic characteristic of these facts, the proof thereof being that it asserts itself as soon as I attempt to resist it. If I attempt to violate the law, it reacts against me so as to prevent my act before its accomplishment, or to nullify my violation by restoring the damage, if it is accomplished and reparable, or to make me expiate it if it cannot be compensated for otherwise.

In the case of purely moral maxims, the public conscience exercises a check on every act which offends it by means of the surveillance it exercises over the conduct of citizens, and the appropriate penalties at its disposal. In many cases the constraint is less violent, but nevertheless it always exists. If I do not submit to the conventions of society, if in my dress I do not conform to the customs observed in my country and in my class, the ridicule I provoke, the social isolation in which I am kept, produce, although in an attenuated form, the same effects as a punishment in the strict sense of the word. The constraint is nonetheless efficacious for being indirect. I am not obliged to speak French with my fellow countrymen nor to use the legal currency, but I cannot possibly do otherwise. If I tried to escape this necessity, my attempt would fail miserably. As an industrialist, I am free to apply the technical methods of former centuries; but by doing so, I should invite certain ruin. Even when I free myself from these rules and violate them successfully, I am always compelled to struggle with them. When finally overcome, they make their constraining power sufficiently felt by the resistance they offer. The enterprises of all innovators, including successful ones, come up against resistance of this kind.

Here, then, is a category of facts with very distinctive characteristics: it consists of ways of acting, thinking, and feeling, external to the individual, and endowed with a power of coercion, by reason of which they control him. These ways of thinking could not be confused with biological phenomena, since they consist of representations and of actions; nor with psychological phenomena, which exist only in the individual consciousness and through it. They constitute, thus, a new variety of phenomena; and it is to them exclusively that the term "social" ought to be applied. And this term fits them quite well, for it is clear that, since their source is not in the individual, their substratum can be no other than society, either the political society as a whole or some one of the partial groups it includes, such as religious denominations, political, literary, and occupational associations, etc. On the other hand, this term "social" applies to them exclusively, for it has a distinct meaning only if it designates exclusively the phenomena which are not included in any of the categories of facts that have already been established and classified. These ways of thinking and acting therefore constitute the proper domain of sociology. It is true that, when we define them with this word "constraint" we risk shocking the zealous partisans of absolute individualism. For those who profess the complete autonomy of the individual, man's dignity is diminished whenever he is made to feel that he is not completely self-determinant. It is generally accepted today, however, that most of our ideas and our tendencies are not developed by ourselves but come to us from without. How can they become a part of us except by imposing themselves upon us? This is the whole meaning of our definition. And it is generally accepted, moreover, that social constraint is not necessarily incompatible with the individual personality.

Since the examples that we have just cited (legal and moral regulations, religious faiths, financial systems, etc.) all consist of established beliefs and practices, one might be led to believe that social facts exist only where there is some social organization. But there are other facts without such crystallized form which have the same objectivity and the same ascendency over the individual. These are called "social currents." Thus the great movements of enthusiasm, indignation, and pity in a crowd do not originate in any one of the particular individual consciousnesses. They come to each one of us from without and can carry us away in spite of ourselves. Of course, it may happen that, in abandoning myself to them unreservedly, I do not feel the pressure they exert upon me. But it is revealed as soon as I try to resist them. Let an individual attempt to oppose one of these collective manifestations, and the emotions that he denies will turn against him. Now, if this power of external coercion asserts itself so clearly in cases of resistance, it must exist also in the first mentioned cases, although we are unconscious of it. We are then victims of the illusion of having ourselves created that which actually forced itself from without. If the complacency with which we permit ourselves to be carried along conceals the pressure undergone, nevertheless it does not abolish it. Thus, air is no less heavy because we do not detect its weight. So, even if we ourselves have spontaneously contributed to the production of the common emotion, the impression we have received differs markedly from that which we would have experienced if we had been alone. Also, once the crowd has dispersed, that is, once these social influences have ceased to act upon us and we are alone again, the emotions which have passed through the mind appear strange to us, and we no longer recognize them as ours. We realize that these feelings have been impressed upon us to a much greater extent than they were created by us. It may even happen that they horrify us, so much were they contrary to our nature. Thus, a group of individuals, most of whom are perfectly inoffensive, may, when gathered in a crowd, be drawn into acts of atrocity. And what we say of these transitory outbursts applies similarly to those more permanent currents of opinion on religious, political, literary, or artistic matters which are constantly being formed around us, whether in society as a whole or in more limited circles.

To confirm this definition of the social fact by a characteristic illustration from common experience, one need only observe the manner in which children are brought up. Considering the facts as they are and as they have always been, it becomes immediately evident that all education is a continuous effort to impose on the child ways of seeing, feeling, and acting which he could not have arrived at spontaneously. From the very first hours of his life, we compel him to eat, drink, and sleep at regular hours; we constrain him to cleanliness, calmness, and obedience; later we exert pressure upon him in order that he may learn proper consideration for others, respect for customs and conventions, the need for work, etc. If, in time, this constraint ceases to be felt, it is because it gradually gives rise to habits and to internal tendencies that render constraint unnecessary; but nevertheless it is not abolished, for it is still the source from which these habits were derived. It is true that, according to Spencer, a rational education ought to reject such methods, allowing the child to act in complete liberty; but as this pedagogic theory has never been applied by any known people, it must be accepted only as an expression of personal opinion, not as a fact which can contradict the aforementioned observations. What makes these facts particularly instructive is that the aim of education is, precisely, the socialization of the human being; the process of education, therefore, gives us in a nutshell the historical fashion in which the social being is constituted. This unremitting pressure to which the child is subjected is the very pressure of the social milieu which tends to fashion him in its own image, and of which parents and teachers are merely the representatives and intermediaries.

It follows that sociological phenomena cannot be defined by their universality. A thought which we find in every individual consciousness, a movement repeated by all individuals, is not thereby a social fact. If sociologists have been satisfied with defining them by this characteristic, it is because they confused them with what one might call their reincarnation in the individual. It is, however, the collective aspects of the beliefs, tendencies, and practices of a group that characterize truly social phenomena. As for the forms that the collective states assume when refracted in the individual, these are things of another sort. This duality is clearly demonstrated by the fact that these two orders of phenomena are frequently found dissociated from one another. Indeed, certain of these social manners of acting and thinking acquire, by reason of their repetition, a certain rigidity which on its own account crystallizes them, so to speak, and isolates them from the particular events which reflect them. They thus acquire a body, a tangible form, and constitute a reality in their own right, quite distinct from the individual facts which produce it. Collective habits are inherent not only in the successive acts which they determine but, by a privilege of which we find no example in the biological realm, they are given permanent expression in a formula which is repeated from mouth to mouth, transmitted by education, and fixed even in writing. Such is the origin and nature of legal and moral rules, popular aphorisms and proverbs, articles of faith wherein religious or political groups condense their beliefs, standards of taste established by literary schools, etc. None of these can be found entirely reproduced in the applications made of them by individuals, since they can exist even without being actually applied.

No doubt, this dissociation does not always manifest itself with equal distinctness, but its obvious existence in the important and numerous cases just cited is sufficient to prove that the social fact is a thing distinct from its individual manifestations. Moreover, even when this dissociation is not immediately apparent, it may often be disclosed by certain devices of method. Such dissociation is indispensable if one wishes to separate social facts from their alloys in order to observe them in a state of purity. Currents of opinion, with an intensity varying according to the time and place, impel certain groups either to more marriages, for example, or to more suicides, or to a higher or lower birthrate, etc. These currents are plainly social facts. At first sight they seem inseparable from the forms they take in individual cases. But statistics furnish us with the means of isolating them. They are, in fact, represented with considerable exactness by the rates of births, marriages, and suicides, that is, by the number obtained by dividing the average annual total of marriages, births, suicides, by the number of persons whose ages lie within the range in which marriages, births, and suicides occur. Since each of these figures contains all the individual cases indiscriminately, the individual circumstances which may have had a share in the production of the phenomenon are neutralized and, consequently, do not contribute to its determination. The average, then, expresses a certain state of the group mind (*l'âme collective*).

Such are social phenomena, when disentangled from all foreign matter. As for their individual manifestations, these are indeed, to a certain extent, social, since they partly reproduce a social model. Each of them also depends, and to a large extent, on the organopsychological constitution of the individual and on the particular circumstances in which he is placed. Thus they are not sociological phenomena in the strict sense of the word. They belong to two realms at once; one could call them socio-psychological. They interest the sociologist without constituting the immediate subject matter of sociology. There exist in the interior of organisms similar phenomena, compound in their nature, which form in their turn the subject matter of the "hybrid sciences," such as physiological chemistry, for example.

The objection may be raised that a phenomenon is collective only if it is common to all members of society, or at least to most of them—in other words, if it is truly general. This may be true; but it is general because it is collective (that is, more or less obligatory), and certainly not collective because general. It is a group condition repeated in the individual because imposed on him. It is to be found in each part because it exists in the whole, rather than in the whole because it exists in the parts. This becomes conspicuously evident in those beliefs and practices which are transmitted to us ready-made by previous generations; we receive and adopt them because, being both collective and ancient, they are invested with a particular authority that education has taught us to recognize and respect. It is, of course, true that a vast portion of our social culture is transmitted to us in this way; but even when the social fact is due in part to our direct collaboration, its nature is not different. A collective emotion which bursts forth suddenly and violently in a crowd does not express merely what all the individual sentiments had in common; it is something entirely different, as we have shown. It results from their being together, a product of the actions and reactions which take place between individual consciousnesses; and if each individual consciousness echoes the collective sentiment, it is by virtue of the special energy resident in its collective origin. If all hearts beat in unison, this is not the result of a spontaneous and preestablished harmony but rather because an identical force propels them in the same direction. Each is carried along by all.

We thus arrive at the point where we can formulate and delimit in a precise way the domain of sociology. It comprises only a limited group of phenomena. A social fact is to be recognized by the power of external coercion which it exercises or is capable of exercising over individuals, and the presence of this power may be recognized in its turn either by the existence of some specific sanction or by the resistance offered against every individual effort that tends to violate it. One can, however, define it also by its diffusion within the group, provided that, in conformity with our previous remarks, one takes care to add as a second and essential characteristic that its own existence is independent of the individual forms it assumes in its diffusion. This last criterion is perhaps, in certain cases, easier to apply than the preceding one. In fact, the constraint is easy to ascertain when it expresses itself externally by some direct reaction of society, as is the case in law, morals, beliefs, customs, and even fashions. But when it is only indirect, like the constraint which an economic organization exercises, it cannot always be so easily detected. Generality combined with externality may, then, be easier to establish. Moreover, this second definition is but another form of the first; for if a mode of behavior whose existence is external to individual consciousnesses becomes general, this can only be brought about by its being imposed upon them.

But these several phenomena present the same characteristic by which we defined the others. These "ways of existing" are imposed on the individual precisely in the same fashion as the "ways of acting" of which we have spoken. Indeed, when we wish to know how a society is divided politically, of what these divisions themselves are composed, and how complete is the fusion existing between them, we shall not achieve our purpose by physical inspection and by geographical observations; for these phenomena are social, even when they have some basis in physical nature. It is only by a study of public law that a comprehension of this organization is possible, for it is this law that determines the organization, as it equally determines our domestic and civil relations. This political organization is, then, no less obligatory than the social facts mentioned above. If the population crowds into our cities instead of scattering into the country, this is due to a trend of public opinion, a collective drive that imposes this concentration upon the individuals. We can no more choose the style of our houses than of our clothing—at least, both are equally obligatory. The channels of communication prescribe the direction of internal migrations and commerce, etc., and even their extent. Consequently, at the very most, it should be necessary to add to the list of phenomena which we have enumerated as presenting the distinctive criterion of a social fact only one additional category, "ways of existing," and as this enumeration was not meant to be rigorously exhaustive, the addition would not be absolutely necessary.

Such an addition is perhaps not necessary, for these "ways of existing" are only crystallized "ways of acting." The political structure of a society is merely the way in which its component segments have become accustomed to live with one another. If their relations are traditionally intimate, the segments tend to fuse with one another, or, in the contrary case, to retain their identity. The type of habitation imposed upon us is merely the way in which our contemporaries and our ancestors have been accustomed to construct their houses. The methods of communication are merely the channels which the regular currents of commerce and migrations have dug, by flowing in the same direction. To be sure, if the phenomena of a structural character alone presented this permanence, one might believe that they constituted a distinct species. A legal regulation is an arrangement no less permanent than a type of architecture, and yet the regulation is a "physiological" fact. A simple moral maxim is assuredly somewhat more malleable, but it is much more rigid than a simple professional custom or a fashion. There is thus a whole series of degrees without a break in continuity between the facts of the most articulated structure and those free currents of social life which are not yet definitely molded. The differences between them are, therefore, only differences in the degree of consolidation they present. Both are simply life, more or less crystallized. No doubt, it may be of some advantage to reserve the term "morphological" for those social facts which concern the social substratum, but only on condition of not overlooking the fact that they are of the same nature as the others. Our definition will then include the whole relevant range of facts if we say: *A social fact is every way of acting, fixed or not, capable of exercising on the individual an external constraint;* or again, *every way of acting which is general throughout a given society, while at the same time existing in its own right independent of its individual manifestations.*

GABRIEL TARDE

For many years a magistrate in the provinces, Gabriel Tarde (1843-1904) became in later life director of criminal statistics in the Ministry of Justice, in Paris, and still later a professor of modern philosophy in the Collège de France. His initial interests were in the fields of criminology and penology and he published books (*La criminalité comparée,* 1886; *La philosophie pénale,* 1890; and *Études pénales et sociales,* 1892) in which he criticized the view of the classical and Italian criminologists, notably Lombroso, that the criminal was an atavistic type marked by distinct physical characteristics. For Tarde criminality was a social phenomenon.

In sociology proper Tarde followed a different line from that of Durkheim, his great opponent, in that he emphasized the importance of psychological factors. Indeed, he is known primarily for developing a theory of imitation, a process in terms of which social interaction is to be explained. In conforming to custom, he said, we are imitating our ancestors, and in conforming to fashion we are imitating our contemporaries. Repetition, opposition, and adaptation are other processes that help to explain the social order.

The selection that follows is taken from lectures delivered at the *Collège libre des sciences sociales* in October, 1897, in which Tarde tried to exhibit the bond that unites his three major works in general sociology (*Les lois de l'Imitation, L'Opposition universelle,* and *La Logique sociale*). So brief an excerpt can provide only the merest flavor of Tarde's brilliant literary style—but the first paragraph in particular expresses what might be called the faith of a sociologist. It is a sentiment at least to which all sociologists subscribe.

From *Social Laws*

When we traverse the gallery of history, and observe its motley succession of fantastic paintings—when we examine in a cursory way the successive races of mankind, all different and constantly changing, our first impression is apt to be that the phenomena of social life are incapable of any general expression or scientific law, and that the attempt to found a system of sociology is wholly chimerical. But the first herdsmen who scanned the starry heavens, and the first tillers of the soil who essayed to discover the secrets of plant life, must have been impressed in much the same way by the sparkling disorder of the firmament, with its manifold meteors, as well as by the exuberant diversity of vegetable and animal forms. The idea of explaining sky or forest by a small number of logically concatenated notions, under the name of astronomy or biology, had it occurred to them, would have appeared in their eyes the height of extravagance. And there is no less complexity—no less real irregularity and apparent caprice—in the world of meteors and in the interior of the virgin forest, than in the recesses of human history.

How is it, then, that in spite of this changing diversity in the domain of sky and forest, among physical objects and living beings, we have seen the birth and gradual growth of the sciences of physics and biology? There are three essential elements involved in the development of these branches, and these must be carefully distinguished before we can form a complete and exact notion of what is meant by a certain noun and adjective that are very widely used, namely, *science* and *scientific*.

In the first place, then, men began to perceive some similarities in the midst of these differences, some *repetitions* among these variations. Such are the periodic return of the same conditions of the heavens, the cycle of the seasons, the regularly repeated succession of ages among living creatures, youth, maturity, and old age, and the traits common to individuals of the same species. There is no science of the individual as such; all science is general; that is, it considers the individual as repeated, or as capable of indefinite repetition.

Science is the coördination of phenomena regarded from the side of their repetitions. But this does not mean that differentiation is not an essential mode of procedure for the scientific mind. It is the duty of science to differentiate, as well as to assimilate; but only to the extent that the object differentiated is a *type* in nature yielding a certain number of copies and capable of indefinite reproduction. A specific type may be discovered and carefully defined; but, if it be found to belong to a single individual only, and to be incapable of transmission to posterity, it fails to interest the scientist, except as a curious monstrosity. Repetition means the production of something that at the same time preserves the original; it implies simple and elementary causation without creation. The effect reproduces the cause point by point, just as in the case of transmission of movement from one body to another, or the transmission of life from a living being to its progeny.

But in addition to the question of *reproduction,* the phenomena involved in *destruction* are of interest to science. And hence, in every sphere of fact to which she directs her attention, science must endeavor to discover, in the second place, the *oppositions* that exist there and are germane to her object. Thus, she must consider the equilibrium of forces, the symmetry of forms, the struggles of living organisms, and the strife among all creatures.

But this is not all, nor even the most important element. The *adaptations* of phenomena, and their relations in creative production, must above all be dealt with. The scientist labors continually to detect, disentangle, and explain these harmonies. With their discovery, he succeeds in establishing a higher adaptation, namely, the harmony of his system of notions and hypotheses with the interrelations of facts.

Thus science consists in viewing any fact whatsoever under three aspects, corresponding respectively, to the repetitions, oppositions, and adaptations which it contains, and which are obscured by a mass of variations, dissymmetries, and disharmonies. The relation of cause to effect, in fact, is not the only element which properly constitutes scientific knowledge. If it were so, pragmatic history, the mere concatenation of causes and effects, which simply teaches that certain battles and certain insurrections had such and such consequences, would be the most perfect example of science. Yet history, as we know, becomes a science only when the relations of causality which it reveals are shown to exist between a general cause, capable of repetition or actually repeating itself, and a general effect, also repeated or capable of repetition.

Again, mathematics never reveals causality in operation. When a cause is postulated under the name of *function,* it is always disguised as an equation. Yet mathematics is certainly a science; in fact, it is the prototype of all science. And why? Because nowhere has a more complete elimination of the dissimilar and individual side of phenomena been effected, and nowhere do they present a more exact and definite repetition, and a more symmetrical opposition. The great fault of mathematics lies in its not perceiving, or taking adequately into account, the adaptations of phenomena. Hence arises that insufficiency of the science, so strongly felt by philosophers, especially the geometricians among them, such as Descartes, Comte, and Cournot.

Repetition, opposition, and adaptation, I repeat, are the three keys which science employs to open up the arcana of the universe. She seeks, before all else, not the mere causes, but the laws that govern the repetition, opposition, and adaptation of phenomena. These are three different species of laws, which must certainly not be confounded; yet they are quite as closely connected as they are distinct. In biology, for example, the tendency of species to multiply in geometric progression (a law of repetition) forms the basis of the struggle for existence and natural selection (a law of opposition); and the appearance of individual variations, the production of various individual aptitudes and harmonies, and the correlation of parts in growth (laws of adaptation) are necessary to the proper functioning of both.

But, of these three keys, the first and third are far more important than the second. The first is the great passkey; while the third, of finer construction, gives access to treasures deeply hidden and most precious. The second, an intermediary, of lesser importance, reveals certain strifes and collisions of temporary utility, which are destined to fade away little by little, though never completely, even this partial disappearance being effected only after numerous transformations and attenuations.

These reflections were needed in order to show what sociology must be, if it is to deserve the name of science, and along what paths sociologists must guide its course, if they wish to see it assume, unchallenged, its proper rank. Like every other science, it will attain this only when it has gained, and is conscious of possessing, its own domain of repetitions, its own domain of oppositions, and its own domain of adaptations, each characteristic of itself and belonging wholly to itself. Sociology can only make progress when it succeeds in substituting true repetitions, oppositions, and harmonies for false ones, as all the other sciences have done before it. And in place of repetitions, oppositions, and adaptations that are true but vague, it must find others that become ever more exact as it advances.

Let us place ourselves at each of these standpoints in turn, first of all to ascertain whether or not the evolution of science in general, and sociology in particular, has taken place in the manner which I have already imperfectly defined, and which I shall be able to define more fully as we proceed; in the second place, to point out the laws of social development under each of these three aspects.

THORSTEIN VEBLEN

Thorstein Veblen (1857-1929), the son of Norwegian immigrants, grew up in a Norwegian community in Wisconsin whose inhabitants had not yet been assimilated and who retained in consequence a feeling of isolation from American culture. He was educated at Carleton College, Johns Hopkins University, Yale (which gave him the Ph.D. degree in 1884), and Cornell. His teaching career, a lively and iconoclastic one, encompassed the University of Chicago, Stanford, the University of Missouri, and, finally, the New School for Social Research in New York City.

In 1899 Veblen published what continues to be his most widely known book, *The Theory of the Leisure Class,* from which the following selection is taken. The orthodox economics of the time, rather thoroughly systematized, had no appeal for him. He tended to regard it, in fact, as little more than an apology for the dominant social order. Nor was he seduced by Marxism, a system too simple and abstract, too little rooted in psychological and sociological realities, especially in its analysis of social class. Veblen functioned, in short, not as a system builder but rather as a social critic and one whose insights have continuing relevance for both economics and sociology. He has had the honor of contributing a number of expressions, such as "conspicuous waste" and "conspicuous consumption," to the American vocabulary. His importance has come to be increasingly recognized since his death.

From *The Theory of the Leisure Class**

CONSPICUOUS CONSUMPTION

In what has been said of the evolution of the vicarious leisure class and its differentiation from the general body of the working classes, reference has been made to a further division of labor—that between different servant classes. One portion of the servant class, chiefly those persons whose occupation is vicarious leisure, come to undertake a new, subsidiary range of duties—the vicarious consumption of goods. The most obvious form in which this consumption occurs is seen in the wearing of liveries and the occupation of spacious servants' quarters. Another, scarcely less obtrusive or less effective form of vicarious consumption, and a much more widely prevalent one, is the consumption of food, clothing, dwelling, and furniture by the lady and the rest of the domestic establishment.

But already at a point in economic evolution far antedating the emergence of the lady, specialized consumption of goods as an evidence of pecuniary strength had begun to work out in a more or less elaborate system. The beginning of a differentiation in consumption even antedates the appearance of anything that can fairly be called pecuniary strength. It is traceable back to the initial phase of predatory culture, and there is even a suggestion that an incipient differentiation in this respect lies back of the beginnings of the predatory life. This most primitive differentiation in the consumption of goods is like the later differentiation with which we are all so intimately familiar, in that it is largely of a ceremonial character, but unlike the latter it does not rest on a difference in accumulated wealth. The utility of consumption as an evidence of wealth is to be classed as a derivative growth. It is an adaptation to a new end, by a selective process, of a distinction previously existing and well established in men's habits of thought.

In the earlier phases of the predatory culture the only economic differentiation is a broad distinction between an honorable

* Reprinted by permission of The Viking Press, Inc.

superior class made up of the able-bodied men on the one side, and a base inferior class of laboring women on the other. According to the ideal scheme of life in force at that time it is the office of the men to consume what the women produce. Such consumption as falls to the women is merely incidental to their work; it is a means to their continued labor, and not a consumption directed to their own comfort and fulness of life. Unproductive consumption of goods is honorable, primarily as a mark of prowess and a perquisite of human dignity; secondarily it becomes substantially honorable in itself, especially the consumption of the more desirable things. The consumption of choice articles of food, and frequently also of rare articles of adornment, becomes tabu to the women and children and if there is a base (servile) class of men, the tabu holds also for them. With a further advance in culture this tabu may change into simple custom of a more or less rigorous character; but whatever be the theoretical basis of the distinction which is maintained, whether it be a tabu or a larger conventionality, the features of the conventional scheme of consumption do not change easily. When the quasi-peaceable stage of industry is reached, with its fundamental institution of chattel slavery, the general principle, more or less rigorously applied, is that the base, industrious class should consume only what may be necessary to their subsistence. In the nature of things, luxuries and the comforts of life belong to the leisure class. Under the tabu, certain victuals, and more particularly certain beverages, are strictly reserved for the use of the superior class.

The ceremonial differentiation of the dietary is best seen in the use of intoxicating beverages and narcotics. If these articles of consumption are costly, they are felt to be noble and honorific. Therefore the base classes, primarily the women, practice an enforced continence with respect to these stimulants, except in countries where they are obtainable at a very low cost. From archaic times down through all the length of the patriarchal regime it has been the office of the women to prepare and administer these luxuries, and it has been the perquisite of the men of gentle birth and breeding to consume them. Drunkenness and the other pathological consequences of the free use of stimulants therefore tend in their turn to become honorific, as being a mark, at the second remove, of the superior status of those who are able to afford the indulgence. Infirmities induced by overindulgence are among some peoples freely recognized as manly attributes. It has even happened that the name for certain diseased conditions of the body arising from such an origin has passed into everyday speech as a synonym for "noble" or "gentle." It is only at a relatively early stage of culture that the symptoms of expensive vice are conventionally accepted as marks of a superior status, and so tend to become virtues and command the deference of the community; but the reputability that attaches to certain expensive vices long retains so much of its force as to appreciably lessen the disapprobation visited upon the men of the wealthy or noble class for any excessive indulgence. The same invidious distinction adds force to the current disapproval of any indulgence of this kind on the part of women, minors, and inferiors. This invidious traditional distinction has not lost its force even among the more advanced peoples of today. Where the example set by the leisure class retains its imperative force in the regulation of the conventionalities, it is observable that the women still in great measure practice the same traditional continence with regard to stimulants.

This characterization of the greater continence in the use of stimulants practiced by the women of the reputable classes may seem an excessive refinement of logic at the expense of common sense. But facts within easy reach of any one who cares to know them go to say that the greater abstinence of women is in some part due to an imperative conventionality; and this conventionality is, in a general way, strongest where the patriarchal tradition—the tradition that the woman is a chattel—has retained its hold in greatest vigor. In a sense which has been greatly qualified in scope and rigor, but which has by no means lost its meaning even yet, this tradition says that the woman, being a chattel, should consume only what is necessary to her sustenance—except so far as her further consumption contributes to the comfort or the good repute of her master. The consumption of luxuries, in the true sense, is a consumption directed to the comfort of the consumer himself, and is, therefore, a mark of the master. Any such consumption by others can take place only on a basis of sufferance. In communities where the popular habits of thought have been profoundly shaped by the patriarchal tradition we may accordingly look for survivals of the tabu on luxuries at least to the extent of a conventional deprecation of their use by the unfree and dependent class. This is more particularly true as regards certain luxuries, the use of which by the dependent class would detract sensibly from the comfort or pleasure of their masters, or which are held to be of doubtful legitimacy on other grounds. In the apprehension of the great conservative middle class of Western civilization the use of these various stimulants is obnoxious to at least one, if not both, of these objections; and it is a fact too significant to be passed over that it is precisely among these middle classes of the Germanic culture, with their strong surviving sense of the patriarchal proprieties, that the women are to the greatest extent subject to a qualified tabu on narcotics and alcoholic beverages. With many qualifications—with more qualifications as the patriarchal tradition has gradually weakened—the general rule is felt to be right and binding that women should consume only for the benefit of their masters. The objection of course presents itself that expenditure on women's dress and household paraphernalia is an obvious exception to this rule; but it will appear in the sequel that this exception is much more obvious than substantial.

During the earlier stages of economic development, consumption of goods without stint, especially consumption of the better grades of goods, ideally all consumption in excess of the subsistence minimum, pertains normally to the leisure class. This restriction tends to disappear, at least formally, after the later peaceable stage has been reached, with private ownership of goods and in an industrial system based on wage labor or on the petty household economy. But during the earlier quasi-peaceable stage, when so many of the traditions through which the institution of a leisure class has affected the economic life of later times were taking form and consistency, this principle has had the force of a conventional law. It has served as the norm to which consumption has tended to conform, and any appreciable departure from it is to be regarded as an aberrant form, sure to be eliminated sooner or later in the further course of development.

The quasi-peaceable gentleman of leisure, then, not only consumes of the staff of life beyond the minimum required for subsistence and physical efficiency, but his consumption also undergoes a specialization as regards the quality of the goods consumed. He consumes freely and of the best, in food, drink, narcotics, shelter, services, ornaments, apparel, weapons and accoutrements, amusements, amulets, and idols or divinities. In the process of gradual amelioration which takes place in the articles of his consumption the motive principle and the proximate aim of innovation is no doubt the higher efficiency of the improved and more elaborate products for personal comfort and well-being. But that does not remain the sole purpose of their consumption. The canon of reputability is at hand and seizes upon such innovations as are, according to its standard, fit to survive. Since the consumption of these more excellent goods is an evidence of wealth, it becomes honorific; and conversely, the failure to consume in due quantity and quality becomes a mark of inferiority and demerit.

This growth of punctilious discrimination as to qualitative excellence in eating, drinking, etc., presently affects not only the manner of life, but also the training and intellectual activity of the gentleman of leisure. He is no longer simply the successful, aggressive male, the man of strength, resource, and intrepidity. In order to avoid stultification he must also cultivate his tastes, for it now becomes incumbent on him to discriminate with some nicety between the noble and the ignoble in consumable goods. He becomes a connoisseur in creditable viands of various degrees of merit, in manly beverages and trinkets, in seemly apparel and architecture, in weapons, games, dancers, and the narcotics. This cultivation of the aesthetic faculty requires time and application, and the demands made upon the gentleman in this direction therefore tend to change his life of leisure into a more or less arduous application to the business of learning how to live a life of ostensible leisure in a becoming way. Closely related to the requirement that the gentleman must consume freely and of the right kind of goods, there is the requirement that he must know how to consume them in a seemly manner. His life of leisure must be conducted in due form. Hence arise good manners in the way pointed out in an earlier chapter. High-bred manners and ways of living are items of conformity to the norm of conspicuous leisure and conspicuous consumption.

Conspicuous consumption of valuable goods is a means of reputability to the gentleman of leisure. As wealth accumulates on his hands, his own unaided effort will not avail to sufficiently put his opulence in evidence by this method. The aid of friends and competitors is therefore brought in by resorting to the giving of valuable presents and expensive feasts and entertainments. Presents and feasts had probably another origin than that of naive ostentation, but they acquired their utility for this purpose very early, and they have retained that character to the present; so that their utility in this respect has now long been the substantial ground on which these usages rest. Costly entertainments, such as the potlatch or the ball, are peculiarly adapted to serve this end. The competitor with whom the entertainer wishes to institute a comparison is, by this method, made to serve as a means to the end. He consumes vicariously for his host at the same time that he is a witness to the consumption of that excess of good things which his host is unable to dispose of single-handed, and he is also made to witness his host's facility in etiquette.

In the giving of costly entertainments other motives, of a more genial kind, are of course also present. The custom of festive gatherings probably originated in motives of conviviality and religion; these motives are also present in the later development, but they do not continue to be the sole motives. The latter day leisure class festivities and entertainments may continue in some slight degree to serve the religious need and in a higher degree the needs of recreation and conviviality, but they also serve an invidious purpose; and they serve it none the less effectually for having a colorable noninvidious ground in these more avowable motives. But the economic effect of these social amenities is not therefore lessened, either in the vicarious consumption of goods or in the exhibition of difficult and costly achievements in etiquette.

As wealth accumulates, the leisure class develops further in function and structures, and there arises a differentiation within the class. There is a more or less elaborate system of rank and grades. This differentiation is furthered by the inheritance of wealth and the consequent inheritance of gentility. With the inheritance of gentility goes the inheritance of obligatory leisure;

and gentility of a sufficient potency to entail a life of leisure may be inherited without the complement of wealth required to maintain a dignified leisure. Gentle blood may be transmitted without goods enough to afford a reputably free consumption at one's ease. Hence results a class of impecunious gentlemen of leisure, incidentally referred to already. These half-caste gentlemen of leisure fall into a system of hierarchical gradations. Those who stand near the higher and the highest grades of the wealthy leisure class, in point of birth, or in point of wealth, or both, outrank the remoter born and the pecuniarily weaker. These lower grades, especially the impecunious, or marginal, gentlemen of leisure, affiliate themselves by a system of dependence or fealty to the great ones; by so doing they gain an increment of repute, or of the means with which to lead a life of leisure, from their patron. They become his courtiers or retainers, servants; and being fed and countenanced by their patron they are indices of his rank and vicarious consumers of his superfluous wealth. Many of these affiliated gentlemen of leisure are at the same time lesser men of substance in their own right; so that some of them are scarcely at all, others only partially, to be rated as vicarious consumers. So many of them, however, as make up the retainers and hangers-on of the patron may be classed as vicarious consumers without qualification. Many of these again, and also many of the other aristocracy of less degree, have in turn attached to their persons a more or less comprehensive group of vicarious consumers in the persons of their wives and children, their servants, retainers, etc.

Throughout this graduated scheme of vicarious leisure and vicarious consumption the rule holds that these offices must be performed in some such manner, or under some such circumstance or insignia, as shall point plainly to the master to whom this leisure or consumption pertains, and to whom therefore the resulting increment of good repute of right inures. The consumption and leisure executed by these persons for their master or patron represents an investment on his part with a view to an increase of good fame. As regards feasts and largesses this is obvious enough, and the imputation of repute to the host or patron here takes place immediately, on the ground of common notoriety. Where leisure and consumption is performed vicariously by henchmen and retainers, imputation of the resulting repute to the patron is effected by their residing near his person so that it may be plain to all men from what source they draw. As the group whose good esteem is to be secured in this way grows larger, more patent means are required to indicate the imputation of merit for the leisure performed, and to this end uniforms, badges, and liveries come into vogue. The wearing of uniforms or liveries implies a considerable degree of dependence, and may even be said to be a mark of servitude, real or ostensible. The wearers of uniforms and liveries may be roughly divided into two classes—the free and the servile, or the noble and the ignoble. The services performed by them are likewise divisible into noble and ignoble. Of course the distinction is not observed with strict consistency in practice; the less debasing of the base services and the less honorific of the noble functions are not infrequently merged in the same person. But the general distinction is not on that account to be overlooked. What may add some perplexity is the fact that this fundamental distinction between noble and ignoble, which rests on the nature of the ostensible service performed, is traversed by a secondary distinction into honorific and humiliating, resting on the rank of the person for whom the service is performed or whose livery is worn. So, those offices which are by right the proper employment of the leisure class are noble; such are government, and the like—in short, those which may be classed as ostensibly predatory employments. On the other hand, those employments which properly fall to the industrious class are ignoble; such as handicraft or other productive labor, menial services, and the like. But a base service performed for a person of very high degree may become a very honorific office; as for instance the office of a Maid of Honor or of a Lady in Waiting to the Queen, or the King's Master of the Horse or his Keeper of the Hounds. The two offices last named suggest a principle of some general bearing. Whenever, as in these cases, the menial service in question has to do directly with the primary leisure employments of fighting and hunting, it easily acquires a reflected honorific character. In this way great honor may come to attach to an employment which in its own nature belongs to the baser sort.

In the later development of peaceable industry, the usage of employing an idle corps of uniformed men-at-arms gradually lapses. Vicarious consumption by dependents bearing the insignia of their patron or master narrows down to a corps of liveried menials. In a heightened degree, therefore, the livery comes to be a badge of servitude, or rather of servility. Something of a honorific character is always attached to the livery of the armed retainer, but this honorific character disappears when the livery becomes the exclusive badge of the menial. The livery becomes obnoxious to nearly all who are required to wear it. We are yet so little removed from a state of effective slavery as still to be fully sensitive to the sting of any imputation of servility. This antipathy asserts itself even in the case of the liveries or uniforms which some corporations prescribe as the distinctive dress of their employees. In this country the aversion even goes the length of discrediting—in a mild and uncertain way—those government employments, military and civil, which require the wearing of a livery or uniform.

With the disappearance of servitude, the number of vicarious consumers attached to any one gentleman tends, on the whole, to decrease. The like is of course true, and perhaps in a still higher degree, of the number of dependents who perform vicarious leisure for him. In a general way, though not wholly nor consistently, these two groups coincide. The dependent who was first delegated for these duties was the wife, or the chief wife; and, as would be expected, in the later development of the institution, when the number of persons by whom these duties are customarily performed gradually narrows, the wife remains the last. In the higher grades of society a large volume of both these kinds of service is required; and here the wife is of course still assisted in the work by a more or less numerous corps of menials. But as we descend the social scale, the point is presently reached where the duties of vicarious leisure and consumption devolve upon the wife alone. In the communities of the Western culture, this point is at present found among the lower middle class.

And here occurs a curious inversion. It is a fact of common observation that in this lower middle class there is no pretence of leisure on the part of the head of the household. Through force of circumstances it has fallen into disuse. But the middle-class wife still carries on the business of vicarious leisure, for the good name of the household and its master. In descending the social scale in any modern industrial community, the primary fact—the conspicuous leisure of the master of the household—disappears at a relatively high point. The head of the middle-class household has been reduced by economic circumstances to turn his hand to gaining a livelihood by occupations which often partake largely of the character of industry, as in the case of the ordinary business man of today. But the derivative fact—the vicarious leisure and consumption rendered by the wife, and the auxiliary vicarious performance of leisure by menials—remains in vogue as a conventionality which the demands of reputability will not suffer to be slighted. It is by no means an uncommon spectacle to find a man applying himself to work with the utmost assiduity, in order that his wife may in due form render for him that degree of vicarious leisure which the common sense of the time demands.

The leisure rendered by the wife in such cases is, of course, not a simple manifestation of idleness or indolence. It almost invariably occurs disguised under some form of work or household duties or social amenities, which prove on analysis to serve little or no ulterior end beyond showing that she does not and need not occupy herself with anything that is gainful or that is of substantial use. As has already been noticed under the head of manners, the greater part of the customary round of domestic cares to which the middle-class housewife gives her time and effort is of this character. Not that the results of her attention to household matters, of a decorative and mundificatory character, are not pleasing to the sense of men trained in middle-class proprieties; but the taste to which these effects of household adornment and tidiness appeal is a taste which has been formed under the selective guidance of a canon of propriety that demands just these evidences of wasted effort. The effects are pleasing to us chiefly because we have been taught to find them pleasing. There goes into these domestic duties much solicitude for a proper combination of form and color, and for other ends that are to be classed as aesthetic in the proper sense of the term; and it is not denied that effects having some substantial aesthetic value are sometimes attained. Pretty much all that is here insisted on is that, as regards these amenities of life, the housewife's efforts are under the guidance of traditions that have been shaped by the law of conspicuously wasteful expenditure of time and substance. If beauty or comfort is achieved—and it is a more or less fortuitous circumstance if they are—they must be achieved by means and methods that commend themselves to the great economic law of wasted effort. The more reputable, "presentable" portion of middle-class household paraphernalia are, on the one hand, items of conspicuous consumption, and on the other hand, apparatus for putting in evidence the vicarious leisure rendered by the housewife.

The requirement of vicarious consumption at the hands of the wife continues in force even at a lower point in the pecuniary scale than the requirement of vicarious leisure. At a point below which little if any pretence of wasted effort, in ceremonial cleanness and the like, is observable, and where there is assuredly no conscious attempt at ostensible leisure, decency still requires the wife to consume some goods conspicuously for the reputability of the household and its head. So that, as the latter-day outcome of this evolution of an archaic institution, the wife, who was at the outset the drudge and chattel of the man, both in fact and in theory, the producer of goods for him to consume, has become the ceremonial consumer of goods which he produces. But still quite unmistakably remains his chattel in theory; for the habitual rendering of vicarious leisure and consumption is the abiding mark of the unfree servant.

This vicarious consumption practiced by the household of the middle and lower classes can not be counted as a direct expression of the leisure-class scheme of life, since the household of this pecuniary grade does not belong within the leisure class. It is rather that the leisure-class scheme of life here comes to an expression at the second remove. The leisure class stands at the head of the social structure in point of reputability; and its manner of life and its standards of worth therefore afford the norm of reputability for the community. The observance of these standards in some degree of approximation, becomes incumbent upon all classes lower in the scale. In modern civilized communities the lines of demarcation between social classes have grown vague and transient, and wherever this happens the norm of reputability imposed by the upper class extends its coercive influence with but slight hindrance down through the social structure to the lowest strata. The result is that the members of each stratum accept as their ideal of decency the scheme of life in vogue in the next higher stratum, and bend their energies to live up to that ideal. On pain of forfeiting their good name and their self-respect in case of failure, they must conform to the accepted code, at least in appearance.

The basis on which good repute in any highly organized industrial community ultimately rests is pecuniary strength; and the means of showing pecuniary strength, and so of gaining or retaining a good name, are leisure and a conspicuous consumption of goods. Accordingly, both of these methods are in vogue as far down the scale as it remains possible; and in the lower strata in which the two methods are employed, both offices are in great part delegated to the wife and children of the household. Lower still, where any degree of leisure, even ostensible, has become impracticable for the wife, the conspicuous consumption of goods remains and is carried on by the wife and children. The man of the household also can do something in this direction, and, indeed, he commonly does; but with a still lower descent into the levels of indigence—along the margin of the slums—the man, and presently also the children, virtually cease to consume valuable goods for appearances, and the woman remains virtually the sole exponent of the household's pecuniary decency. No class of society, not even the most abjectly poor, foregoes all customary conspicuous consumption. The last items of this category of consumption are not given up except under stress of the direst necessity. Very much of squalor and discomfort will be endured before the last trinket or the last pretence of pecuniary decency is put away. There is no class and no country that has yielded so abjectly before the pressure of physical want as to deny themselves all gratification of this higher or spiritual need.

EDWARD A. ROSS

Edward Alsworth Ross (1866-1951) was one of the liveliest—and longest-lived—of American sociologists. He was graduated from Coe College, in Iowa, in 1886, studied at Berlin, and received his Ph.D. from The Johns Hopkins University in 1891. He taught at Indiana, Cornell, Stanford, Nebraska, and, finally, from 1906 to his retirement in 1937, at the University of Wisconsin—one of the longest teaching careers in American academic life. He was also a world traveler, visiting at times Mexico, China, Russia, Sweden, India, and other countries. He was fifth president of the American Sociological Society and the last man to be elected for a second year, serving in the post in both 1914 and 1915.

Ross was both a sociologist and a social reformer. In the latter capacity, in fact, he lost his job at Stanford University. He was also, according to common report, one of the most colorful and interesting of university lecturers in the field of sociology. His many books exhibit both his scholarly and scientific interests on the one hand and his reformist tendencies on the other. In the former groups four books are outstanding—*Social Control,* 1901; *The Foundations of Sociology,* 1905; *Social Psychology,* 1908 (the first book ever written in that field); and *The Principles of Sociology,* 1920 (revised 1930). The first of these, *Social Control,* is a clear classic in the literature of sociology, surveying as it does "the foundations of order" in society. It is from this book that the following selection is taken.

From *Social Control*

A condition of order at the junction of crowded city thoroughfares implies primarily an absence of collisions between men or vehicles that interfere one with another. Order cannot be said to prevail among people going in the same direction at the same pace, because there is no interference. It does not exist when persons are constantly colliding one with another. But when all who meet or overtake one another in crowded ways take the time and pains needed to avoid collision, the throng is *orderly*. Now, at the bottom of the notion of social order lies the same idea. The members of an orderly community do not go out of their way to aggress upon one another. Moreover, whenever their pursuits interfere they make the adjustment necessary to escape collision, and make it according to some conventional rule. If the weaker of two hunters that have brought down the same stag avoids a fight by yielding up the game, there is peace, but no order. But if the dispute is settled according to the rule that "first struck" decides the ownership of game, the solution is an orderly one. Similarly, there is order when teamsters shun collision by conforming to "the law of the road," or miners settle the ownership of claims according to priority of "pegging out."

The denser the traffic that is handled without confusion at a busy corner, the higher is the grade of order. Likewise, the more that the smooth running of social machinery implies the frequent breaking off or turning aside of individual activities, the more perfect is the social order. *Successful cooperation,* therefore, bespeaks a high grade of social order, inasmuch as each of the cooperators must unfold specific activities within precise limits, and the results therefrom are enjoyed or shared according to some recognized principle. *Hierarchical organization* is still more a test of orderliness, inasmuch as in the sharing of unlike burdens and the division of unequal benefits men are more apt to fall afoul of one another.

The severest test of the regime of order occurs when, as in

war or government, individuals are incited to a common effort, the benefits of which are shared in common. The sacrificing of one corps of an army to save the rest, or the placing of the public burdens upon the nongoverning classes, is recognized as putting the severest strain on discipline. In general, the absence of hostile encounter is a mark of social order, since it implies that interferences are adjusted according to some rule. But extreme division of social labor and high organization is the surest sign of order, since it requires the nice adjustment of multifarious activities according to some prearranged plan.

The readiness of men to disturb the peace or to violate rules in the pursuit of their personal interests depends upon their mental make-up. The peaceable turn aside from collision, while the pugnacious welcome it. The easily contented readily accommodate their desires and actions to the customary restrictions, but the enterprising are always pressing against and trampling upon barriers. The passive strive only to satisfy old wants, and are therefore much stronger in resistance than in offence. The aggressive are insatiate and put forth as much energy to seize what they have not, as to keep what they have. In a passive race, once order is established, the individual keeps to his prescribed orbit from sheer inertia. In an aggressive race order is perpetually endangered by the unruliness of the individual, and can be maintained only through the unremitting operation of certain social forces.

Now, it is the purpose of this inquiry to ascertain how men of the West-European breed are brought to live closely together, and to associate their efforts with that degree of harmony we see about us. Social order, even among the passive, unambitious Hindoos, presents a problem for solution. But it is a much more serious problem among the dolichocephalic blonds of the West. The restless, striving, doing Aryan, with his personal ambition, his lust for power, his longing to wreak himself, his willingness to turn the world upside down to get the fame, or the fortune, or the woman, he wants, is under no easy discipline. The existence of order among men of this daring and disobedient breed challenges explanation. Especially is this true of the European man in America or Australia. The same selective migrations that made the Teuton more self-assertive than the docile Slav or the quiescent Hindoo, have made the American more strong-willed and unmanageable than even the West-European.

To many, no doubt, a survey of the foundations of social order will appear superfluous. Most of us take order for granted, and are hardly more aware of it than we are of the air we breathe. Order being the universal and indispensable condition of all our social structures, we give no more thought to it than to the force of cohesion that keeps our machinery from flying into bits. Those to whom the fact is brought home by the persistence of a delinquent class assume, nevertheless, that the social fabrics rest on a law-abiding disposition which is natural to all but the slant-browed few.

But it would be, in truth, much juster to assume a state of disorder. We ought to take for granted that men living in propinquity will continually fall afoul of one another. We ought to expect in the normal person not, it is true, the malice, lust, or ferocity of the born criminal, but certainly a natural unwillingness to be checked in the hot pursuit of his ends. Whenever men swarm in new places—Dutch Flat, Kimberly, Siberia, Skagway —the man-to-man struggle stands out naked and clear, and the slow emergence of order out of disorder and violence presents itself as the attainment of a difficult and artificial condition. Could we abstract from such communities the training received in older societies, the thrift that recognizes disorder as a blight upon prosperity, and the ready revolver which discourages aggression by equalizing men, we might arrive at a notion of the state in which the men of today, despite their high facial angle, would find themselves, if they were remanded to the zero point of social development.

Starting from this point, we must face the problem. By what means is the human struggle narrowed and limited? How has violence been purged away from it? How has the once brawling torrent of conflicting personal desires been induced to flow smoothly in the channels of legitimate rivalry, or even for a time to vanish underground in those numerous cooperations where conflict is absent until it comes to dividing the results?

It is a common delusion that order is to be explained by the person's inherited equipment for good conduct, rather than by any control that society exercises over him. Once it was held that normal human beings are born with a set of commandments etched upon the soul. When evidence accumulated as to the startling contrasts in the moral ideas of different times and peoples, the moralists contented themselves with declaring that the soul is, at least, endowed with a sense of *oughtness*. When the emptiness of this theory was demonstrated, and formalism was convicted of overlooking the emotional elements that lie behind conduct, there arose the theory that man's nature is constituted out of egoism and altruism. This in time was seen to be much the same as defining milk as a combination of whey and curd. Then came the charming tales of the mutual aid of ants, beavers, and prairie dogs, suggesting the existence of certain social instincts which moralists found it very convenient to use in explaining human society.

We are not yet sure, however, that man is the "good ape" Buffon supposed him to be. There is reason to believe that our social order is by no means a mere hive or herd order. It seems to be a *fabric,* rather than a *growth.*

But, in any case, it is important to know what human nature can furnish in the cause of social harmony. The gulf between private ends and public ends, between the aims of the individual and the aims of his fellows, is bridged from both sides, and we must know what abutments and spans are provided by the individual himself, if we are to measure the extent of the moral engineering that must be undertaken by society. It is our business, therefore, before entering upon the consideration of the social factors of order, to take stock of the moral capital of the person. We shall, first of all, ascertain the role of *sympathy,* of *sociability,* of *the sense of justice,* and of *resentment,* in establishing and maintaining social order. . . .

A control that we have any right to call *social* has behind it practically the whole weight of society. But still this control often wells up and spreads out from certain centres which we might term *the radiant points of social control.* Uniform as it is to the eye, the social substance when tested resolves itself into froth and liquid, into chaff and wheat, into protoplasm and nuclei. Our task now is to fix upon the nuclei that determine the principal lines social control may take. In plain terms, the question before us is, What is the ultimate seat of authority? Where resides the will that guides the social energies? Who hold the levers which set in motion the social checks or stimuli that hold a man back or push him on?

That frequently these checks and stimuli are managed by a rather small knot of persons should not for a moment lead the reader to confuse social control with class control. Often enough, indeed, a minority, in virtue of its superior strength, courage, craft, or organization, seizes the reins of power; but such domination always entails a rupture of social consciousness. While outwardly there is but one society, there are in reality two or more societies which happen to interpenetrate as to substance. Between leaders and led, there is a bond of good will and trust. Between drones and workers, parasites and hosts, come distrust and hate, and their clash of interests is liable to pass at any moment into the clash of arms. In history the relations of Venetians and Cypriotes, Normans and Sicilians, Franks and Gauls, betray the presence of class control.

Totally different from class control in origin is the power of a minority to direct social control. Each category of people in society has its own point of view, and consequently its own way of envisaging the problems of conduct. Now, one of these views can prevail only in case the others are withdrawn. If a class finds itself leading the march at the head of the social procession, it is only because the other classes have more confidence in it than they have in themselves. *Social power is concentrated or diffused in proportion as men do or do not feel themselves in need of guidance or protection.* When it is concentrated it lodges in that class of men in which the people feel the most confidence. The many transfer their allegiance from one class to another—from elders to priests, or from priests to savants—when their supreme need changes, or when they have lost confidence in the old guidance. When they begin to feel secure and able to cope with evils in their own strength and wisdom, the many resume self-direction and the monopoly of social power by the few ceases.

Such is the underlying law of the transformations and displacements of power. The immediate cause of the location of power is prestige. The class that has the most prestige will have the most power. The prestige of *numbers* gives ascendency to the crowd. The prestige of *age* gives it to the elders. The prestige of *prowess* gives it to the war chief, or to the military caste. The prestige of *sanctity* gives it to the priestly caste. The prestige of *inspiration* gives it to the prophet. The prestige of *place* gives it to the official class. The prestige of *money* gives it to the capitalists. The prestige of *ideas* gives it to the élite. The prestige of *learning* gives it to the mandarins. The absence of prestige and the faith of each man in himself gives weight to the individual and reduces social control to a minimum.

In some cases there exists an appropriate name for the régime. When the priest guides, we call it *clericalism.* When the fighting caste is deferred to, we call it *militarism.* When the initiative lies with the minions of the state, we call it *officialism.* The leadership of the moneyed men is *capitalism.* That of the men of ideas is *liberalism.* The reliance of men upon their own wisdom and strength is *individualism.*

These distinctions, I need hardly add, are far deeper than distinctions, like *aristocracy, monarchy, republic,* which relate merely to the form of government. For the location of social power expresses much more truly the inner constitution of society than does the location of political power. And so the shiftings of power within the state, far from having causes of their own, are apt to follow and answer to the shiftings of power within society. Yet since political power is palpable and lies near the surface of things, political science long ago ascertained its forms and laws; while social power, lying hidden in the dim depths, has hardly even yet drawn the attention of social science.

When picked men flock together in a settlement or mining camp, authority resides at first in the Crowd. The mass is the sole seat of social power, and the mass meeting, in which one man is as good as another, expresses the will of the community. When in the course of time neighbors learn to know and appraise one another, men of superior character, sagacity, or disinterestedness come to influence their fellows more than they are influenced by them. The seat of the common will, then, is no longer the crowd, but the Public. In this organization of minds every man counts for something, but one man does not always count for as much as another.

When, on the other hand, a group is formed by the natural

increase of families, the first seat of authority is the Elders. The long years of dependence on the parent make it difficult even for grown sons to throw off the paternal yoke. This prestige of the father becomes the prestige of *age* when ancestor worship teaches men that the old stand nearest to the Unseen, and will themselves soon become spirits, able to ban or to bless.

Like the kinship bond, the ascendency of the elders is all but universal in the childhood of societies. But one place where the graybeard is always at a disadvantage is in the fight. So when, as with lusty barbarians, fighting becomes the chief business of life, the war leader quite outshines the council of elders. Prowess finally surpasses age in prestige, just as from the same cause the bond of comradeship becomes stronger than the tie of blood. Warriors of fine qualities and brilliant exploits get together the biggest bands for foray, and so are able to amass wealth, keep retainers, and get looked upon as "noble." In the days of permanent conquest these men of social power become the captains of the host, the heads of the state, and the sole possessors of political power.

It is clear, then, that the Military Caste does not get social weight just because it is able to bully the rest of the people. Terrify men and they cling to the skirts of those powerful to save. When violence is loose the hind creeps under the castle wall, the trembling burgher pours out his florins for protection, and the Soldier strikes the dominant note in social opinion. When peace makes broad her wings the fighting man, becoming less necessary, becomes less influential.

In proportion as men do not understand the play of natural forces, they are likely to connect their fate with the good will or the ill will of unseen beings. If now, in an ignorant age, among imaginative men who see pain, disease, and death lurking on every hand, there arises a class of men who claim to enjoy high consideration with these unseen beings, that class will acquire enormous social power. Whether or not they finger the machinery of the state, their curse will be dreaded, their commands obeyed, and their intercessions sought by all men. It is no wonder, then, that the Priesthood, which in the civilized Roman Empire was the minister of society, became its master when this organization of intelligent men had only benighted, fanciful barbarians to deal with. The fact that between the sixth and the thirteenth centuries about one-third of the soil of Europe passed by free offering into the hands of religious corporations, while the best talent of the age turned to the monastic life, tells what confidence men had in the supernatural powers of the sacred caste.

The layman is far less supple to the will of the priest if there lie to hand written directions and formulas for controlling or pleasing the Unseen. An open Sacred Book, therefore, has saved both the Jew and the Mohammedan from the excesses of priestly domination; and when Luther and the Reformers sought to break the sacerdotal spell, they gave men the Bible, and bade them look therein for the way of life.

After safety from foes and from the Unseen, man's next desire is for the security of his daily bread. For most men this depends upon the willingness of some one to buy their wares or their labor, i.e. upon patronage. The Wealthy, then, who, as luxurious idlers, spend money and make trade, or, as captains of industry and lords of enterprise, employ the labor and organize the prosperity of kingdoms, will never be without great social power. From the dependence of the working many upon the moneyed few flows a patronal authority which sends its tinge far into law, religion, morals, and policy. For when any class of men play the part of earthly Providence to the multitude, their views as to what ought to be praised or blamed, commanded or forbidden, cannot but affect the character of social control.

The State is, in theory at least, a channel and not a source of control. It is supposed to be a device by which social power is collected, transmitted, and applied *so as to do work*. But, as a matter of fact, the state, when it becomes paternal and develops on the administrative side, is able in a measure to guide the society it professes to obey. With its hierarchy of officials and its army of functionaries, the state gets a glamour of its own, and becomes an independent centre of social power. And here again we can see that such a concentration of influence is a measure of man's need and trust. For the prestige of officialdom is not wholly a matter of numbers and pay. The more the state helps the citizen when he cannot help himself, protecting him from disease, foes, criminals, rivals abroad and monopolists at home, the more he will look to it for guidance. While, conversely, the more he uses it merely as a convenient alternative to self-help or free association, the less will he accept its lead.

Another radiant point in society is the Mandarinate, or the body of scholarly or learned men who have in some formal way been tested, accredited, and labelled. Such are the mandarins of China, the pundits of India, the *Gelehrte* of Germany, the academicians and professors in France, the clergy of nonsacerdotal bodies like the Reformed churches, and the rabbis of the Jewish congregations. The mandarinate ought to include the wisest and best in society; but the false worth that attaches to purely conventional learning, and the sifting and promoting of the learned by tests that are artificial and futile, are likely to prevent it.

The Élite, or those distinguished by ideas and talent, are the natural leaders of society, inasmuch as their ascendency depends on nothing false or factitious. Usually they appear as a small knot of persons who, united by allegiance to some group of ideas, are able to persuade the majority without allowing themselves, in turn, to be infected by vulgar prejudices. The Greek Philosophers, the Stoics, the Fathers, the Schoolmen, the Humanists, the Reformers, the Pietists, the Encyclopedists, the Liberals, are examples of an active leaven able to leaven the whole lump.

Finally, there is the Genius, who, as founder of religion, prophet, reformer, or artist, is able to build up a vast personal authority and sway the multitude at pleasure. Society can dispense with the guidance of the Élite and the genius only when the way is straight and the path is clear. A people creeping gradually across a vast empty land, as we Americans have been doing this century, may safely belittle leadership and deify the spirit of self-reliance. But when population thickens, interests clash, and the difficult problems of mutual adjustment become pressing, it is foolish and dangerous not to follow the lead of superior men.

The impulses streaming out from each of the eight principal centres we have described do not, of course, meet a perfectly yielding mass. The power of the Few to take the role of social cerebrum depends entirely upon how far the Many capitulate to it. The radiation of control from the elders is limited by the reaction of the young men, that from the priests is limited by the reaction of the laity, that from the bureaucracy is limited by the reaction of the citizens, that from the élite is limited by the reaction of the vulgar. When the energy of the resistance comes to equal that of the impulses, the class ceases to be a controlling centre and loses itself in the social mass.

What keeps social commands from multiplying and choking up life, as the rank growth of swamp weed chokes up water-courses, is, of course, the resistance of the individual. Naturally a man prefers to do as he pleases, and not as society pleases to have him do. The more, then, that social power dwells in the mass of persons whose necks are galled by social requirement, the more the yoke of the law will be lightened. On the other hand, the more distinct those who apply social pressure from those who must bear it, the more likely is regulation to be laid on lavishly in obedience to some class ideal. Hence we arrive at the law that *the volume of social requirement will be greater when social power is concentrated than when it is diffused.*

When the laws, standards, and ideals a man is required to conform to, spring up among the plain people, they will be ahead of the community, but not very far ahead. But when they originate with the few, they may be very far in advance of the community and so hurrying it forward, or they may be far in the rear and hence holding it back. It is a well-known fact that we never find a legal or moral code pitched high above the natural inclination of a people without signs of minority domination. It is safe, then, to frame the law, *the greater the ascendency of the few, the more possible is it for social control to affect the course of the social movement.*

Social control takes the tinge of the source from which it springs. When the reverend seniors monopolize power, much will be made of filial respect and obedience, infanticide will be a small offence, while parricide will be punished with horrible torments. Let the priests get the upper hand, and chastity, celibacy, humility, unquestioning belief, and scrupulous observance will be the leading virtues. The ascendency of the military caste shifts the accent to obedience, loyalty, pugnacity, and sensitiveness to personal honor. When the moneyed man holds the baton, we hear much of industriousness, thrift, sobriety, probity, and civility. The mandarins and *literati* have no moral programme of their own, but they are sure to exalt reverence for order, precedent, and rank. The élite, whatever ideal they champion, will be sure to commend the ordering of one's life according to ideas and principles, rather than according to precedent and tradition. For only by fostering the radical spirit can they hope to lead men into untrodden paths. We may, then, lay it down as a law that *the character of social requirement changes with every shifting of social power.*

Classes differ in readiness to twist social control to their own advantage. Elders, élite, or genius have rarely abused their social power. But ecclesiasticism claims exemptions and privileges for the clergy, makes the word of the priest binding even when he is living in open sin, and grants for money indulgence to commit the most horrible crimes. When the fighting caste guides social opinion, it is permissible to mulct the husbandman and the merchant, and to condone the violence and sensuality of the men of the camp. Under the ascendency of the rich and leisured, property becomes more sacred than person, moral standards vary with pecuniary status, and it is felt that "God will think twice before He damns a person of quality." In general, *the more distinct, knit together, and self-conscious the influential minority, the more likely is social control to be colored with class selfishness.*

WILLIAM GRAHAM SUMNER

Born in Paterson, New Jersey, the son of an English immigrant, William Graham Sumner (1840-1910) was trained for the ministry both at Oxford and at Yale, and served as deacon, assistant, and rector of churches in New York City and in New Jersey. He discovered early in his career, however, that he was drawn more to economic and social subjects than to theological ones and therefore welcomed the opportunity to return to Yale as a professor of political and social science, a post he held throughout his lifetime. At one point his university career was endangered when he was accused of using as a text an "atheistic" book, namely Spencer's *Principles of Sociology*.

Sumner made his most enduring mark as a teacher and indeed it may be said that for many generations of Yale students he was an institution. He preached in the classroom no less than he had formerly done in the pulpit, and the new preaching was in favor of such social and economic doctrines as laissez-faire, "hard money," and the survival of the fittest. He was opposed to all forms of unscientific sentimentality and for two intellectual disciplines—metaphysics and psychology—he had little use. His books reflect the social Darwinism to which he was heir. The specifically sociological works among them include the now classic *Folkways* (1907), from which the following brief selections are taken, and *The Science of Society* (4 volumes, 1927) which his devoted colleague A. G. Keller painstakingly put together with the assistance of his student Maurice R. Davie after Sumner's death. Sumner succeeded Ward in the presidency of the American Sociological Society and served during the two years 1908 and 1909.

From *Folkways**

Definition and mode of origin of the Folkways. If we put together all that we have learned from anthropology and ethnography about primitive men and primitive society, we perceive that the first task of life is to live. Men begin with acts, not with thoughts. Every moment brings necessities which must be satisfied at once. Need was the first experience, and it was followed at once by a blundering effort to satisfy it. It is generally taken for granted that men inherited some guiding instincts from their beast ancestry, and it may be true, although it has never been proved. If there were such inheritances, they controlled and aided the first efforts to satisfy needs. Analogy makes it easy to assume that the ways of beasts had produced channels of habit and predisposition along which dexterities and other psychophysical activities would run easily. Experiments with newborn animals show that in the absence of any experience of the relation of means to ends, efforts to satisfy needs are clumsy and blundering. The method is that of trial and failure, which produces repeated pain, loss, and disappointments. Nevertheless, it is a method of rude experiment and selection. The earliest efforts of men were of this kind. Need was the impelling force. Pleasure and pain, on the one side and the other, were the rude constraints which defined the line on which efforts must proceed. The ability to distinguish between pleasure and pain is the only physical power which is to be assumed. Thus ways of doing things were selected, which were expedient. They answered the purpose better than other ways, or with less toil and pain. Along the course in which efforts were compelled to go, habit, routine, and skill were developed. The struggle to maintain existence was carried on, not individually, but in groups. Each profited by the other's experience; hence there was concurrence towards that which proved to be most expedient. All at last adopted the same way

* From *Folkways* by William Graham Sumner, by permission of Ginn and Company.

for the same purpose; hence the ways turned into customs and became mass phenomena. Instincts were developed in connection with them. In this way folkways arise. The young learn them by tradition, imitation, and authority. The folkways, at a time, provide for all the needs of life then and there. They are uniform, universal in the group, imperative, and invariable. As time goes on, the folkways become more and more arbitrary, positive, and imperative. If asked why they act in a certain way in certain cases, primitive people always answer that it is because they and their ancestors always have done so. A sanction also arises from ghost fear. The ghosts of ancestors would be angry if the living should change the ancient folkways.

The folkways are a societal force. The operation by which folkways are produced consists in the frequent repetition of petty acts, often by great numbers acting in concert or, at least, acting in the same way when face to face with the same need. The immediate motive is interest. It produces habit in the individual and custom in the group. It is, therefore, in the highest degree original and primitive. By habit and custom it exerts a strain on every individual within its range; therefore it rises to a societal force to which great classes of societal phenomena are due. Its earliest stages, its course, and laws may be studied; also its influence on individuals and their reaction on it. It is our present purpose so to study it. We have to recognize it as one of the chief forces by which a society is made to be what it is. Out of the unconscious experiment which every repetition of the ways includes, there issues pleasure or pain, and then, so far as the men are capable of reflection, convictions that the ways are conducive to societal welfare. These two experiences are not the same. The most uncivilized men, both in the food quest and in war, do things which are painful, but which have been found to be expedient. Perhaps these cases teach the sense of social welfare better than those which are pleasurable and favorable to welfare. The former cases call for some intelligent reflection on experience. When this conviction as to the relation to welfare is added to the folkways they are converted into mores, and, by virtue of the philosophical and ethical element added to them, they win utility and importance and become the source of the science and the art of living.

Folkways are made unconsciously. It is of the first importance to notice that, from the first acts by which men try to satisfy needs, each act stands by itself, and looks no further than the immediate satisfaction. From recurrent needs arise habits for the individual and customs for the group, but these results are consequences which were never conscious, and never foreseen or intended. They are not noticed until they have long existed, and it is still longer before they are appreciated. Another long time must pass, and a higher stage of mental development must be reached, before they can be used as a basis from which pressure can be foreseen. The folkways, therefore are not creations of human purpose and wit. They are like products of natural forces which men unconsciously set in operation, or they are like the instinctive ways of animals, which are developed out of experience, which reach a final form of maximum adaptation to an interest, which are handed down by tradition and admit of no exception or variation, yet change to meet new conditions, still within the same limited methods, and without rational reflection or purpose. From this it results that all the life of human beings, in all ages and stages of culture, is primarily controlled by a vast mass of folkways handed down from the earliest existence of the race, having the nature of the ways of other animals, only the top-most layers of which are subject to change and control, and have been somewhat modified by human philosophy, ethics, and religion, or by other acts of intelligent reflection. We are told of savages that "It is difficult to exhaust the customs and small ceremonial usages of a savage people. Custom regulates the whole of a man's actions,—his bathing, washing, cutting his hair, eating, drinking, and fasting. From his cradle to his grave he is the slave of ancient usage. In his life there is nothing free, nothing original, nothing spontaneous, no progress towards a higher and better life, and no attempt to improve his condition, mentally, morally, or spiritually." All men act in this way with only a little wider margin of voluntary variation.

The aleatory interest. If we should try to find a specimen society in which expedient ways of satisfying needs and interests were found by trial and failure, and by long selection from experience, as broadly described above, it might be impossible to find one. Such a practical and utilitarian mode of procedure, even when mixed with ghost sanction, is rationalistic. It would not be suited to the ways and temper of primitive men. There was an element in the most elementary experience which was irrational and defied all expedient methods. One might use the best known means with the greatest care, yet fail of the result. On the other hand, one might get a great result with no effort at all. One might also incur a calamity without any fault of his own. This was the aleatory element in life, the element of risk and loss, good or bad fortune. This element is never absent from the affairs of men. It has greatly influenced their life philosophy and policy. On one side, good luck may mean something for nothing, the extreme case of prosperity and felicity. On the other side, ill luck may mean failure, loss, calamity, and disappointment, in spite of the most earnest and well-planned endeavor. The minds of men always dwell more on bad luck. They accept ordinary prosperity as a matter of course. Misfortunes arrest their attention and remain in their memory. Hence the ills of life are the mode of manifestation of the aleatory element which has most affected life policy. Primitive men ascribed all incidents to the agency of men or of ghosts and spirits. Good and ill luck were attributed to the superior powers, and were supposed to be due to their pleasure or displeasure at the conduct of men. This group of notions constitutes goblinism. It furnishes a complete world philosophy. The element of luck is always present in the struggle for existence. That is why primitive men never could carry on the struggle for existence, disregarding the aleatory element and employing a utilitarian method only. The aleatory element has always been the connecting link between the struggle for existence and religion. It was only by religious rites that the aleatory element in the struggle for existence could be controlled. The notions of ghosts, demons, another world, etc., were all fantastic. They lacked all connection with facts, and were arbitrary constructions put upon experience. They were poetic and developed by poetic construction and imaginative deduction. The nexus between them and events was not cause and effect, but magic. They therefore led to delusive deductions in regard to life and its meaning, which entered into subsequent action as guiding faiths, and imperative notions about the conditions of success. The authority of religion and that of custom coalesced into one indivisible obligation. Therefore the simple statement of experiment and expediency in the first paragraph above is not derived directly from actual cases, but is a product of analysis and inference. It must also be added that vanity and ghost fear produced needs which man was as eager to satisfy as those of hunger or the family. Folkways resulted for the former as well as for the latter.

CHARLES HORTON COOLEY

Except for two brief intervals, one of which he spent abroad and the other at the Census Bureau in Washington, Charles Horton Cooley (1864-1929) lived his entire lifetime in Ann Arbor, Michigan. The son of a distinguished jurist of that state, he was graduated from the University of Michigan in 1887 and took his Ph.D. degree there in 1894. He was an assistant in political science from 1892 to 1895, taught economics in the rank of assistant professor from 1899 to 1904, and served as professor of sociology from 1904 to 1929. He was president of the American Sociological Society in 1918.

If Cooley is quoted more often than any American sociologist it is because he introduced two concepts into the literature that have become standard components of the corpus of sociological thought. The first of these is the concept of the primary group and the second is the "looking glass" concept of the self. The primary group is that intimate, face-to-face group which is the nuclear group in human society. It is discussed in the selection that follows, from *Social Organization,* which Cooley published in 1909. The looking glass concept of the self focuses attention upon the social determination of personality and means, in brief, that I am not what I think I am, nor what you think I am, but what I think you think I am. This concept received its preliminary treatment in *Human Nature and the Social Order,* which appeared in 1902. Cooley's other books include *Personal Competition* (1899), *Social Process* (1918), *Life and the Student* (1927), and *Sociological Theory and Social Research* (1930).

*Primary Groups**

Meaning of Primary Groups—Family, Playground, and Neighborhood—How Far Influenced by Larger Society—Meaning and Permanence of "Human Nature"—Primary Groups the Nursery of Human Nature.

By primary groups I mean those characterized by intimate face-to-face association and cooperation. They are primary in several senses, but chiefly in that they are fundamental in forming the social nature and ideals of the individual. The result of intimate association, psychologically, is a certain fusion of individualities in a common whole, so that one's very self, for many purposes at least, is the common life and purpose of the group. Perhaps the simplest way of describing this wholeness is by saying that it is a "we"; it involves the sort of sympathy and mutual identification for which "we" is the natural expression. One lives in the feeling of the whole and finds the chief aims of his will in that feeling.

It is not to be supposed that the unity of the primary group is one of mere harmony and love. It is always a differentiated and usually a competitive unity, admitting of self-assertion and various appropriative passions; but these passions are socialized by sympathy, and come, or tend to come, under the discipline of a common spirit. The individual will be ambitious, but the chief object of his ambition will be some desired place in the thought of the others, and he will feel allegiance to common standards of service and fair play. So the boy will dispute with his fellows a place on the team, but above such disputes will place the common glory of his class and school.

The most important spheres of this intimate association and cooperation—though by no means the only ones—are the fam-

* Reprinted from *Social Organization* by Charles Horton Cooley with permission of Charles Scribner's Sons.

ily, the play-group of children, and the neighborhood or community group of elders. These are practically universal, belonging to all times and all stages of development; and are accordingly a chief basis of what is universal in human nature and human ideals. The best comparative studies of the family, such as those of Westermarck or Howard, show it to us as not only a universal institution, but as more alike the world over than the exaggeration of exceptional customs by an earlier school had led us to suppose. Nor can any one doubt the general prevalence of play-groups among children or of informal assemblies of various kinds among their elders. Such association is clearly the nursery of human nature in the world about us, and there is no apparent reason to suppose that the case has anywhere or at any time been essentially different.

As regards play, I might, were it not a matter of common observation, multiply illustrations of the universality and spontaneity of the group discussion and cooperation to which it gives rise. The general fact is that children, especially boys after about their twelfth year, live in fellowships in which their sympathy, ambition and honor are engaged even more, often, than they are in the family. Most of us can recall examples of the endurance by boys of injustice and even cruelty, rather than appeal from their fellows to parents or teachers—as, for instance, in the hazing so prevalent at schools, and so difficult, for this very reason, to repress. And how elaborate the discussion, how cogent the public opinion, how hot the ambitions in these fellowships.

Nor is this facility of juvenile association, as is sometimes supposed, a trait peculiar to English and American boys; since experience among our immigrant population seems to show that the offspring of the more restrictive civilizations of the continent of Europe form self-governing playgrounds with almost equal readiness. Thus Miss Jane Addams, after pointing out that the "gang" is almost universal, speaks of the interminable discussion which every detail of the gang's activity receives, remarking that "in these social folkmotes, so to speak, the young citizen learns to act upon his own determination."

Of the neighborhood group it may be said, in general, that from the time men formed permanent settlements upon the land, down, at least, to the rise of modern industrial cities, it has played a main part in the primary, heart-to-heart life of the people. Among our Teutonic forefathers the village community was apparently the chief sphere of sympathy and mutual aid for the commons all through the "dark" and middle ages, and for many purposes it remains so in rural districts at the present day. In some countries we still find it with all its ancient vitality, notably in Russia, where the mir, or self-governing village group, is the main theatre of life, along with the family, for perhaps fifty millions of peasants.

In our own life the intimacy of the neighborhood has been broken up by the growth of an intricate mesh of wider contacts which leaves us strangers to people who live in the same house. And even in the country the same principle is at work, though less obviously, diminishing our economic and spiritual community with our neighbors. How far this change is a healthy development, and how far a disease, is perhaps still uncertain.

Besides these almost universal kinds of primary association, there are many others whose form depends upon the particular state of civilization; the only essential thing, as I have said, being a certain intimacy and fusion of personalities. In our own society, being little bound by place, people easily form clubs, fraternal societies and the like, based on congeniality, which may give rise to real intimacy. Many such relations are formed at school and college, and among men and women brought together in the first instance by their occupations—as workmen in the same trade, or the like. Where there is a little common interest and activity, kindness grows like weeds by the roadside.

But the fact that the family and neighborhood groups are ascendant in the open and plastic time of childhood makes them even now incomparably more influential than all the rest.

Primary groups are primary in the sense that they give the individual his earliest and completest experience of social unity, and also in the sense that they do not change in the same degree as more elaborate relations, but form a comparatively permanent source out of which the latter are ever springing. Of course they are not independent of the larger society, but to some extent reflect its spirit; as the German family and the German school bear somewhat distinctly the print of German militarism. But this, after all, is like the tide setting back into creeks, and does not commonly go very far. Among the German, and still more among the Russian, peasantry are found habits of free cooperation and discussion almost uninfluenced by the character of the state; and it is a familiar and well-supported view that the village commune, self-governing as regards local affairs and habituated to discussion, is a very widespread institution in settled communities, and the continuator of a similar autonomy previously existing in the clan. "It is man who makes monarchies and establishes republics, but the commune seems to come directly from the hand of God."

In our own cities the crowded tenements and the general economic and social confusion have sorely wounded the family and the neighborhood, but it is remarkable, in view of these conditions, what vitality they show; and there is nothing upon which the conscience of the time is more determined than upon restoring them to health.

These groups, then, are springs of life, not only for the individual but for social institutions. They are only in part moulded by special traditions, and, in larger degree, express a universal nature. The religion or government of other civilizations may seem alien to us, but the children or the family group wear the common life, and with them we can always make ourselves at home.

By human nature, I suppose, we may understand those sentiments and impulses that are human in being superior to those of lower animals, and also in the sense that they belong to mankind at large, and not to any particular race or time. It means, particularly, sympathy and the innumerable sentiments into which sympathy enters, such as love, resentment, ambition, vanity, hero worship, and the feeling of social right and wrong.

Human nature in this sense is justly regarded as a comparatively permanent element in society. Always and everywhere men seek honor and dread ridicule, defer to public opinion, cherish their goods and their children, and admire courage, generosity, and success. It is always safe to assume that people are and have been human.

It is true, no doubt, that there are differences of race capacity, so great that a large part of mankind are possibly incapable of any high kind of social organization. But these differences, like those among individuals of the same race, are subtle, depending upon some obscure intellectual deficiency, some want of vigor, or slackness of moral fibre, and do not involve unlikeness in the generic impulses of human nature. In these all races are very much alike. The more insight one gets into the life of savages, even those that are reckoned the lowest, the more human, the more like ourselves, they appear. Take for instance the natives of Central Australia, as described by Spencer and Gillen, tribes having no definite government or worship and scarcely able to count to five. They are generous to one another, emulous of virtue as they understand it, kind to their children and to the aged, and by no means harsh to women. Their faces as shown in the photographs are wholly human and many of them attractive.

And when we come to a comparison between different stages in the development of the same race, between ourselves, for instance, and the Teutonic tribes of the time of Caesar, the difference is neither in human nature nor in capacity, but in organization, in the range and complexity of relations, in the diverse expression of powers and passions essentially much the same.

There is no better proof of this generic likeness of human nature than in the ease and joy with which the modern man makes himself at home in literature depicting the most remote and varied phases of life—in Homer, in the Nibelung tales, in the Hebrew Scriptures, in the legends of the American Indians, in stories of frontier life, of soldiers and sailors, of criminals and tramps, and so on. The more penetratingly any phase of human life is studied the more an essential likeness to ourselves is revealed.

To return to primary groups: the view here maintained is that human nature is not something existing separately in the individual, but a *group-nature or primary phase of society,* a relatively simple and general condition of the social mind. It is something more, on the one hand, than the mere instinct that is born in us —though that enters into it—and something less, on the other, than the more elaborate development of ideas and sentiments that makes up institutions. It is the nature which is developed and expressed in those simple, face-to-face groups that are somewhat alike in all societies; groups of the family, the playground, and the neighborhood. In the essential similarity of these is to be found the basis, in experience, for similar ideas and sentiments in the human mind. In these, everywhere, human nature comes into existence. Man does not have it at birth; he cannot acquire it except through fellowship, and it decays in isolation.

If this view does not recommend itself to commonsense, I do not know that elaboration will be of much avail. It simply means the application at this point of the idea that society and individuals are inseparable phases of a common whole, so that wherever we find an individual fact we may look for a social fact to go with it. If there is a universal nature in persons there must be something universal in association to correspond to it.

What else can human nature be than a trait of primary groups? Surely not an attribute of the separate individual—supposing there were any such thing—since its typical characteristics, such as affection, ambition, vanity, and resentment, are inconceivable apart from society. If it belongs, then, to man in association, what kind of degree of association is required to develop it? Evidently nothing elaborate, because elaborate phases of society are transient and diverse, while human nature is comparatively stable and universal. In short the family and neighborhood life is essential to its genesis and nothing more is.

Here as everywhere in the study of society we must learn to see mankind in psychical wholes, rather than in artificial separation. We must see and feel the communal life of family and local groups as immediate facts, not as combinations of something else. And perhaps we shall do this best by recalling our own experience and extending it through sympathetic observation. What, in our life, is the family and the fellowship; what do we know of the we-feeling? Thought of this kind may help us to get a concrete perception of that primary group-nature of which everything social is the outgrowth.

FRANKLIN H. GIDDINGS

Franklin H. Giddings (1855-1931) is ranked by Howard Odum with Ward, Sumner, and Small among the first four names in American sociology. Certainly he as much as anyone was on the frontier, founding as he did the Columbia department and teaching there both sociology and the history of civilization. Giddings was born in Connecticut, began his academic career at Bryn Mawr College in 1888, was appointed lecturer at Columbia in 1892, and achieved the professorship two years later in 1894. He was third president of the American Sociological Society, serving in the two years 1910 and 1911, was president also of the *Institut International de Sociologie,* and Fellow of the American Statistical Association and of the American Association for the Advancement of Science. He held honorary degrees from Union, North Carolina, Columbia, and Iowa.

Giddings was not a system-builder in the science to which he devoted so much of his energy and talent, and his ideas, as would be expected, changed somewhat during the interval from the publication of his first major work, *Principles of Sociology,* in 1896 to his *Civilization and Society* in 1932. In between he wrote such other works as *Elements of Sociology* (1898), *Inductive Sociology* (1901), *Studies in the Theory of Human Society* (1922), and *The Scientific Study of Human Society* (1924). Giddings emphasized throughout his career, however, the importance of statistical methods and of an objective approach to social phenomena. The selection that follows, from *The Scientific Study of Human Society,* indicates what Giddings meant by the scientific method in relation to sociology.

From *The Scientific Study of Human Society**

For practical reasons even more than for merely intellectual ones, we need rigorously scientific studies of human society and of our individual relations to it. In particular we need such studies of the societal interests that are labeled "public policy," "education," "missions," and "social work." I am aware that this proposition is resented by men and women who suffer from an anti-"academic" complex and worry lest "the human touch," "the ways of the neighborhood" and the naïve thinking of "plain people" shall have spontaneity squeezed out of them by theory. This is an unfortunate misapprehension of what science is and of what it does for us. It ought not to be necessary at this late day, but it is necessary, to tell the general public that science is nothing more nor less than getting at facts, and trying to understand them, and that what science does for us is nothing more nor less than helping us to face facts. Facing the facts that the physical and biological sciences have made known to us has enabled us to live more comfortably and longer than men once did. Facing the facts that the social sciences are making known to us, and will make better known, should enable us to diminish human misery and to live more wisely than the human race has lived hitherto. In particular it should enable us to take the kinks out of our imperfect codes of conduct. It will be discovered one day that the chief value of social science, far from being academic, is moral.

Let me sharpen the point by illustrations. I have on my desk the latest report of an organization which purports to ameliorate prison life and to reform convicts. Little exact information is given. Instead, the pages are filled with autobiographical tales by "reformed" felons. These tell us that neglected childhood, evil communications, unemployment (for which the narrators were not to blame) or other hard luck, drove these unhappy persons

* Reprinted by permission of the University of North Carolina Press.

into careers of crime which they would have followed to the end of their days if the beneficent organization had not discovered their inherent goodness and obtained for them, by parole or otherwise, "another chance." Conceivably one or two of the tales may be true, but no proof is offered that any of them is. If verification of any sort has been attempted there is no mention of the fact in this self-glorifying report. Therefore, in all human probability, the organization has experimentally satisfied itself that there are enough rich morons in the world to sustain its merciful activities without asking embarrassing questions.

An active worker in an organization of wide reach, which devotes itself to the religious and moral guardianship of young men, read a seminar paper on the "program" which the association attempts to carry out. It appeared that four great lines of work had been projected and are being followed. Young men are being made physically "fit"; they are being intellectually "developed"; their religious life is being "deepened"; and they are being trained to be of "service." I asked the reader to describe the methods of checking up which the association employs to satisfy itself that these admirable objects are being attained. He was unable to enlighten us, and I therefore made my questions specific. Are the young men physically examined and rated from time to time by medical or other experts? No. Is their intellectual progress tested from time to time, as the progress of public school pupils is, or in any other way? No. Is the "depth" of religious life now and then sounded, or otherwise measured? No. Are tangible evidences of "service" obtained and recorded? No.

Another seminar paper, read on another occasion, set forth the well-advertised social work of an "influential" metropolitan church. A chief item was the relief and "oversight" of more than one hundred indigent families. The writer of the paper (an unfeeling wretch) had asked the almoner what procedure was followed to ascertain that the families were deserving. Not satisfied with the answer received he had gone to the records of a charity organization society and had learned that more than ninety per cent of the families in question were "notorious" cases of professional mendicancy, each of them "working" from two or three to eight to ten sources of income.

My readers may object that these illustrations of irresponsible social work are not representative, presuming that they are discreditable survivals of traditions and practices now passing. Up to date social work, they may insist, is both more intelligently and more responsibly conducted.

I want to believe that it is, but then, *is it,* always or generally? Does anybody *know* that it usually is, or is everybody just *saying* that it is? If anybody does know he is more wicked than the servant who hid his lord's treasure in a napkin, if he keeps the information much longer to himself. Frankly, I doubt if the information is obtainable. I have made more attempts to get it than I can count, and without success. One thing is certain. Our social workers and our uplift organizations do not know what results they are getting, and by what methods they are getting them, in the same rigorous sense in which a well-managed business corporation knows what it is getting out of its personnel, its machines, and its methods.

This brings us back to my main contention, that the major value of a scientific study of society is moral. It is only by the methods of making sure (which constitute scientific study) that we ever can know what our public policies, our educational procedures, our religious endeavors and our social work are accomplishing. Therefore nothing but the scientific study of society can save us from the sin, the scandal and the humiliation of obtaining money under false pretenses, for the attainment of righteous ends which, like enough, we are not in fact attaining.

The scientific study of any subject is a substitution of business-like ways of "making sure" about it for the lazy habit of "taking it for granted" and the worse habit of making irresponsible assertions about it. To make sure, it is necessary to have done with a careless "looking into it" and to undertake precise observations, many times repeated. It is necessary to make measurements and accountings, to substitute realistic thinking (an honest dealing with facts as they are) for wishful or fanciful or other self deceiving thinking and to carry on a systematic "checking up." At every step we must make sure that the methods which we use and rely on have been accredited by exhaustive criticism and trial, and are applicable to the investigation in hand.

Inasmuch then, as science, as was said, "is nothing more nor less than getting at facts, and trying to understand them" the discovery of facts *which prove to be facts* is initial scientific activity. In the nature of things it continues more or less fortuitously, however systematic we try to make it. The *scrutiny* of alleged facts to determine whether or not they *are* facts, is the fundamental *systematic* work of science.

We make acquaintance with a fact as an individual instance of something or other which arrests attention. A hundred other things, quite as obvious, quite as important, and possibly more significant, we may not see at all. If we reflect for a moment on this circumstance we discover that the assortment of facts which we carry in our heads and build into the structure of knowledge must be smaller than the assortment which makes up the world of actuality, and differently arranged. So, right at the beginning of inquiry, we are warned to watch our steps. Relativity, it seems, is a factor in reality.

The particular instance of something or other which has arrested our attention looks like a unit or item, detached or detachable, and so we think of it for the moment. Then we make further discoveries. Our instance is a unit as far as its relations with other instances like itself or different happen to go, but if we leave them out of our field of vision and forget them, and look intently at our particular instance we see it resolve into a multitude of lesser items, arranged perhaps in clusters or patterns, and, like enough, moving about. Each of these items in turn, we presently ascertain, is composite, and so on, without end.

Human society abounds in examples and the social worker encounters them. He may be interested chiefly in a mill town, or chiefly in a neighborhood, or chiefly in certain families. At one time he will be most concerned about what the mill town or the neighborhood or a family *does*. At another time he will be most concerned about what it *is*. As long as he is attending to what the mill town does he thinks of it as a whole. It is a community. He compares it with other communities as wholes. He observes similarities and differences of activity and achievement. These observations may lead him to ask why such similarities and differences exist, how they are to be accounted for. Trying to answer this question, he finds himself inquiring what his mill town is, and from that moment he is resolving it into components. He is discovering that it is made up of corporations, trade unions, churches, schools, shops and markets, professional men and business men, skilled mechanics and unskilled laborers, native born folk and foreign born folk of various nationalities; in fine, of inhabitants arranged in bewildering clusters and patterns. If he is interested chiefly in a neighborhood or in a family he has a like experience. He thinks of it as a unit while he is learning what it does. He necessarily thinks of it as a composite when he tries to learn what it is.

A particular instance, then, is a unit or not as we happen, or have occasion, to see it, and we have occasion to see it in the one or the other way according to the nature of the investigation that we attempt to make. If it is our purpose to learn how our particular instance is related to other instances like itself, or behaves toward them or with them, or enters into combination with them to make up a bigger whole; or how it is related to things (that is to say instances) unlike itself, and behaves toward them or with them, or enters into combination with them—our instance is a unit, and we deal with it as such. But if our purpose is to learn what it *is,* if we are attempting to account for it, and to understand it, our unit of investigation must obviously be an item of lower order. Practically it must be an item of the next lower order. In accounting for things we must go back step by step.

Here it is important to understand that in so viewing the particular instance, and in so choosing a unit of investigation, we are not acting arbitrarily. In books on scientific method, and most often, perhaps, in books on statistical method, we encounter the statement that we do take our unit arbitrarily, or pragmatically. This is a shorthand expression, a talk saving device, and harmless enough if we do not take it too literally. Speaking strictly, our choice is determined by a logical necessity. We take the particular instance as a unit if we are investigating what it does. We do not take it as a unit, but resolve it into units of the next lower order if we are investigating what it is.

What is the practical value of all this for the social worker, or for the investigator? It is the same for both, and it lies in an admonition. Don't mix up things that should be discriminated, and don't take your knowledge for something that it is not. Do not deceive yourself with the notion that you can understand what your nation, or your town, or your neighborhood, or your family, *does,* or why it does it, until you have had the patience to learn what it *is,* or with the notion that you can learn what it is in any other way than by painstakingly resolving it into component units and scrutinizing them. Short cuts to a knowledge of society and to proficiency in helping it through tribulations will yield you nothing, and get you nowhere.

When we have determined whether the particular instance of something or other which has arrested our attention, and in which we have become interested, shall be regarded for our further purposes as doing something, or as being or becoming something, and thereby have chosen our unit subject, it is good scientific practice to ascertain next, as accurately as may be necessary for our further purposes, its position in time and in space. To place a thing roughly in its time and space relations to other things is usually not difficult. To place it accurately is another matter. This operation takes patience, energy, time and money. Unfortunately, in the study of societal variables these costs are often almost prohibitive. It is therefore highly important that the investigator should bring good practical judgment to the task of deciding how precise he ought to be; in other words, how much precision is worth while. He is likely to find that this depends upon the shifting, that is to say, the variability, of the position which he is observing. If the variability is negligible—as it is, for example, in the case of a town as old as London or even as San Francisco; or as it is in the case of one of those French peasant families that have lived continuously on the same piece of land for more than five hundred years—the problem is relatively simple. But it is not at all simple in the case of one of those colonies of Italians or of Jews that are moving continuously from one end of one side of Manhattan Island to the other, or of a migrating church, or school, or shopping district. It is least of all simple in the case of a migrating wage-earning family, or dependent family, or criminal family. Yet it is precisely in these cases that accurate determination of position in space and in time is imperative for purposes of identification.

Similar requirements of scientific scrutiny apply to our determination of other categorical matters, including the conditions attaching to persistence in one or another place or in one or another succession of events; the identifying marks and attributes of the thing, individual, or group in which we are interested; its form or changing forms; its magnitudes or varying magnitudes, and its reactions, that is to say, its behavior. Here should be noted certain important differences between the task of the physicist or of the biologist, on the one hand, and that of the sociologist, on the other. Form and magnitude are, in general, of more immediate and continuing concern to the physicist and the biologist than they are to the sociologist, although they never can be neglected by the latter. Again, the forms which the physical and biological sciences have to do with are relatively definite and constant patterns, while those that sociology has to do with are somewhat less definite and more variable patterns. Magnitudes also offer striking contrasts. The magnitudes with which physics and chemistry have to do are inconceivably minute, and can be measured only with instruments of the utmost precision. Those with which astronomy has to do are inconceivably vast, but their calculation is made possible by means of the fine measurements of physics. The magnitudes with which sociology has to do lie within the ranges of everyday observation, and they are measured by commonplace counting, and by subsequent statistical operations. Accurate counting, however, is not always as easy as it looks, and costly investigations are too often invalidated by untrustworthy enumerations. And statistical methods are fine-edged tools. The sociologist and the social worker should acquire expertness in counting, under varying circumstances, including the coming and going of not too large crowds, and they must get a sound, if not necessarily extensive, knowledge of statistics.

When it comes to the scrutiny of qualities and reactions, as much painstaking and precision are necessary in sociology as in the physical sciences or in biology. Carelessness and error are fatal. It is above all important to discriminate between those relatively unvarying ways in which things, individuals and groups impinge upon our consciousness—and which we call their traits, properties, characters or characteristics, or, collectively, their qualities—and those relatively variable ways of impinging which we call their changes, activities, reactions, or behavior. Among qualities it is necessary to discriminate between those which are usually, but not always, associated with their subjects, and those which, always inseparable from them, we call their attributes. In human beings inherited qualities only are attributes.

The behavior in which the social psychologist is interested is the reaction of an individual or of an intimate group to a fellow individual or to another intimate group. It may take the form of indifference or of interest; of fear or of trust; of liking or of disliking; of anger or of sympathy; of envy, jealousy, malice or hate, or of rejoicing in another's good fortune; of respect, reverence or affection. It may be aloofness or coöperation. The social worker is every moment dealing with social or unsocial behavior. He should thoroughly know his social psychology.

The behaviour in which the sociologist is interested, as was shown in our first chapter, is the approximately simultaneous reaction of a considerable number of individuals that happen to be in the same situation or circumstance. Their reactions may be alike or different; equally or unequally alert and persistent. This behavior we called multi-individual or pluralistic. It develops into group ways, class ways, and folk ways, and into organization. The social worker is at all times in contact with it and dealing with it. He should thoroughly know his sociology.

Pluralistic behavior can be seen or heard, or both seen and heard, and no further acquaintance with it is necessary to satisfy us of its occurrence, but to check up our knowledge of a particular instance of occurrence, so that it shall be reasonably complete and accurate, it is necessary to do more or less counting. Only by counting can we know how much more effective in provoking pluralistic reaction a given stimulus is at one time than at another, or in one place than in another. Counting for this purpose has become an important factor in determining the relative attractiveness of residential areas, of occupations, recreations, styles, and a hundred other interests of everyday life. Business and professional men make or lose money by their attention or indifference to it. To determine the relative efficacy of alternative stimuli in calling forth pluralistic response, for example in shop work, or in school work, the counting must be accurate. So, also, it must be to determine alertness and persistence of response to varying stimuli. By no other means can we certainly know, for example, whether the percentage of workers at their places within three minutes after the whistle blows in the morning is equal to the percentage outside the door within three minutes after it blows at noon, or the effect upon these ratios of such devices as fines and bonuses. Persisting reaction and its extent can be ascertained in no other way than by counting, which is always resorted to for measuring the effectiveness of religious and of political activity, but too often stops short of satisfying completeness. I have before me an account of the revival meetings which Dwight L. Moody conducted in one of the larger American cities. It says: "A careful computation puts the total attendance at 900,000 and the converts at 4,000." We are not told how many of the 4,000 converts (they were less than three tenths of one per cent of the attendance) *continued* to live a "sober, righteous, and godly life."

The *consciousness of kind* is obvious enough as a state of mind which continually obtrudes itself into our relations with other persons, but our notion of it may be vague. A simple counting of a few items will clarify and define. Write down the names of twenty-five acquaintances of your own sex and color race whom you like and associate with, and twenty-five names of persons who annoy you so that you dislike them and, whenever possible, avoid them. Go over each list and note in which one you find more persons who are like yourself in coloring (blondness or brunetness); in which one you find more who are like yourself in being conventional or unconventional in dress and in manners; in which one you find more whose notions about right and wrong are like your own; in which one you find more whose tastes and interests are yours. Now get a considerable number of careful persons to make similar lists and comparisons. The more lists you can get the better, but fifty is a good number. Assemble the results, and you will make interesting discoveries. Similarity or contrast of coloring within the same color race is a negligible factor in your likings and dislikings. You may have been told or taught otherwise. Similar or dissimilar notions of right and wrong have a good deal of influence, but the big factors are similarities or dissimilarities of manners, tastes and interests.

We observe concerted volition of a spontaneous, or at least unorganized, kind whenever we see a mob bent on mischief, or watch the proceedings of a public meeting which adopts resolutions, or participates in a referendum election. These casual observations, however, tell us only that people actually do these things. By counting certain combinations of items we make further discoveries. For example, not everybody participates who might; the number of qualified voters answering to a roll call varies from question to question, from resolution to resolution, and you do not have to make an impossible number of countings to learn that the constant factor affecting the number of votes is the degree of mental equipment[1] required, not to *understand* the question, but to be *interested* in it. It will not be long before the data made available in states which have referendum voting on questions will afford a convincing confirmation of other hotly discussed results of mentality tests.

Pluralistic behavior, complicated by the *consciousness of kind,* and becoming concerted volition, is over and over repeated. Through repetition it acquires form or mode. It is subject to faultfinding and disapproval. Forms or modes that are usually approved survive. They become conventions or customs, that is to say, group ways, class ways and folk ways. That each of these is followed more or less, and disregarded more or less, is familiar knowledge; but in order to know which ones are most followed and which ones most disregarded, in particular to know to what extent each one is followed and each one disregarded, it is necessary to do a good deal of counting. This proposition will not be disputed, and I need not say more about it now.

The particular instance of something or other in which one is interested may be amenable to experimental control, which is the best of all the ways of scientific scrutiny, or it may not be. It has generally been held that the phenomena of human society are too complicated for a strictly scientific experimental investigation. It is true, of course, that we are all the time making social and societal experiments. In no other field do we make so many, but these are not usually of the scientific sort. In scientific experimentation we control everything that happens. We determine when it shall occur and where. We arrange circumstances and surroundings; atmospheres and temperatures; possible ways of getting in

[1] I use here the term "mental equipment" instead of "intelligence" because as yet we are unable to test intelligence unmixed with habit, knowledge, and familiarity, irrespective of native intelligence. Mental equipment includes the factor intelligence, the factors familiarity and practice, and the factor knowledge.

and possible ways of getting out. We take out something that has been in, or put in something that has been out, and see what happens. At every step we describe what we do and the things that we deal with, with accurate specifications. We count, measure and weigh, and make records. To manage all this in societal experimentation cannot be easy. Is it at all possible?

Among unnecessary ways of being mistaken none is more unnecessary or more discredited by experience than to assume that something or other can not be done.

As far as I know there is no record of a strictly scientific societal experiment completely carried through on a large scale, but there have been many tentative and partial experiments (experiments in experimenting, if one may call them that) and they are multiplying. The more promising ones have been and are being made in workshops and in schools and by a few intelligently managed corporations, industrial or philanthropic. The more disappointing, although often sincerely attempted ones, have been made by neighborhood houses and by churches. The cause of failure, in many instances, has been a commendable aversion to anything that has looked like prying into private affairs and keeping tab on them. This aversion I share and unqualifiedly approve; but in the environment of every settlement and of every church there are opportunities for social and societal experimentation that would not require intrusiveness or meddling. That these have not been more successfully exploited must be explained, I am afraid, by aversion to the tedium of counting and recording, to note books and statistics.

Among small but insignificant societal experiments which, without question, could be conducted in a strictly scientific manner and carried through to indisputable results, are a few rigorous and crucial ones to determine what are the best ways and means of awakening group, class, or neighborhood interest, and of holding it. Settlements and churches are continually trying out these ways and means, practical ones and fantastic ones, sane ones and crazy ones, but their results are astonishingly meagre. Their reports, with commendable exceptions, are a flotsam of unverified assertions, uncritical impressions, and optimistic forecasts, made, not to establish a fact, but to wheedle money for more loose work of the same kind. It is possible to do this work in a scientific and convincing way, and it ought to be so done. A good many schools and a good many employers of wage earners are making carefully conducted experiments in the formation of group and class habits. The results are of great and increasing value. Year by year they are being checked up and extended. Big corporations managed by men of vision are making experiments in organization. These, too, are of increasing value.

The final verification of an alleged fact (its conclusive establishment as a fact) is attained only through much repeating of observations and measurements. Not until we can safely challenge anybody to go over our work and discover errors in it can we be quite sure that we *know* anything. As I have heretofore insisted a fact in the scientific sense of the word "is the close agreement of many observations or measurements of the same phenomenon." Error creeps into observation in unaccountable ways, and different observers make different mistakes. Precise measurement by one person at one time and in one place is next to impossible. The nearest approximation to accuracy is made by taking the average of many measurements made by many measurers and calculating its probable error. Physicists and chemists, astronomers and geologists, biologists and psychologists, are tirelessly repeating their observations and their measurements of presumptive fact. Social psychologists and sociologists must get this habit.

GEORG SIMMEL

Georg Simmel (1858-1918) was a philosopher rather than a sociologist, in the sense in which we should make the distinction today, and his sociological writings proper comprise only a part of his work. He had in addition a strong interest in art, literature, and history. Born in Berlin, he became a *Privatdozent* in philosophy at the University of Berlin at the age of twenty-seven, a post he retained until 1914 when, at the age of fifty-six, he became professor of philosophy at the University of Strassburg. He taught there until his death in 1918.

Simmel is known as a "formal" sociologist. That is, he dealt with the pure forms of interaction in society—forms divorced as far as possible from the concrete actuality in which they occur. By thus working and thinking on a most abstract level he was able to define sociology as a science of form, a discipline interested in investigating the various categories of order in independence of the particular societies in which they might be manifested. Such phenomena, for example, as superordination and subordination, majorities and minorities, the division of labor, and the formation of parties, occur wherever men interact with men and it is these phenomena, in consequence, that become the subject matter of sociology. For Simmel, then, sociology is a social, not a cultural, science in our contemporary terminology. The following selection, in which this point of view is elaborated, is from his *Soziologie,* published in 1908 and translated by Kurt H. Wolff of the Ohio State University in 1950.

*The Field of Sociology**

The first difficulty which arises if one wants to make a tenable statement about the science of sociology is that its claim to *be* a science is not undisputed. Further, there is a chaotic multitude of opinions concerning its contents and aims. There are so many contradictions and confusions, that one doubts again and again whether one deals with a scientifically justifiable problem at all here. The lack of an undisputed and clear definition would not be so bad if it were made up for by the existence of a certain number of specific problems which are not, or not exhaustively, treated in other disciplines and which contain the fact or concept of "society" as their common element and point of contact. They might be too different from one another in content, orientation, and method of solution to be treated as if they amounted to a homogeneous field of inquiry. Yet even then, they could at least find a preliminary refuge under the heading of "sociology"; at least superficially, it would be clear where to look for them. In such a scheme, sociology would resemble technology, a tag quite legitimately attached to an immense range of tasks whose understanding and solution are not too greatly helped by the suggestion (through the name "technology") that they have some feature in common.

SOCIETY AND KNOWLEDGE OF SOCIETY

Such a tenuous tie among heterogeneous problems might hold out the promise of their unity at a deeper level. Yet even this tenuous tie appears impossible because of the problematic character of the only concept that holds these problems together—"society." In fact, all existing denials of the possibility of sociology as a science arise on the basis of this problematic character. It

* From *The Sociology of George Simmel,* translated, edited, and with an introduction by Kurt H. Wolff. Reprinted by permission of The Free Press.

is remarkable that the denials either minimize or exaggerate this concept. Existence, we hear, is an exclusive attribute of individuals, their qualities and experiences. "Society," by contrast, is an abstraction. Although indispensable for practical purposes and certainly very useful for a rough and preliminary survey of the phenomena that surround us, it is no real *object.* It does not exist outside and in addition to the individuals and the processes among them. After each of these individuals is investigated in his natural and historical characteristics, nothing is left by way of subject matter for a particular science.

For this sort of critique, "society," obviously, is too slight a matter to constitute a field of science. For another kind of critique, however, it is too big: for on the other hand it is said all that men are and do occurs within society, is determined by society, and is part of its life; there is no science of man that is not science of society. The science of society thus ought to replace the artificially compartmentalized special disciplines, historical, psychological, and normative. It ought to make it evident that it is *sociation* which synthesizes all human interests, contents, and processes into concrete units. But, obviously, this definition, which wants to give sociology everything, takes as much away from it as did the first conception that left it nothing. For jurisprudence and philology, political science and literary criticism, psychology and theology, and all the other disciplines that have divided up the study of human life among themselves, will certainly continue to exist. Nothing is gained by throwing their sum total into a pot and sticking a new label on it: "sociology."

The trouble is that the science of society, in contrast to other sciences that are well established, is in the unfortunate position of still having to prove its right to exist. Yet this is fortunate, too, for sociology's struggle for existence is bound to lead to a clarification of its basic concepts (which is good and necessary in itself) and to the establishment of its specific manner of investigating reality.

Let us grant for the moment that only individuals "really" exist. Even then, only a false conception of science could infer from this "fact" that any knowledge which somehow aims at synthesizing these individuals deals with merely speculative abstractions and unrealities. Quite on the contrary, human thought always and everywhere synthesizes the given into units that serve as subject matters of the sciences. They have no counterpart whatever in immediate reality. Nobody, for instance, hesitates to talk of the development of the Gothic style. Yet nowhere is there such a thing as "Gothic style," whose existence could be shown. Instead, there are particular works of art which along with individual elements, also contain stylistic elements; and the two cannot be clearly separated. The Gothic style as a topic of historical knowledge is an *intellectual* phenomenon. It is abstracted from reality; it is not itself a given reality. Innumerable times, we do not even want to know how individual things behave in all detail: we form new units out of them. When we inquire into the Gothic style, its laws, its development, we do not describe any particular cathedral or palace. Yet the *material* that makes up the unit we are investigating—"Gothic style"—we gain only from a study of the details of cathedrals and palaces. Or, we ask how the "Greeks" and the "Persians" behaved in the battle of Marathon. If it were true that only individuals are "real," historical cognition would reach its goal only if it included the behavior of each individual Greek and each individual Persian. If we knew his whole life history, we could psychologically understand his behavior during the battle. Yet even if we could manage to satisfy such a fantastic claim, we would not have solved our problem at all. For this problem does not concern this or that individual Greek or Persian; it concerns all of them. The notion, "the Greeks" and "the Persians," evidently constitutes a totally different phenomenon, which results from a certain intellectual synthesis, not from the observation of isolated individuals. To be sure, each of these individuals was led to behave as he did by a development which is somehow different from that of every other individual. In reality, none of them behaved precisely like any other. And, in no one individual, is what he shares with others clearly separable from what distinguishes him from others. Both aspects, rather, form the inseparable unity of his personal life. Yet in spite of all this, out of all these individuals we form the more comprehensive units, "the Greeks" and "the Persians."

Even a moment's reflection shows that similar concepts constantly supersede individual existences. If we were to rob our cognition of all such intellectual syntheses because only individuals are "real," we would deprive human knowledge of its least dubious and most legitimate contents. The stubborn assertion that after all there exist nothing but individuals which alone, therefore, are the concrete objects of science, cannot prevent us from speaking of the histories of Catholicism and Social Democracy, of cities, and of political territories, of the feminist movement, of the conditions of craftsmen, and of thousands of other synthetic events and collective phenomena—and, therefore, of society in general. It certainly is an abstract concept. But each of the innumerable articulations and arrangements covered by it is an object that can be investigated and is worth investigation. And none of them consists of individual existences that are observed in all their details.

This whole consideration, however, might be due, simply, to an imperfect grasp of the matter at issue. It might merely be a (perhaps) necessary preliminary that would, potentially or actually, be overcome by a more intimate knowledge of the individuals as the ultimately concrete elements. Yet if we examine "individuals" more closely, we realize that they are by no means such ultimate elements or "atoms" of the human world. For the unit denoted by the concept "individual" (and which, as a matter of fact, perhaps is insoluble, as we shall see later) is not an object of cognition at all, but only of experience. The way in which each of us, in himself and in others, knows of this unit, cannot be compared to any other way of knowing. What we know about man *scientifically* is only single characteristics. They may exist once, or they may stand in a relation of reciprocal influence to one another; but each of them requires its special investigation and derivation, which leads to innumerable influences of the physical, cultural, personal environment—influences that come from everywhere and extend infinitely in time. Only by isolating and grasping them and by reducing them to increasingly simple, covert and remote elements do we approach what is really "ultimate," that is, what is real in the rigorous sense of the word. This "real" alone must form the basis for any higher intellectual synthesis. Color molecules, letters, particles of water indeed "exist"; but the painting, the book, the river are synthesis: they are units that do not exist in objective reality but only in the consciousness which constitutes them. But what is more, even *these* so-called elements are highly synthetic phenomena. It is, therefore, not true that reality can be attributed only to properly ultimate units, and not to phenomena in which these units find their forms. Any form (and a form always is a synthesis) is something added by a synthesizing subject. Thus, a conception that considers only individuals as "real" lets what *should* be considered real get out of hand. It is perfectly arbitrary to stop the reduction, which leads to ultimately real elements, at the individual. For this reduction is interminable. In it, the individual appears as a composite of single qualities, and destinies, forces and historical derivations, which in comparison to the individual himself have the same character of elementary realities as do the individuals in comparison to society.

In other words, the alleged realism that performs this sort of critique of the concept of society, and thus of sociology, actually eliminates all knowable reality. It relegates it into the infinite and looks for it in the realm of the inscrutable. As a matter of fact, cognition must be conceived on the basis of an entirely different structural principle. This principle is the abstraction, from a given complex of phenomena, of a number of heterogeneous objects of cognition that are nevertheless recognized as equally definitive and consistent. The principle may be expressed by the symbol of different *distances* between such a complex of phenomena and the human mind. We obtain different pictures of an object when we see it at a distance of two, or of five, or of ten yards. At each distance, however, the picture is "correct" in its particular way and only in this way. And the different distance also provides different margins for error. For instance, if the minute detail of a painting that we gain at very close range were injected into a perspective gained at a distance of several yards, this perspective would be utterly confused and falsified. And yet on the basis of a superficial conception, one might assert that the detailed view is "truer" than the more distant view. But even this detailed perception involves some distance whose lower limit is, in fact, impossible to determine. All we can say is that a view gained at any distance whatever has its own justification. It cannot be replaced or corrected by any other view emerging at another distance.

In a similar way, when we look at human life from a certain distance, we see each individual in his precise differentiation from all others. But if we increase our distance, the single individual disappears, and there emerges, instead, the picture of a "society" with its own forms and colors—a picture which has its own possibilities of being recognized or missed. It is certainly no less justified than is the other in which the parts, the individuals, are seen in their differentiation. Nor is it by any means a mere preliminary of it. The difference between the two merely consists in the difference between purposes of cognition; and this difference, in turn, corresponds to a difference in distance.

The right to sociological study thus is not in the least endangered by the circumstance that all real happenings only occur in individuals. Yet the independence of sociology from this circumstance can be argued even more radically. For it is not true that the cognition of series of individual occurrences grasps immediate reality. This reality, rather, is given to use as a complex of images, as a surface of contiguous phenomena. We articulate this datum —which is our only truly primary datum—into something like the destinies of individuals. Or we reduce its simple matter-of-factness to single elements that are designed to catch it as if they were its nodal points. Clearly, in either case there occurs a process which *we* inject into reality, an *ex-post-facto* intellectual *transformation* of the immediately given reality. Because of constant habit, we achieve this almost automatically. We almost think it is no transformation at all, but something given in the natural order of things. Actually, this transformation is exactly as subjective—but also, since it yields valid cognition, exactly as objective—as is the synthesis of the given under the category of society. Only the particular purpose of cognition determines whether reality, as it emerges or is experienced in its immediacy, is to be investigated in a personal or in a collective frame of reference. Both frames of reference, equally, are "standpoints." Their relation to one another is not that of reality to abstraction. Rather, since both are interpretations, though different ones, both are detached from "reality," which itself cannot be the immediate subject matter of science. It becomes amenable to cognition only by means of categories such as, for instance, "individual," or "society."

Nor is the concept of society invalidated by the fact that, if we look at it from still another angle, we must admit that human existence is real only in individuals. If the concept "society" is taken in its most general sense, it refers to the psychological interaction among individual human beings. This definition must not be jeopardized by the difficulties offered by certain marginal phenomena. Thus, two people who for a moment look at one another or who collide in front of a ticket window, should not on these grounds be called sociated. Yet even here, where interaction is so superficial and momentary, one could speak, with some justification, of sociation. One has only to remember that interactions of this sort merely need become more frequent and intensive and join other similar ones to deserve properly the name of sociation. It is only a superficial attachment to linguistic usage (a usage quite adequate for daily practice) which makes us want to reserve the term "society" for *permanent* interactions only. More specifically, the interactions we have in mind when we talk about "society" are crystallized as definable, consistent structures such as the state and the family, the guild and the church, social classes and organizations based on common interests.

But in addition to these, there exists an immeasurable number of less conspicuous forms of relationship and kinds of interaction. Taken singly, they may appear negligible. But since in actuality they are inserted into the comprehensive and, as it were, official social formations, they alone produce society as we know it. To confine ourselves to the large social formations resembles the older science of anatomy with its limitation to the major, definitely circumscribed organs such as heart, liver, lungs, and stomach, and with its neglect of the innumerable, popularly unnamed or unknown tissues. Yet without these, the more obvious organs could never constitute a living organism. On the basis of the major social formations—the traditional subject matter of social science—it would be similarly impossible to piece together the real life of society as we encounter it in our experience. Without the interspersed effects of countless minor syntheses, society would break up into a multitude of discontinuous systems. Sociation continuously merges and ceases and emerges again. Even where its eternal flux and pulsation are not sufficiently strong to form organizations proper, they link individuals together. That people look at one another and are jealous of one another; that they exchange letters or dine together; that irrespective of all tangible interests they strike one another as pleasant or unpleasant; that gratitude for altruistic acts makes for inseparable union; that one asks another man after a certain street, and that people dress and adorn themselves for one another—the whole gamut of relations that play from one person to another and that may be momentary or permanent, conscious or unconscious, ephemeral or of grave consequence (and from which these illustrations are quite casually chosen), all these incessantly tie men together. Here are the interactions among the atoms of society. They account for all the toughness and elasticity, all the color and consistency of social life, that is so striking and yet so mysterious.

The large systems and the superindividual organizations that customarily come to mind when we think of society, are nothing but immediate interactions that occur among men constantly, every minute, but that have become crystallized as permanent fields, as autonomous phenomena. As they crystallize, they attain their own existence and their own laws, and may even confront or oppose spontaneous interaction itself. At the same time, society, as its life is constantly being realized, always signifies that individuals are connected by mutual influence and determination. It is, hence, something functional, something individuals do and suffer. To be true to this fundamental character of it, one should properly speak, not of society, but of sociation. Society merely is the name for a number of individuals, connected by interaction. It is because of their interaction that they are a unit—just as a system of bodily masses is a unit whose reciprocal effects wholly determine their mutual behavior. One may, of course, insist that only these masses are true "realities," and that their mutually stimulated movements and modifications are something intangible, and thus only secondary realities, so to speak, for they have their locus only in the concrete bodies themselves. The so-called unit merely is the synopsis of these materially separated existences: after all, the impulses and formations they receive and produce remain in *them*. In the same sense one may insist that ultimately it is the human individuals that are the true realities. But this adds nothing to our argument. In accordance with it, society certainly is not a "substance," nothing concrete, but an *event:* it is the function of receiving and effecting the fate and development of one individual by the other. Groping for the tangible, we find only individuals; and between them, only a vacuum, as it were. Later, we shall consider the consequences of this conception. At any rate, if it leaves "existence" (more strictly speaking) only to individuals, it must nevertheless accept the process and the dynamics of acting and suffering, by which the individuals modify one another, as something "real" and explorable.

THE ABSTRACT CHARACTER OF SOCIOLOGY

Under the guidance of its particular conception, any science extracts only one group or aspect out of the totality or experienced immediacy of phenomena. Sociology does so, too. It acts no less legitimately than does any other science if it analyzes individual existences and recomposes them in the light of its own conception. Sociology asks what happens to men and by what rules they behave, not insofar as they unfold their understandable individual existences in their totalities, but insofar as they form groups and are determined by their group existence because of interaction. It treats the history of marriage without analyzing particular couples; the principle underlying the organization of offices, without describing a "typical day" at a particular office; the laws and consequences of the class struggle, without dealing with the development of a particular strike or of particular wage negotiations. The topics of its researches certainly arise in a process of abstraction. But this feature does not distinguish sociology from such sciences as logic or economic theory. They, too, under the guidance of certain conceptions (such as cognition and economics, respectively) produce, out of reality, interrelated phenomena that do not exist as something experienceable but whose laws and evolution they discover.

Sociology thus is founded upon an abstraction from concrete reality, performed under the guidance of the concept of society. We have already noted the invalidity of the accusation of unreality, which was derived from the assertion of the exclusive reality of individuals. But this realization also protects our discipline from the exaggeration that I have mentioned, earlier, as an equally grave danger for its existence as a science. To repeat: since man in all aspects of his life and action is determined by the fact that he is a social being, all sciences of him are reduced to parts of the science of social life. All subject matters of these sciences are nothing more than particular channels, as it were, in which social life, the only bearer of all energy and of all significance, flows. I have shown that all this conception does is to yield a new common name for all the branches of knowledge that will continue to exist anyway, unperturbed and autonomous, with all their specific contents and nomenclatures, tendencies and methods. Nevertheless, this erroneous exaggeration of the concepts "society" and "sociology" is based upon a fact of great significance and consequence. For, the recognition that man in his whole nature and in all his manifestations is determined by the circumstance of living in interaction with other men, is bound to lead to a new viewpoint that must make itself felt in all so-called human studies.

As recent a period as the eighteenth century explained the great contents of historical life—language, religion, the formation of states, material culture—essentially, as inventions of single individuals. Where the reason and interests of the individual were not adequate explanations, transcendental forces were resorted to. The "genius" of the single inventor, incidentally, served as a link between the two explanatory principles: it suggested that the known and understandable forces of the individual did not suffice to produce the phenomenon in question. Thus, language was either the invention of individuals or a divine gift; religion (as a historical event), the invention of shrewd priests or divine will; moral laws were either inculcated into the mass by heroes or bestowed by God, or were given to man by "nature," a no less mystical hypostasis. These two insufficient alternatives were replaced by the notion of societal production, according to which all these phenomena emerge in interactions among men, or sometimes, indeed, *are* such interactions. They cannot be derived from the individual considered in isolation. In addition to the two earlier possibilities, therefore, we now have a third: the production of phenomena through social life. This production occurs in a twofold manner. In the first place, there is the simultaneity of interacting individuals which in each produces what cannot be explained on the basis of him alone. In the second place, there is the succession of generations. The inheritance and tradition of this succession inseparably fuse with the acquisitions made by the individual himself: social man, in contrast to all subhuman animals, is not only a successor but also an heir.

SOCIOLOGY AS A METHOD

The notion of societal production lies, as it were, somewhere between the notions of purely individual and transcendental production. It has provided all human studies with a genetic method, with a new tool for the solution of their problems, whether they concern the state or church organization, language or moral conditions. Sociology thus is not only a science with its own subject matter that is differentiated, by division of labor, from the subject matters of all other sciences. It also has become a *method* of the historical disciplines and of the human studies in general. Yet in order to use it, these sciences by no means need abandon their own particular viewpoints. They need not become mere parts of sociology, as that fantastic exaggeration of its idea, which I mentioned earlier, would make us believe. Rather, sociology adapts itself to each specific discipline—economics, history of culture, ethics, theology, or what not. In this respect, it is essentially like induction. At its time, induction, as a new principle of investigation, penetrated into all kinds of problem areas. It thus contributed new solutions for tasks well established in these areas. The parallel suggests that sociology is no more a special science than induction is (and surely, it is not an all-embracing science). Insofar as it is based on the notions that man must be understood as a social animal and that society is the medium of all historical events, sociology contains no subject matter that is not already treated in one of the extant sciences. It only opens up a new avenue for all of them. It supplies them with a scientific method which, precisely because of its applicability to all problems, is not a science with its own content.

In its very generality, this method is apt to form a common basis for problem areas that previously, in the absence of their mutual contact, lacked a certain clarity. The universality of sociation, which makes for the reciprocal shaping of the individuals, has its correspondence in the singleness of the sociological way of cognition. The sociological approach yields possibilities of solution or of deeper study which may be derived from fields of knowledge contentually quite different (perhaps) from the field of the particular problem under investigation. I will mention three examples, which range from the most specific to the most general.

(1) The criminologist may learn much concerning the nature of so-called mass crimes from a sociological investigation of the psychology of the theatre audience. For here, the stimulus of a collective-impulsive behavior can still be clearly ascertained. Furthermore, this behavior occurs in the sphere of art which, as it were, is abstract and precisely delimited. Thus here—and this is very important for the problem of guilt in regard to "mass crimes"—the extent to which the individual can be determined by a mass in physical proximity with him, and the extent to which subjective and objective value judgments can be eliminated under the impact of contagion, may be observed under conditions that are as purely experimental and crucial as scarcely anywhere else.

(2) The student of religion is often inclined to explain the life of the religious community and its readiness to sacrifice in terms of their devotion to an ideal that is common to all members. He may tend to ascribe the conduct of life, inspired as it is by the hope in a perfect state beyond the lives of the existing individuals, to the strength in content of the religious faith. Yet the members of a Social-Democratic labor union may exhibit the same traits in their common and mutual behavior. If the student of religion notes this similarity, he may learn that religious behavior does not exclusively depend on religious contents, but that it is a generally human form of behavior which is realized under the stimulus not only of transcendental objects but also of other motivations. He will also gain insight into something even more important to him. This is the fact that, even in its autonomy, religious life contains elements that are not specifically religious, but social. Certainly, these elements—particular kinds of reciprocal attitude and behavior—are fused organically with the religious mood itself. But only when they are isolated by means of the sociological method, will they show what within the whole complex of religious behavior may legitimately be considered purely religious, that is, independent of anything social.

(3) I will give one last example of the mutual fertilization of problem areas that is suggested by the common involvement of

human sociation in all of them. The contemporary student of political or cultural history is often inclined, for instance, to derive the character of the domestic policy pursued by a given country from its economic conditions and processes as sufficient causes. Suppose he explains the strong individualism of early Italian Renaissance political constitutions as the effect of the liberation of economic life from guild and church ties. Here it is an observation of the historian of art that may greatly qualify his conception. The observation is that already in the beginning of the epoch under discussion there was an immense spread of naturalistic and individualistic portrait busts. Thus the general attention appears to have shifted from what men have in common (and what therefore can easily be relegated into somewhat more abstract and ideal spheres) to what must be left to the *individual.* Attention is focused on the significance of personal strength; the concrete is preferred to the general law that is valid "on the whole." And this discovery suggests that the observed economic individualism is the manifestation of a fundamental sociological change which has found its expression in the fields of art and politics as well. It suggests that none of these immediately caused the other.

Perhaps, in fact, sociological analyses of this sort are apt quite generally to point the way toward a conception of history which is more profound than historical materialism, and which may even supersede it. Historical changes, at their properly effective level, are possibly changes in sociological forms. It is perhaps the way in which individuals and groups behave toward one another; in which the individual behaves toward his group; in which value accents, accumulations, prerogatives, and similar phenomena shift among the elements of society—perhaps it is *these* things which make for truly epochal events. And if economics seems to determine all the other areas of culture, the truth behind this tempting appearance would seem to be that it itself is determined—determined by sociological shifts which similarly shape all other cultural phenomena. Thus, the form of economics, too, is merely a "superstructure" on top of the conditions and transformations in the purely sociological structure. And this sociological structure is the ultimate historical element which is bound to determine all other contents of life, even if in a certain parallelism with economics.

THE PROBLEM AREAS OF SOCIOLOGY

(a) *The Sociological Study of Historical Life ("General Sociology")*

These considerations afford a glimpse, beyond the mere concept of sociological *method,* at the first basic *problem area* of sociology. Although it covers almost all of human existence, it does not therefore lose that character of one-sided abstraction that no science can get rid of. For however socially determined and permeated, as it were, each item in the economic and intellectual, political and juridical, even religious and generally cultural spheres may be, nevertheless, in the actuality of concrete life, this social determination is interwoven with other determinations that stem from other sources. Above all, from the circumstance that things also have a purely objective character. It is always some objective content—technical, dogmatic, intellectual, physiological—which channels the development of the social forces and which, by virtue of its own character, logic, and law, keeps it within certain directions and limits. Any social phenomenon, no matter in what material it realize itself, must submit to the natural laws of this material. Any intellectual achievement is tied, in however various ways, to the laws of thought and to the behavior of objects. Any creation in the fields of art, politics, law, medicine, philosophy, or in any other field of invention, observes a certain order that we can understand in terms of the objective situation of its contents and that is characterized by such relations as intensification, connection, differentiation, combination, etc. No human wish or practice can take arbitrary steps, jump arbitrary distances, perform arbitrary syntheses. They must follow the intrinsic logic of things.

Thus, one could very well construct the history of art, as a perfectly understandable development, by presenting works of art themselves, anonymously, in their temporal sequence and stylistic evolution; or the development of law, as the sequence of particular institutions and laws; or that of science, as the mere series, historical or systematic, of its results; etc. Here, as in the cases of a song that is analyzed in terms of its musical value, or of a physical theory in terms of its truth, or of a machine in terms of its efficiency, we realize that all contents of human life, even though they materialize only under the conditions and in the dynamics of social life, nevertheless permit interpretations ignoring it. Objects embody their own ideas; they have significance, laws, value standards which are independent of both the social and the individual life and which make it possible to define and understand them in their own terms. In comparison with full reality, of course, even this understanding involves abstraction, since no objective content is realized by its own logic alone but only through the cooperation of historical and psychological forces. Cognition cannot grasp reality in its total immediacy. What we call objective content is something conceived under a specific category.

Under one of these categories, the history of mankind appears as the behavior and product of *individuals*. One may look at a work of art only in regard to its artistic significance; one may place it, as if it had fallen from the sky, within a series of artistic products. Yet one may also understand it in terms of the artist's personality and development, his experiences and tendencies. One may interpret it as a pulsation or immediate experience of individual life. Thus viewed, the work of art remains within the bounds of the individual and his continuity. Certain cultural data —above all art and, in general, everything that has the breath of creativity—appear more easily graspable in such a perspective than do other data. Quite generally, to look at the world as something that is carried by the active and receptive, typical or unique subject, is one of the possibilities of translating the unity of all human creation into understandability. The manifestation of the individual strikes us as an active element everywhere. Its laws permit us to form a plane, as it were, on which to project reality in all its fullness.

The purpose of this discussion is to show that there exists *not only* social life as a basis for the life of mankind and as a formula of it. This life may also be derived from the objective significance of its contents, and be interpreted in *these* terms. And it may finally be conceived in the framework of the nature and creativity of the individual. Perhaps there are other interpretive categories that have not yet been clearly developed. At any rate, all these analyses and structuralizations of our immediate life and creativity experience this life as a unity. They lie on the same plane and have the same right to be heard. Therefore—and this is the point—no one of them can claim to be the only or the only adequate manner of cognition. Naturally, neither can such a claim be made by the approach which proceeds in terms of the social form of our existence. It, too, is limited; and it supplements other approaches by which in turn it is supplemented. With this qualification, however, it can, in principle, offer a possibility of cognition in front of the totality of human existence.

The facts of politics, religion, economics, law, culture styles, language, and innumerable others can be analyzed by asking how they may be understood, not as individual achievements or in their objective significance, but as products and developments of society. Nor would the absence of an exhaustive and undisputed definition of the nature of society render the cognitive value of this approach illusory. For it is a characteristic of the human mind to be capable of erecting solid structures, while their foundations are still insecure. Physical and chemical propositions do not suffer from the obscure and problematical character of the concept of matter; juridical propositions, not from the quarrel over the nature of law and of its first principles; psychological ones, not from the highly questionable "nature of the soul." If, therefore, we apply the "sociological method" to the investigation of the fall of the Roman Empire or of the relation between religion and economics in the great civilizations or of the origin of the idea of the German national state or of the predominance of the Baroque style; if, that is, we view these and similar phenomena as the result of indistinguishable contributions made by the interaction of individuals, or as life stages in the lives of superindividual groups; then we are, in point of fact, conducting our investigations according to the sociological method. And these investigations may be designated as sociology.

Yet from these sociological investigations there emerges a further abstraction that may well be characterized as the result of a highly differentiated scientific culture. This abstraction yields a group of sociological problems in the narrower sense of this term. If we study all kinds of life data in terms of their development within and by means of social groups, we must assume that they have common elements in their materialization (even though different elements, under different circumstances). These common elements emerge if, and only if, social life itself emerges as the origin or the subject of these data. The question thus arises whether perhaps it is possible to find, in the most heterogeneous historical developments that share nothing but the fact that they are exhibited by one particular group, a common law, or a rhythm, that is fully derivable from this one fact.

It has been maintained, for instance, that all historical developments pass through three phases. The first is the undifferentiated unity of manifold elements. The second is the differentiated articulation of these elements, that have become alienated from one another. The third is a new unity, the harmonious interpenetration of the elements that have been preserved, however, in their specific characters. More briefly, the road of all completed developments leads from an undifferentiated unity through a differentiated manifoldness to a differentiated unity. Another conception of historical life sees it as a process which progresses from organic commonness to mechanical simultaneousness. Property, work, and interests originally grow out of the solidarity of the individuals, the carriers of the group life; but later are distributed among egoists each of whom seeks only his own benefit and, only because of this motive, enters into relations with others. The first stage is the manifestation of an unconscious will which inheres in the very depth of our nature and becomes evident only as a feeling; the second stage, by contrast, is the product of an arbitrary will and of the calculating intellect. According to a still different conception, it is possible to ascertain a definite relation, in any given epoch, between its intellectual world view and its social conditions: both equally are manifestations, in some sense, of biological development. Finally, there is the notion that human cognition, on the whole, must go through three stages. In the first, or theological stage, natural phenomena are explained by recourse to the arbitrary will of all kinds of entities. In the second, metaphysical stage, the supernatural causes are replaced by laws which, however, are mystical and speculative (as, for instance, "vital force," "ends of nature," etc.). Finally, the third, or positive stage corresponds to modern experimental and exact science. Each particular branch of knowledge develops by passing through these three stages; and the knowledge of this fact removes the enigmatic character of social development, which pervades areas of all kinds.

A further sociological question under this category is the problem concerning conditions of group *power,* as distinguished from individual power. The conditions for the power of individuals are immediately evident: intelligence, energy, an apt alternation between consistency and elasticity, etc.; but to account for the historical power of such extraordinary phenomena as Jesus, on the one hand, and Napoleon, on the other, there must also exist as yet unexplained forces which are by no means clarified by labels like "power of suggestion," "prestige," and so forth. But in the exercise of power by groups, both over their members and over other groups, there operate still other factors. Some of these are the faculty of rigid concentration, as well as of diversion into independent activities by individual group members; conscious faith in leading minds; groping toward expansion; egoism of the individual paralleled by sacrificial devotion to the whole; fanatic dogmatism, as well as thoroughly critical intellectual freedom. All these are effective in the rise (and, negatively, in the decay) not only of political nations but also of countless economic and religious, partylike and family groups. In all investigations of group power, the question, clearly, is not the origin of sociation as such, but the fate of society as something already constituted. And this fate is ascertained inductively.

Another question that arises out of the sociological consideration of conditions and events is that of the *value* relations between collective and individual conduct, action, and thought. Which differences of level, as measured by certain ideal standards, exist between social and individual phenomena? The inner, fundamental structure of society itself here becomes as little the central problem as it did in connection with the preceding question. Again, this structure is already presupposed, and the data are considered on the basis of this presupposition. The question, rather, is: which general principles are revealed in these data if they are considered in this particular perspective? In the next chapter, this problem of levels will be examined as an example of a sociological type that may be called "general sociology."

(b) *The Study of Societal Forms ("Pure, or Formal, Sociology")*

Scientific abstraction cuts through the full concreteness of social phenomena from yet a different angle. It thereby connects all that is "sociological"—"sociological" in a sense that will be discussed presently and that appears to me to be the most decisive sense of the term. In doing this, scientific abstraction produces a consistent manner of cognition. Yet it fully realizes that in actuality, sociological phenomena do not exist in such isolation and recomposition, but that they are factored out of this living reality by means of an added concept. It will be remembered that societal facts are not *only* societal. It is always an objective content (sense-perceived or intellectual, technical or physiological) which is socially embodied, produced, or transmitted, and which only thus produces the totality of social life. Yet this societal formation of contents itself can be investigated by a science. Geometrical abstraction investigates only the spatial forms of bodies, although empirically, these forms are given merely as the forms of some material content. Similarly, if society is conceived as interaction among individuals, the description of the forms of this interaction is the task of the science of society in its strictest and most essential sense.

The first problem area of sociology, it will be remembered, consisted of the whole of historical life insofar as it is formed societally. Its societal character was conceived as an undifferentiated whole. The second problem area now under consideration, consists of the societal forms themselves. These are conceived as constituting society (and societies) out of the mere sum of living men. The study of this second area may be called "pure sociology," which abstracts the mere element of sociation. It isolates it inductively and psychologically from the heterogeneity of its contents and purposes, which, in themselves, are not societal. It thus proceeds like grammar, which isolates the pure forms of language from their contents through which these forms, nevertheless, come to life. In a comparable manner, social groups which are the most diverse imaginable in purpose and general significance, may nevertheless show identical forms of behavior toward one another on the part of their individual members. We find superiority and subordination, competition, division of labor, formation of parties, representation, inner solidarity coupled with exclusiveness toward the outside, and innumerable similar features in the state, in a religious community, in a band of conspirators, in an economic association, in an art school, in the family. However diverse the interests are that give rise to these sociations, the *forms* in which the interests are realized may yet be identical. And on the other hand, a contentually identical interest may take on form in very different sociations. Economic interest is realized both in competition and in the planned organization of producers, in isolation against other groups as well as in fusion with them. The religious contents of life, although they remain identical, sometimes demand an unregulated, sometimes a centralized form of community. The interests upon which the relations between the sexes are based are satisfied by an almost innumerable variety of family forms; etc.

Hence, not only may the form in which the most divergent contents are realized be identical; but inversely, the content, too, may persist, while its medium—the interactions of the individuals—adopts a variety of forms. We see, then, that the analysis in terms of form and content transforms the facts—which, in their immediacy, present these two categories as the indissoluble unity of social life—in such a way as to justify the sociological problem. This problem demands the identification, the systematic ordering, the psychological explanation, and the historical development of the pure forms of sociation. Obviously, in terms of its subject matter, sociology thus seen is not a special science, as it was in terms of the first problem area. Yet in terms of its clearly specified way of asking questions, it is a special science even here. The discussion of "sociability," in the third chapter of the present sketch, will offer an example that may serve to symbolize the total picture of the investigations in "pure sociology."

(c) *The Study of the Epistemological and Metaphysical Aspects of Society ("Philosophical Sociology")*

The modern scientific attitude toward facts finally suggests a third complex of questions concerning the fact "society." Insofar as these questions are adjacent (as it were) to the upper and lower limits of this fact, they are sociological only in a broad sense of the term; more properly, they are philosophical. Their *content* is constituted by this fact itself. Similarly, nature and art, out of which we develop their *immediate* sciences, also supply us with the subject matters of their philosophies, whose interests and methods lie on a different level. It is the level on which factual details are investigated concerning their significance for the totality of mind, life, and being in general, and concerning their justification in terms of such totality.

Thus, like every other exact science which aims at the immediate understanding of the given, social science, too, is surrounded by two *philosophical* areas. One of these covers the conditions, fundamental concepts, and presuppositions of concrete research, which cannot be taken care of by research itself since it is based on them. In the other area, this research is carried toward completions, connections, questions, and concepts that have no place in experience and in immediately objective knowledge. The first area is the epistemology, the second, the metaphysics of the particular discipline.

The tasks of the special social sciences—the study of economics and of institutions, the history of morals and of parties, population theory, and the discussion of occupational differentiation—could not be carried out at all if they did not presuppose certain concepts, postulates, and methods as axiomatic. If we did not assume a certain drive toward egoistic gain and pleasure, but at the same time the limitability of this drive through coercion, custom, and morals; if we did not claim the right to speak of the moods of a mass as a unit, although many of the members of this mass are only its superficial followers or even dissenters; if we did not declare the development within a particular sphere of culture understandable by recreating it as an evolution with a psychological logic—if we did not proceed in this way, we should be utterly unable to cast innumerable facts into a social picture. In all these and in countless other situations, we operate with methods of thinking that use particular events as raw materials from which we derive social scientific knowledge. Sociology proceeds like physics, which could never have been developed without grasping external phenomena on the basis of certain assumptions concerning space, matter, movement, and enumerability. Every special social science customarily and quite legitimately accepts without question such a basis of itself. Within its own domain, it could not even come to grips with it; for, in order to do so, obviously it would also have to take all other social sciences into consideration. Sociology thus emerges as the epistemology of the special social sciences, as the analysis and systematization of the bases of their forms and norms.

If these problems go beneath the concrete knowledge of social life, others, as it were, go beyond it. They try, by means of hypothesis and speculation, to supplement the unavoidably fragmentary character of the empirical facts (which always are fragmentary) in the direction of a closed system. They order the chaotic and accidental events into a series that follow an idea or approach a goal. They ask where the neutral and natural sequences of events might provide these events or their totality with *significance*. They assert or doubt—and both assertion and doubt, equally, derive from a superempirical world view—that the play of social historical phenomena contains a religious significance, or a relation (to be known or at least sensed) to the metaphysical ground of being. More particularly, they ask questions such as these: Is society the purpose of human existence, or is it a means for the individual? Does the ultimate value of social development lie in the unfolding of personality or of association? Do meaning and purpose inhere in social phenomena at all, or exclusively in individuals? Do the typical stages of the development of societies show an analogy with cosmic evolutions so that there might be a general formula or rhythm of development in general (as, for instance, the fluctuation between differentiation and integration), which applies to social and material data alike? Are social movements guided by the principle of the conservation of energy? Are they directed by material or by ideological motives?

Evidently, this type of question cannot be answered by the ascertainment of facts. Rather, it must be answered by interpretations of ascertained facts and by efforts to bring the relative and problematical elements of social reality under an overall view. Such a view does not compete with empirical claims because it serves needs which are quite different from those answered by empirical propositions.

The investigation of such problems, clearly, is more strictly based on differences in world views, individual and party valuations, and ultimate, undemonstrable convictions than is the investigation within the other two, more strictly fact-determined branches of sociology. For this reason, the discussion of a single problem as an example could not be as objective and could not as validly suggest the whole type of similar problems here, as is possible in the case of the other two branches. It therefore seems to me more advisable to trace, in the last chapter, a line of pertinent theories as they have been developed, in the course of many controversies, during a particular period of general intellectual history.

MAX WEBER

Max Weber (1864-1920), probably the greatest of the German sociologists, began his academic career in the law and became a *Privatdozent* in jurisprudence at the University of Berlin. In 1893, at the age of twenty-nine, he was appointed professor of economics at the University of Freiburg and a few years later succeeded the historical economist Karl Knies at Heidelberg. His career was interrupted by a serious illness in 1900, however, and he was forced to resign his professorship—although he maintained his residence in Heidelberg and continued to work there. Later on, in 1918, he was a visiting professor at the University of Vienna and in the following year became a regular professor of economics at Munich. In his second semester of teaching at Munich he died suddenly of pneumonia.

Weber was known first in the United States as an economic historian and he made to be sure many contributions to that field of inquiry. Much of his work, both in economics and sociology, was published in article form and collected by his students after his death. The work in sociology falls into three large divisions, the first dealing with the methodology of the social sciences (*Gesammelte Aufsätze zur Wissenschaftslehre*), the second with the sociology of religion (*Gesammelte Aufsätze zur Religionssoziologie*), and finally the uncompleted treatise on general theory (*Wirtschaft und Gesellschaft*). The selection that follows is part of the most famous of all the essays on the sociology of religion, *The Protestant Ethic and the Spirit of Capitalism,* translated by Talcott Parsons in 1930. It has been called the most distinguished piece of sociological research ever accomplished.

The Spirit of Capitalism[*]

In the title of this study is used the somewhat pretentious phrase, the *spirit* of capitalism. What is to be understood by it? The attempt to give anything like a definition of it brings out certain difficulties which are in the very nature of this type of investigation.

If any object can be found to which this term can be applied with any understandable meaning, it can only be an historical individual, i.e., a complex of elements associated in historical reality which we unite into a conceptual whole from the standpoint of their cultural significance.

Such an historical concept, however, since it refers in its content to a phenomenon significant for its unique individuality, cannot be defined according to the formula *genus proximum, differentia specifica,* but it must be gradually put together out of the individual parts which are taken from historical reality to make it up. Thus the final and definitive concept cannot stand at the beginning of the investigation, but must come at the end. We must, in other words, work out in the course of the discussion, as its most important result, the best conceptual formulation of what we here understand by the spirit of capitalism, that is the best from the point of view which interests us here. This point of view (the one of which we shall speak later) is, further, by no means the only possible one from which the historical phenomena we are investigating can be analyzed. Other standpoints would, for this as for every historical phenomenon, yield other characteristics as the essential ones. The result is that it is by no means necessary to understand by the spirit of capitalism only what it will come to mean to us for the purposes of our analysis. This is a necessary result of the nature of historical concepts

* Reprinted from *The Protestant Ethic and the Spirit of Capitalism* by Max Weber, translated by Talcott Parsons (1930). Used by permission of Charles Scribner's Sons, New York, and George Allen & Unwin, Ltd., London.

which attempt for their methodological purposes not to grasp historical reality in abstract general formula, but in concrete genetic sets of relations which are inevitably of a specifically unique and individual character.

Thus, if we try to determine the object, the analysis and historical explanation of which we are attempting, it cannot be in the form of a conceptual definition, but at least in the beginning only a provisional description of what is here meant by the spirit of capitalism. Such a description is, however, indispensable in order clearly to understand the object of the investigation. For this purpose we turn to a document of that spirit which contains what we are looking for in almost classical purity, and at the same time has the advantage of being free from all direct relationship to religion, being thus, for our purposes, free of preconceptions.

"Remember, that time is money. He that can earn ten shillings a day by his labor, and goes abroad, or sits idle one half of that day, though he spends but sixpence during his diversion or idleness, ought not to reckon that the only expense; he has really spent, or rather thrown away, five shillings besides.

"Remember, that credit is money. If a man lets his money lie in my hands after it is due, he gives me the interest, or so much as I can make of it during that time. This amounts to a considerable sum where a man has good and large credit, and makes good use of it.

"Remember, that money is of the prolific, generating nature. Money can beget money, and its offspring can beget more, and so on. Five shillings turned is six, turned again it is seven and threepence, and so on, till it becomes a hundred pounds. The more there is of it, the more it produces every turning, so that the profits rise quicker and quicker. He that kills a breeding sow, destroys all her offspring to the thousandth generation. He that murders a crown, destroys all that it might have produced, even scores of pounds."

"Remember this saying, The good paymaster is Lord of another man's purse. He that is known to pay punctually and exactly to the time he promises, may at any time, and on any occasion, raise all the money his friends can spare. This is sometimes of great use. After industry and frugality, nothing contributes more to the raising of a young man in the world than punctuality and justice in all his dealings; therefore never keep borrowed money an hour beyond the time you promised, lest a disappointment shut up your friend's purse for ever.

"The most trifling actions that affect a man's credit are to be regarded. The sound of your hammer at five in the morning, or at eight at night, heard by a creditor, makes him easy six months longer; but if he sees you at a billiard table, or hears your voice at a tavern, when you should be at work, he sends for his money the next day; demands it, before he can receive it, in a lump.

"It shows, besides, that you are mindful of what you owe; it makes you appear a careful as well as an honest man, and that still increases your credit.

"Beware of thinking all your own that you possess, and of living accordingly. It is a mistake that many people who have credit fall into. To prevent this, keep an exact account for some time both of your expenses and your income. If you take the pains at first to mention particulars, it will have this good effect: you will discover how wonderfully small, trifling expenses mount up to large sums, and will discern what might have been, and may for the future be saved, without occasioning any great inconvenience."

"For six pounds a year you may have the use of one hundred pounds, provided you are a man of known prudence and honesty.

"He that spends a groat a day idly, spends idly above six pounds a year, which is the price for the use of one hundred pounds.

"He that wastes idly a groat's worth of his time per day, one day with another, wastes the privilege of using one hundred pounds each day.

"He that idly loses five shillings' worth of time, loses five shillings, and might as prudently throw five shillings into the sea.

"He that loses five shillings, not only loses that sum, but all the advantage that might be made by turning it in dealing, which by the time that a young man becomes old, will amount to a considerable sum of money."

It is Benjamin Franklin who preaches to us in these sentences, the same which Ferdinand Kurnberger satirizes in his clever and malicious *Picture of American Culture* as the supposed confession of faith of the Yankee. That it is the spirit of capitalism which here speaks in characteristic fashion, no one will doubt, however little we may wish to claim that everything which could be understood as pertaining to that spirit is contained in it. Let us pause a moment to consider this passage, the philosophy of which Kurnberger sums up in the words, "They make tallow out of cattle and money out of men." The peculiarity of this philosophy of avarice appears to be the ideal of the honest man of recognized credit, and above all the idea of a duty of the individual toward the increase of his capital, which is assumed as an end in itself. Truly what is here preached is not simply a means of making one's way in the world, but a peculiar ethic. The infraction of its rules is treated not as foolishness but as forgetfulness of duty. That is the essence of the matter. It is not mere business astuteness; that sort of thing is common enough, it is an ethos. *This* is the quality which interests us.

When Jacob Fugger, in speaking to a business associate who had retired and who wanted to persuade him to do the same, since he had made enough money and should let others have a chance, rejected that as pusillanimity and answered that "he (Fugger) thought otherwise, he wanted to make money as long as he could," the spirit of his statement is evidently quite different from that of Franklin. What in the former case was an expression of commercial daring and a personal inclination morally neutral, in the latter takes on the character of an ethically coloured maxim for the conduct of life. The concept *spirit of capitalism* is here used in this specific sense, it is the spirit of modern capitalism. For that we are here dealing only with Western European and American capitalism is obvious from the way in which the problem was stated. Capitalism existed in China, India, Babylon, in the classic world, and in the Middle Ages. But in all these cases, as we shall see, this particular ethos was lacking.

Now, all Franklin's moral attitudes are colored with utilitarianism. Honesty is useful, because it assures credit; so are punctuality, industry, frugality, and that is the reason they are virtues. A logical deduction from this would be that where, for instance, the appearance of honesty serves the same purpose, that would suffice, and an unnecessary surplus of this virtue would evidently appear to Franklin's eyes as unproductive waste. And as a matter of fact, the story in his autobiography of his conversion to those virtues, or the discussion of the value of a strict maintenance of the appearance of modesty, the assiduous belittlement of one's own deserts in order to gain general recognition later, confirms this impression. According to Franklin, those virtues, like all others, are only in so far virtues as they are actually useful to the individual, and the surrogate of mere appearance is always sufficient when it accomplishes the end in view. It is a conclusion which is inevitable for strict utilitarianism. The impression of many Germans that the virtues professed by Americanism are pure hypocrisy seems to have been confirmed by this striking case. But in fact the matter is not by any means so simple. Benjamin Franklin's own character, as it appears in the really unusual candidness of his autobiography, belies that suspicion. The circumstance that he ascribes his recognition of the utility of virtue to a divine revelation which was intended to lead him in the path of righteousness, shows that something more than mere garnishing for purely egocentric motives is involved.

In fact, the *summum bonum* of this ethic, the earning of more and more money, combined with the strict avoidance of all spontaneous enjoyment of life, is above all completely devoid of any eudemonistic, not to say hedonistic, admixture. It is thought of so purely as an end in itself, that from the point of view of the happiness of, or utility to, the single individual, it appears entirely transcendental and absolutely irrational. Man is dominated by the making of money, by acquisition as the ultimate purpose of his life. Economic acquisition is no longer subordinated to man as the means for the satisfaction of his material needs. This reversal of what we should call the natural relationship, so irrational from a naïve point of view, is evidently a definitely leading principle of capitalistic influence. At the same time it expresses a type of feeling which is closely connected with certain religious ideas. If we thus ask, why should "money be made out of men," Benjamin Franklin himself, although he was a colorless deist, answers in his autobiography with a quotation from the Bible, which his strict Calvinistic father drummed into him again and again in his youth: "Seest thou a man diligent in his business? He shall stand before kings" (Prov. xxii. 29). The earning of money within the modern economic order is, so long as it is done legally, the result and the expression of virtue and proficiency in a calling; and this virtue and proficiency are, as it is now not difficult to see, the real Alpha and Omega of Franklin's ethic, as expressed in the passages we have quoted, as well as in all his works without exception.

And in truth this peculiar idea, so familiar to us today, but in reality so little a matter of course, of one's duty in a calling, is what is most characteristic of the social ethic of capitalistic culture, and is in a sense the fundamental basis of it. It is an obligation which the individual is supposed to feel and does feel towards the content of his professional activity, no matter in what it consists, in particular no matter whether it appears on the surface as a utilization of his personal powers, or only of his material possessions (as capital).

Of course, this conception has not appeared only under capitalistic conditions. On the contrary, we shall later trace its origins back to a time previous to the advent of capitalism. Still less, naturally, do we maintain that a conscious acceptance of these ethical maxims on the part of the individuals, entrepreneurs or laborers, in modern capitalistic enterprises, is a condition of the further existence of present-day capitalism. The capitalistic economy of the present day is an immense cosmos into which the individual is born, and which presents itself to him, at least as an individual, as an unalterable order of things in which he must live. It forces the individual, in so far as he is involved in the system of market relationships, to conform to capitalistic rules of action. The manufacturer who in the long run acts counter to these norms, will just as inevitably be eliminated from the economic scene as the worker who cannot or will not adapt himself to them will be thrown into the streets without a job.

Thus the capitalism of today, which has come to dominate economic life, educates and selects the economic subjects which it needs through a process of economic survival of the fittest. But here one can easily see the limits of the concept of selection as a means of historical explanation. In order that a manner of life so well adapted to the peculiarities of capitalism could be selected at all, i.e. should come to dominate others, it had to originate somewhere, and not in isolated individuals alone, but as a way of life common to whole groups of men. This origin is what really needs explanation. Concerning the doctrine of the more naive historical materialism, that such ideas originate as a reflection or superstructure of economic situations, we shall speak more in detail below. At this point it will suffice for our purpose to call attention to the fact that without doubt, in the country of Benjamin Franklin's birth (Massachusetts), the spirit of capitalism (in the sense we have attached to it) was present before the capitalistic order. There were complaints of a peculiarly calculating sort of profit-seeking in New England, as distinguished from other parts of America, as early as 1632. It is further undoubted that capitalism remained far less developed in some of the neighboring colonies, the later Southern States of the United States of America, in spite of the fact that these latter were founded by large capitalists for business motives, while the New England colonies were founded by preachers and seminary graduates with the help of small bourgeois, craftsmen and yeomen, for religious reasons. In this case the causal relation is certainly the reverse of that suggested by the materialistic standpoint.

But the origin and history of such ideas is much more complex than the theorists of the superstructure suppose. The spirit of capitalism, in the sense in which we are using the term, had to fight its way to supremacy against a whole world of hostile forces. A state of mind such as that expressed in the passages we have quoted from Franklin, and which called for the applause of a whole people, would both in ancient times and in the Middle Ages have been proscribed as the lowest sort of avarice and as an attitude entirely lacking in self-respect. It is, in fact, still regularly thus looked upon by all those social groups which are least involved in or adapted to modern capitalistic conditions. This is not wholly because the instinct of acquisition was in those times unknown or undeveloped, as had often been said. Nor because the *auri sacra fames,* the greed for gold, was then, or now, less powerful outside of bourgeois capitalism than within its peculiar sphere, as the illusions of modern romanticists are wont to believe. The difference between the capitalistic and pre-capitalistic spirits is not to be found at this point. The greed of the Chinese Mandarin, the old Roman aristocrat, or the modern peasant, can stand up to any comparison. And the *auri sacra fames* of a Neopolitan cab driver or *barcaiuolo,* and certainly of Asiatic representatives of similar trades, as well as of the craftsmen of southern European or Asiatic countries, is, as anyone can find out for himself, very much more intense, and especially more unscrupulous than that of, say, an Englishman in similar circumstances.

The universal reign of absolute unscrupulousness in the pursuit of selfish interests by the making of money has been a specific characteristic of precisely those countries whose bourgeois-capitalistic development, measured according to Occidental standards, has remained backward. As every employer knows, the lack of *coscienziosita* of the laborers of such countries, for instance Italy as compared with Germany, has been, and to a certain extent still is, one of the principal obstacles to their capitalistic development. Capitalism cannot make use of the labor of those who practise the doctrine of undisciplined *liberum arbitrium,* any more than it can make use of the business man who seems absolutely unscrupulous in his dealings with others, as we can learn from Franklin. Hence the difference does not lie in the degree of development of any impulse to make money. The *auri sacra fames* is as old as the history of man. But we shall see that those who submitted to it without reserve as an uncontrolled impulse, such as the Dutch sea-captain who "would go through hell for gain, even though he scorched his sails," were by no means the representatives of that attitude of mind from which the specifically modern capitalistic spirit as a mass phenomenon is derived, and that is what matters. At all periods of history, wherever it was possible, there has been ruthless acquisition, bound to no ethical norms whatever. Like war and piracy, trade has often been unrestrained in its relations with foreigners and those outside the group. The double ethic has permitted here what was forbidden in dealings among brothers.

Capitalistic acquisition as an adventure has been at home in all types of economic society which have known trade with the use of money and which have offered it opportunities, through *comenda,* farming of taxes, State loans, financing of wars, ducal courts and officeholders. Likewise the inner attitude of the adventurer, which laughs at all ethical limitations, has been universal. Absolute and conscious ruthlessness in acquisition has often stood in the closest connection with the strictest conformity to tradition. Moreover, with the breakdown of tradition and the more or less complete extension of free economic enterprise, even to within the social group, the new thing has not generally been ethically justified and encouraged, but only tolerated as a fact. And this fact has been treated either as ethically indifferent or as reprehensible, but unfortunately unavoidable. This has not only been the normal attitude of all ethical teachings, but, what is more important, also that expressed in the practical action of the average man of pre-capitalistic times, pre-capitalistic in the sense that the rational utilization of capital in a permanent enterprise and the rational capitalistic organization of labor had not yet become dominant forces in the determination of economic activity. Now just this attitude was one of the strongest inner obstacles which the adaptation of men to the conditions of an ordered bourgeois-capitalistic economy has encountered everywhere. . . .

VILFREDO PARETO

The Italian sociologist Vilfredo Pareto (1848-1923) enjoyed an extraordinary vogue in this country, at Harvard, during the early and middle nineteen-thirties, primarily because his work, though well known to American sociologists, attracted the attention there of the influential physiologist, Lawrence J. Henderson. Henderson organized a public seminar, including both professors and the laity, to study Pareto's writings and it was at this time that his formidable opus, *Trattato di sociologia generale* (1915), was translated into English as *The Mind and Society* (4 volumes, 1935) by Arthur Livingston of Columbia—a translation so excellent that someone has remarked that it is superior to the original work.

In any event, Pareto was the son of an Italian nobleman and a French mother. Trained originally as an engineer, his early career included several important positions with the Italian railways and in mining. He became interested in mathematical economics, however, and in 1893 received an appointment at the University of Lausanne. From economics it was another short step to sociology, a science that had hitherto failed of maturity, in Pareto's opinion, because its practitioners had been insufficiently dedicated to experience and observation and had been led astray by such notions as progress, humanity, and democracy. It was Pareto's demand that sociology become a logico-experimental science using exactly the same methods that had proven to be successful in physics and celestial mechanics. His views on the subject are illustrated by the following selection from *The Mind and Society*.

*Sociology as a Science**

A logico-experimental study merely relates facts with facts. If that is done directly, merely describing facts that are observable simultaneously, we get pure empiricism. Empiricism may serve to discover uniformities if, by observation or experiment, one succeeds in distinguishing not more than two categories of facts that stand in correlation. Once the categories multiply and effects become involved, it proves to be very difficult, and more often impossible, to find uniformities with the tool of pure empiricism. The sum of effects has somehow to be unsnarled. In certain cases that can be done materially by experiment. In others, experiment is out of the question or else fails to unravel the complication. Then one can only resort to hypothetical abstractions, now to one, now to another, testing each in turn with the idea of solving ideally what cannot be solved materially, accepting finally that hypothesis among the many which yields results that accord with experience. The manner in which the hypothesis has been reached may be absurd. That is of little if any importance; for the value of the hypothesis is tested not by the manner in which it has been conceived, but by the verifications that can be made of it.

But if the hypothesis has been inferred in the first place from certain facts, A, B . . . . P, that circumstance in itself is a first step towards verification; for since the hypothesis has been inferred from those facts, they certainly will appear among the results it will yield. What remains to be seen is whether it will also yield the facts Q, R . . . . V, which have not yet been taken into the reckoning.

In these volumes, therefore, we might have followed a deductive method, positing our residues and derivations at the very

* From *The Mind and Society,* Volume IV, by Vilfredo Pareto, translated by Andrew Bongiorno and Arthur Livingston, copyright, 1935, by Harcourt, Brace and Company, Inc.

outset as mere hypotheses, without explaining how we came by them, thence going on to show that they yielded results which accorded with the facts. Instead we elected to follow the inductive method, deriving our residues and derivations from facts in very large numbers. So, as far as those facts were concerned, the verification was made then and there, and all that remained was to extend the verification to other facts not as yet considered. That verification we proceeded to make and are still making. In a word, then, what we have been doing, and are still doing, is to establish relations between facts.

There is nothing peculiar about such a method. It is the method general in all the sciences. Oftentimes in the sciences a hypothesis serves for a certain length of time and promotes progress in a particular science; then it is replaced by another, which performs the same function until, in its turn, it gives way to still a third; and so on. Sometimes a hypothesis may hold its ground for a long time, as was the case with the hypothesis of universal gravitation.

The logico-experimental sciences are made up of a sum of theories that are like living creatures, in that they are born, live, and die, the young replacing the old, the group alone enduring. As is the case with living beings, the lifetimes of theories vary in length and not always are the long-lived ones the ones that contribute most to the advancement of knowledge. Faith and metaphysics aspire to an ultimate, eternal resting place. Science knows that it can attain only provisory, transitory positions. Every theory fulfils its function, and nothing more can be asked of it.

If such succession in doctrines is in great part determined by a single force, the successive stages may constantly approach a certain limit; their curve may have an asymptote. That is what is happening in the logico-experimental sciences. The force, and if not the only one at least the chief one, that is now influencing those sciences is the investigation of correspondences between theories and experience. Theories therefore are constantly getting closer to experimental reality; whereas in a day gone by other forces were at work and prevented attainment of that result. Economic and social doctrines are still subject to such forces, and for that reason they continue to be at variance with experimental reality, sometimes to very considerable degrees, and it is doubtful whether there be any asymptote for their oscillations.

If the succession of doctrines is determined by a large number of forces of approximately equal intensities, the movement revealed in the succession may be so complicated as to make it impossible to find any general expression for it. But if such forces, without being so few as one, are at least not many, there are cases in which we can discover such an expression. We may, for instance, recognize movements as oscillating about a given point, whether tending towards an equilibrium in that position or continuing on indefinitely without any tendency of the kind. We have seen movements of that sort taking place under the pressure of two forces in the main: correspondences with experimental reality and social utility.

Only in a first approximation can the numberless forces operating in a concrete case be reduced to two. If, to carry an investigation farther, new forces are brought into consideration as an addition to the two main ones, we get movements that grow increasingly complicated and are harder and harder to manage. In these volumes we have succeeded in taking a few steps along that road, but it bristles with obstacles, and they are too numerous to permit us to go as far as we should have liked.

Kepler's discovery that the orbit of Mars was an ellipse with one of its foci coinciding with the centre of the Sun was purely empirical, providing a summary description of the situation. In that case, owing to the imperfect observations available, it was possible to distinguish the movement of one planet with respect to the Sun from the movements of the other planets. Had the observations been more nearly exact, no such distinction could have been made, Kepler would have found no ellipse, and that would have been a serious obstacle to the advancement of astronomy.

Two cases have to be considered in this connexion:

1. As regards our solar system, the obstacle might have been overcome without great difficulty. Some scientists would have observed that if the curve traversed by Mars was not an ellipse, it was in any case not far from an ellipse; and he could have suggested the *hypothesis* that if Mars and the Sun were consid-

ered apart from the other planets, the curve had to be an ellipse, and that if that was not the case, it was because the Sun and Mars were not considered apart from the other planets.

2. The obstacle would have been much greater and perhaps insuperable if instead of our solar system, where the central body has an enormously greater mass than any of its planets, a system of stars and planets of no very appreciable differences in mass had been in question.

Sometimes, though unfortunately very rarely, the facts correlated by statistics may be brought under the first case just mentioned: that is to say, by interpolation, a certain hypothetical curve can be found from which the real curve can be inferred by assuming perturbations. But much more often the facts of economics, and to a still greater extent of sociology, are to be brought under the second case.

Newton advanced a hypothesis, known as the theory of universal gravitation, whereby if the Sun is assumed to be stationary with a planet revolving around it, one gets a curve something like the curve discovered by Kepler—an ellipse.

That hypothesis has one peculiar merit that is rarely met with in other hypotheses of the kind. The relation between the hypothesis and the facts can be inverted. If it be assumed that a planet is moving in an ellipse about a stationary Sun, a law of gravitation results that is Newton's law exactly. Generally, in economics and sociology, a hypothesis may indeed imply the existence of certain facts, but those facts may lend themselves to many other hypotheses.

Newton's hypothesis has also another very great merit, that so far at least (1914), taking the Sun and its planets as a whole, it has been adequate for explaining all the perturbations that have been observed in the movements of the celestial bodies. If that has not been the case, Newton's hypothesis might have stood, but it would have had to be supplemented with other hypotheses, the hypothesis, for instance, that the attraction exerted by the planets upon one another is different from the attraction between the planets and the Sun.

Needless to say, neither economics nor sociology possess simple hypotheses as widely applicable as Newton's.

In political economy and sociology, therefore, it is indispensable to consider many different elements in the complex phenomena that are directly recorded by observation. The simplest thing one can say in economics is that the economic equilibrium results from the conflict between tastes and obstacles; but the simplicity is only apparent, since one then has to go on and take account of an intricate variety of tastes and obstacles. The complications in sociology are greater still and by far. There, in addition to logical conduct, which is alone envisaged in economics, one has to deal with nonlogical conduct, and then again, in addition to logical thinking, with derivations.

The laws, so called, of supply and demand cannot be deduced from statistics as to the quantities and prices of a commodity produced or brought to market. When economists said that an increase in supply brings a drop in price, they stated the law of an ideal situation that is rarely observable in the concrete. In working out theories in economics it is an illusion to believe that we get any closer to the concrete by starting with the laws of supply and demand than we do by starting with the "utility" of the early economists, or with the "marginal utility," the "rarity," or the "ophelimity," of more recent economists. Whatever we do, we are resorting to abstraction, and we cannot do otherwise. Theoretically one may start with any one of those considerations or indeed with any others; but however we start, we must use certain cautions that are overlooked by many writers who talk political economy without knowing the first thing about it. From the theoretical standpoint, again, one must not forget that consumptions of commodities are not independent, as not a few of the founders of pure economics assumed them to be. Nor can the undulatory movements of economic phenomena be disregarded, nor a great many other circumstances, such as speculation, which change the simpler form of the phenomena that, for purposes of convenience, was the one considered first.

All that has just been said applies *a fortiori* to sociology. Little or nothing can be inferred directly from the mere description, and in that sense the apothegm that "history never repeats itself" is very true. Concrete phenomena have to be broken up into ideal phenomena that are simpler, that we may so arrive at something more nearly constant than the complex and ever shifting thing we have before us in the concrete. In these volumes we have sought these less variable, these more constant, elements in residues and derivations. They might very well be sought in other directions. That is not so important as to be careful that wherever one goes looking for them, elements and forms that lead away from objective reality are not introduced. That "history never repeats itself" identically is just as certain as it is that history is "always repeating itself" in certain respects that we may call the main respects. It would be inconceivably absurd to imagine that history could produce an event identically repeating the Peloponnesian War, in the sense of being an exact copy of it. But then again, history shows that that war, which arose in the rivalry between Athens and Sparta, is only one item in an endless series of similar wars that have been brought on by similar causes, that in that sense there are numberless copies of it that are likenesses, to some extent at least, from the wars that arose in the rivalries between Carthage and Rome down to all the other wars that have been fought in all periods of history between then and now. In his *Politica,* V, 3, 7 (Rackham, p. 305) Aristotle says: "Finally, it must be evident that those who have been the cause of power (to a city), whether they be private citizens, magistrates, clans, or in short, any part of a people, are responsible for insurrections." In those words he was describing one of the main elements in the great many facts that were known to him, and he was foreseeing a great many other facts that were to come true after his time, the cases of Cromwell and Napoleon, to mention examples closer to our own times.

The main element in such happenings is in fact supplied by sentiments (residues), which have varied but slightly between Aristotle's time and our own. The same may be said of many maxims of Machiavelli, which hold as true today as they were in his time. Classes of residues vary but slightly and but slowly, and they may therefore be counted among the elements that determine the constant, virtually constant, or at least not very variable element in historical phenomena. The separate genera in a class of residues vary to a far greater degree and much more rapidly than the class as a whole, and we must therefore be cautious in giving them any such position. Derivations vary widely and very rapidly; and they are generally to be counted, therefore, only among the subordinate elements that determine secondary, variable, and for the most part negligible phases in a phenomenon. What we have just been saying furnishes the key also to a fact to which we have had frequent occasion to allude—that in a quest for sociological uniformities, too many facts, details too minute, may be a hindrance rather than a help; for if one dwells on all the petty circumstances that figure in a situation, one can easily lose one's way, like a person traveling in a thick underbrush; one is prevented from assigning proper indices to the various elements, mistaking what is secondary for what is principal, what is very variable for what is quasi-constant, and so one ends by writing a piece of literature that is devoid of the slightest scientific value.

In the practice of the social sciences one must especially be on one's guard against intrusions of personal sentiments; for a writer is inclined to look not for what is and nothing else, but for what *ought* to be in order to fit in with his religious, moral, patriotic, humanitarian or other sentiments. The quest for uniformities is an end in itself. Once they have been found, they may be made to serve other purposes. But to mix the two researches is harmful to both, and is in any case a serious and oftentimes insuperable obstacle to the discovery of experimental uniformities. As long as the natural sciences had to deal with such obstacles, they made little or no progress, and only as the obstacles became fewer in number and finally disappeared did they make the marvellous progress they show today. If, accordingly, one would remould the social sciences on the model of the natural sciences, one must proceed in them as in the natural sciences, reducing highly complicated concrete phenomena to simpler theoretical phenomena, being exclusively guided all the while by the intent to discover experimental uniformities, and judging the efficacy of what one has done only by the experimental verifications that may be made of it.

V · *Recent Sociology*

W. I. THOMAS

William Isaac Thomas (1863-1947) was known for many years before his death as the dean of American sociologists. He was educated first at the University of Tennessee, where for a time he taught Greek, Latin, French, German, and English. After graduate study at Berlin and Göttingen he returned to the United States to teach English and Germanic philology at Oberlin. After five years at Oberlin he left for the new University of Chicago, where he took his doctorate in 1896, became assistant professor in 1897, associate professor in 1900, and professor in 1910. In 1918 he resigned and thereafter held no permanent academic post, though he lectured on occasion at the New School for Social Research and served as visiting professor at Harvard during the year 1936-1937. A robust and vibrant man, Thomas's interests were by no means limited to sociology. He lived with zest and was in addition an inventor of some consequence. He was president of the American Sociological Society in 1927.

In sociology Thomas's interests turned in the direction of social psychology. He was particularly interested in the psychological aspects of culture and was responsible, more than any one, for introducing into sociological research the use of personal documents like life histories and autobiographies. These interests are reflected in the monumental five-volume work (with Znaniecki), *The Polish Peasant in Europe and America* (1918-21), a work that has been called the one sure classic of American sociology. Thomas wrote in addition *Sex and Society* (1907), *Source Book for Social Origins* (1909), *The Unadjusted Girl* (1923), *The Child in America* (with Dorothy S. Thomas, 1928), and *Primitive Behavior* (1937).

The "Methodological Note" to *The Polish Peasant*, from which the following excerpt is taken, is required reading for anyone who aspires to be a sociologist. A brief biographical account of the coauthor, Florian Znaniecki, appears on p. 449.

From *The Polish Peasant*

The ideal of social theory, as of every other nomothetic science, is to interpret as many facts as possible by as few laws as possible, that is, not only to explain causally the life of particular societies at particular periods, but to subordinate these particular laws to general laws applicable to all societies at all times—taking into account the historical evolution of mankind which continually brings new data and new facts and thus forces us to search for new laws in addition to those already discovered. But the fact that social theory as such cannot test its results by the laboratory method, but must rely entirely on the logical perfection of its abstract analysis and synthesis, makes the problem of control of the validity of its generalizations particularly important. The insufficient realization of the character of this control has been the chief reason why so many sociological works bear a character of compositions, intermediary between philosophy and science and fulfilling the demands of neither.

We have mentioned above the fact that social theory as nomothetic science must be clearly distinguished from any philosophy of social life which attempts to determine the essence of social reality or to outline the unique process of social evolution. This distinction becomes particularly marked when we reach the problem of testing the generalizations. Every scientific law bears upon the empirical facts themselves in their whole variety, not upon their underlying common essence, and hence every new discovery in the domain which it embraces affects it directly and immediately, either by corroborating it or by invalidating it. And, as scientific laws concern facts which repeat themselves, they automatically apply to the future as well as to the past, and new happenings in the domain embraced by the law must be taken into consideration as either justifying or contradicting the generalization based upon past happenings, or demanding that this generalization be supplemented by a new one.

And thus the essential criterion of social science as against social philosophy is the direct dependence of its generalizations on new discoveries and new happenings. If a social generalization is not permanently qualified by the assumption that at any moment a single new experience may contradict it, forcing us either to reject it or to supplement it by other generalizations, it is not scientific and has no place in social theory, unless as a general principle helping to systematize the properly scientific generalizations. The physicist, the chemist, and the biologist have learned by the use of experiment that their generalizations are scientifically fruitful only if they are subject to the check of a possible experimental failure, and thus the use of experiment has helped them to pass from the mediaeval *philosophia naturalis* to the modern natural science. The social theorician must follow their example and methodically search only for such generalizations as are subject to the check of a possible contradiction by new facts and should leave the empirically unapproachable essences and meanings where they properly belong, and where they have a real though different importance and validity—in philosophy.

The ultimate test of social theory, as we have emphasized throughout the present note, will be its application in practice, and thus its generalizations will be also subject in the last resort to the check of a possible failure. However, practical application is not experimentation. The results of the physical sciences are also ultimately tested by their application in industry, but this does not alter the fact that the test is made on the basis of laboratory experiments. The difference between experiment and application is twofold: (1) The problems themselves usually differ in complexity. The experiment by which we test a scientific law is artificially simplified in view of the special theoretic problem, whereas in applying scientific results to attain a practical purpose we have a much more complex situation to deal with, necessitating the use of several scientific laws and the calculation of their interference. This is a question with which we shall deal presently. (2) In laboratory experiments the question of the immediate practical value of success or failure is essentially excluded for the sake of their theoretical value. Whether the chemist in trying a new combination will spoil his materials and have to buy a new supply, whether the new combination will be worth more or less money than the elements used, are from the standpoint of science completely irrelevant questions; and even a failure if it puts the scientist on the trail of a new law will be more valuable than a success if it merely corroborates once more an old and well-established law. But in applying scientific results in practice we have essentially the practical value of success or failure in view. It is unthinkable that a chemist asked to direct the production of a new kind of soap in a factory should test his theory by direct application and risk the destruction of a hundred thousand dollars worth of material, instead of testing it previously on a small scale by laboratory experiments. Now in all so-called social experiments, on however small a scale, the question of practical value is involved, because the objects of these experiments are men; the social scientist cannot exclude the question of the bearing of his "experiments" on the future of those who are affected by them. He is therefore seldom or never justified in risking a failure for the sake of testing his theory. Of course he does and can take risks, not as a scientist, but as a practical man; that is, he is justified in taking the risk of bringing some harm if there are more chances of benefit than of harm to those on whom he operates. His risk is then the practical risk involved in every application of an idea, not the special theoretic risk involved in the mere testing of the idea. And, in order to diminish this practical risk, he must try to make his theory as certain and applicable as possible before trying to apply it in fact, and he can secure this result and hand over to the social practitioner generalizations at least approximately as applicable as those of physical science, only if he uses the check of contradiction by new experience. This means that besides using only such generalizations as can be contradicted by new experiences he must not wait till new experiences impose themselves on him by accident, but must search for them, must institute a systematic method of *observation*. And, while it is only natural that a scientist in order to form a hypothesis and to give it some amount of probability has to search first of all for such experiences as may corroborate it, his hypothesis cannot be considered fully tested until he has made subsequently a systematic search for such experiences as may contradict it, and proved those contradictions to be only seeming, explicable by the interference of definite factors.

Assuming now that social theory fulfils its task satisfactorily and goes on discovering new laws which can be applied to regulate social becoming, what will be the effect of this on social practice? First of all, the limitations with which social practice has struggled up to the present will be gradually removed. Since it is theoretically possible to find what social influences should be applied to certain already existing attitudes in order to produce certain new attitudes, and what attitudes should be developed with regard to certain already existing social values in order to make the individual or the group produce certain new social values, there is not a single phenomenon within the whole sphere of human life that conscious control cannot reach sooner or later. There are no objective obstacles in the nature of the social world or in the nature of the human mind which would essentially prevent social practice from attaining gradually the same degree of efficiency as that of industrial practice. The only obstacles are of a subjective kind.

There is, first, the traditional appreciation of social activity as meritorious in itself, for the sake of its intentions alone. There must, indeed, be some results in order to make the good intentions count, but, since anything done is regarded as meritorious, the standards by which the results are appreciated are astonishingly low. Social practice must cease to be a matter of merit and be treated as a necessity. If the theorician is asked to be sure of his generalizations before trying to apply them in practice, it is at least strange that persons of merely good will are permitted to try out on society indefinitely and irresponsibly their vague and perhaps sentimental ideas.

The second obstacle to the development of a perfect social practice is the well-known unwillingness of the common-sense man to accept the control of scientific technique. Against this unwillingness there is only one weapon—success. This is what the history of industrial technique shows. There is perhaps not a single case where the first application of science to any field of practice held by common sense and tradition did not provoke the opposition of the practitioner. It is still within the memory of man that the old farmer with his common-sense methods laughed at the idea that the city chap could teach him anything about farming, and was more than skeptical about the application of the results of soil analysis to the growing of crops. The fear of new things is still strong even among cultivated persons, and the social technician has to expect that he will meet at almost every step this old typical hostility of common sense to science. He can only accept it and interpret it as a demand to show the superiority of his methods by their results.

But the most important difficulty which social practice has to overcome before reaching a level of efficiency comparable to that of industrial practice lies in the difficulty of applying scientific generalizations. The laws of science are abstract, while the practical situations are concrete, and it requires a special intellectual activity to find what are the practical questions which a given law may help to solve, or what are the scientific laws which may be used to solve a given practical question. In the physical sphere this intellectual activity has been embodied in technology, and it is only since the technologist has intervened between the scientist and the practitioner that material practice has acquired definitely the character of a self-conscious and planfully developing technique and ceased to be dependent on irrational and often unreasonable traditional rules. And if material practice needs a technology in spite of the fact that the generalizations which physical science hands over to it have been already experimentally tested, this need is much more urgent in social practice where the application of scientific generalizations is their first and only experimental test.

We cannot enter here into detailed indications of what social technology should be, but we must take into account the chief point of its method—the general form which every concrete problem of social technique assumes. Whatever may be the aim of social practice—modification of individual attitudes or of social institutions—in trying to attain this aim we never find the elements which we want to use or to modify isolated and passively waiting for our activity, but always embodied in active practical *situations,* which have been formed independently of us and with which our activity has to comply.

The situation is the set of values and attitudes with which the individual or the group has to deal in a process of activity and with regard to which this activity is planned and its results appreciated. Every concrete activity is the solution of a situation. The situation involves three kinds of data: (1) The objective conditions under which the individual or society has to act, that is, the totality of values—economic, social, religious, intellectual, etc.—which at the given moment affect directly or indirectly the conscious status of the individual or the group. (2) The pre-existing attitudes of the individual or the group which at the given moment have an actual influence upon his behavior. (3) The definition of the situation, that is, the more or less clear conception of the conditions and consciousness of the attitudes. And the definition of the situation is a necessary preliminary to any act of the will, for in given conditions and with a given set of attitudes an indefinite plurality of actions is possible, and one definite action can appear only if these conditions are selected, interpreted, and combined in a determined way and if a certain systematization of these attitudes is reached, so that one of them becomes predominant and subordinates the others. It happens, indeed, that a certain value imposes itself immediately and unreflectively and leads at once to action, or that an attitude as soon as it appears excludes the others and expresses itself unhesitatingly in an active process. In these cases, whose most radical examples are found in reflex and instinctive actions, the definition is already given to the individual by external conditions or by his own tendencies. But usually there is a process of reflection, after which either a ready social definition is applied or a new personal definition worked out.

Let us take a typical example out of the fifth volume of the present work, concerning the family life of the immigrants in America. A husband, learning of his wife's infidelity, deserts her. The objective conditions were: (1) the social institution of marriage with all the rules involved; (2) the wife, the other man, the children, the neighbors, and in general all the individuals constituting the habitual environment of the husband and, in a sense, given to him as values; (3) certain economic conditions; (4) the fact of the wife's infidelity. Toward all these values the husband had certain attitudes, some of them traditional, others recently developed. Now, perhaps under the influence of the discovery of his wife's infidelity, perhaps after having developed some new attitude toward the sexual or economic side of marriage, perhaps simply influenced by the advice of a friend in the form of a rudimentary scheme of the situation helping him to "see the point," he defines the situation for himself. He takes certain conditions into account, ignores or neglects others, or gives them a certain interpretation in view of some chief value, which may be his wife's infidelity, or the economic burdens of family life of which this infidelity gives him the pretext to rid himself, or perhaps some other woman, or the half-ironical pity of his neighbors, etc. And in this definition some one attitude—sexual jealousy, or desire for economic freedom, or love for the other woman, or offended desire for recognition—or a complex of these attitudes, or a new attitude (hate, disgust) subordinates to itself the others and manifests itself chiefly in the subsequent action, which is evidently a solution of the situation, and fully determined both in its social and in its individual components by the whole set of values, attitudes, and reflective schemes which the situation included. When a situation is solved, the result of the activity becomes an element of a new situation, and this is most clearly evidenced in cases where the activity brings a change of a social institution whose unsatisfactory functioning was the chief element of the first situation.

Now, while the task of science is to analyze by a comparative study the whole process of activity into elementary facts, and it must therefore ignore the variety of concrete situations in order to be able to find laws of causal dependence of abstractly isolated attitudes or values on other attitudes and values, the task of technique is to provide the means of a rational control of concrete situations. The situation can evidently be controlled either by a change of conditions or by a change of attitudes, or by both, and in this respect the role of technique as application of science is easily characterized. By comparing situations of a certain type, the social technician must find what are the predominant values or the predominant attitudes which determine the situation more than others, and then the question is to modify these values or these attitudes in the desired way by using the knowledge of social causation given by social theory. Thus, we may find that some of the situations among the Polish immigrants in America resulting in the husband's desertion are chiefly determined by the wife's infidelity, others by her quarrelsomeness, others by bad economic conditions, still others by the husband's desire for freedom, etc. And, if in a given case we know what influences to apply in order to modify these dominating factors, we can modify the situation accordingly, and ideally we can provoke in the individual a behavior in conformity with any given scheme of attitudes and values.

To be sure, it may happen that, in spite of an adequate scientific knowledge of the social laws permitting the modification of those factors which we want to change, our efforts will fail to influence the situation or will produce a situation more undesirable than the one we wished to avoid. The fault is then with our technical knowledge. That is, either we have failed in determining the relative importance of the various factors, or we have failed to foresee the influence of other causes which, interfering with our activity, produce a quite unexpected and undesired effect. And since it is impossible to expect from every practitioner a complete scientific training and still more impossible to have him work out a scientifically justified and detailed plan of action for every concrete case in particular, the special task of the social technician is to prepare, with the help of both science and practical observation, thorough schemes and plans of action for all the various *types* of situations which may be found in a given line of social activity, and leave to the practitioner the subordination of the given concrete situation to its proper type. This is actually the role which all the organizers of social institutions have played, but the technique itself must become more conscious and methodically perfect, and every field of social activity should have its professional technicians. The evolution of social life makes necessary continual modifications and developments of social technique, and we can hope that the evolution of social theory will continually put new and useful scientific generalizations within the reach of the social technician; the latter must therefore remain in permanent touch with both social life and social theory, and this requires a more far-going specialization than we actually find.

But, however efficient this type of social technique may become, its application will always have certain limits beyond which a different type of technique will be more useful. Indeed, the form of social control outlined above presupposes that the individual—or the group—is treated as a passive object of our activity and that we change the situations for him, from case to case, in accordance with our plans and intentions. But the application of this method becomes more and more difficult as the situations grow more complex, more new and unexpected from case to case, and more influenced by the individual's own reflection. And, indeed, from both the moral and the hedonistic standpoints and also from the standpoint of the level of efficiency of the individual and of the group, it is desirable to develop in the individuals the ability to control spontaneously their own activities by conscious reflection. To use a biological comparison, the type of control where the practitioner prescribes for the individual a scheme of activity appropriate to every crisis as it arises corresponds to the tropic or reflex type of control in animal life, where the activity of the individual is controlled mechanically by stimulations from without, while the reflective and individualistic control corresponds to the type of activity characteristic of the higher conscious organism, where the control is exercised from within by the selective mechanism of the nervous system. While, in the early tribal, communal, kinship, and religious groups, and to a large extent in the historic state, the society itself provided a rigoristic and particularistic set of definitions in the form of "customs" or "mores," the tendency to advance is associated with the liberty of the individual to make his own definitions.

We have assumed throughout this argument that if an adequate technique is developed it is possible to produce any desirable attitudes and values, but this assumption is practically justified only if we find in the individual attitudes which cannot avoid response to the class of stimulations which society is able to apply to him. And apparently we do find this disposition. Every individual has a vast variety of wishes which can be satisfied only by his incorporation in a society. Among his general patterns of wishes we may enumerate: (1) the desire for new experience, for fresh stimulations; (2) the desire for recognition, including, for example, sexual response and general social appreciation, and secured by devices ranging from the display of ornament to the demonstration of worth through scientific attainment; (3) the desire for mastery, or the "will to power," exemplified by ownership, domestic tyranny, political despotism, based on the instinct of hate, but capable of being sublimated to laudable ambition; (4) the desire for security, based on the instinct of fear and exemplified negatively by the wretchedness of the individual in perpetual solitude or under social taboo. Society is, indeed, an agent for the repression of many of the wishes in the individual; it demands that he shall be moral by repressing at least the wishes which are irreconcilable with the welfare of the group, but nevertheless it provides the only medium within which any of his schemes or wishes can be gratified. And it would be superfluous to point out by examples the degree to which society has in the past been able to impose its schemes of attitudes and values on the individual. Professor Sumner's volume, *Folkways,* is practically a collection of such examples, and, far from discouraging us as they discourage Professor Sumner, they should be regarded as proofs of the ability of the individual to conform to any definition, to accept any attitude, provided it is an expression of the public will or represents the appreciation of even a limited group. To take a single example from the present, to be a bastard or the mother of a bastard has been regarded heretofore as anything but desirable, but we have at this moment reports that one of the warring European nations is officially impregnating its unmarried women and girls and even married women whose husbands are at the front. If this is true (which we do not assume) we have a new definition and a new evaluation of motherhood arising from the struggle of this society against death, and we may anticipate a new attitude—that the resulting children and their mothers will be the objects of extraordinary social appreciation. And even if we find that the attitudes are not so tractable as we have assumed, that it is not possible to provoke all the desirable ones, we shall still be in the same situation as, let us say, physics and mechanics: we shall have the problem of securing the highest degree of control possible in view of the nature of our materials.

WILLIAM FIELDING OGBURN

William Fielding Ogburn (1886-1959) was born in Georgia and received his first academic degree at Mercer University, a denominational school in that state. He took his M.A. in 1909 and his Ph.D. in 1912 as a student of Giddings at Columbia University. He taught sociology first at Reed College, in Oregon, and was professor of that subject at Columbia from 1919 to 1927. In the latter year he moved to the University of Chicago and taught there continuously until his retirement in 1951. In addition he taught at various times at Oxford, Calcutta, New Delhi, Florida State, and the University of Washington, and held important posts in the Federal Government. He was president both of the American Sociological Society (1929) and of the American Statistical Association (1931) and a vice president of the American Association for the Advancement of Science (1932).

Like the other sociologists represented in this volume, Ogburn was the author, coauthor, and editor of many books. Among the most important of these are *Social Change* (1922; rev. 1950), *The Social Sciences and Their Interrelations* (1927), *American Marriage and Family Relationships* (1928), *Recent Social Trends* (1933), *Social Characteristics of Cities* (1937), *Sociology* (with Meyer F. Nimkoff, 1940; rev. 1950, 1958), and *The Social Effects of Aviation* (1946). He was editor or associate editor of at least four learned journals and he published over two hundred articles in various periodicals.

In his approach to sociology Ogburn insisted on the importance of such criteria as reliability and verifiability and preferred to leave theory and system-building to others. It is somewhat ironic, therefore, that the contribution destined to be linked with his name is a concept, the concept of cultural lag, which he introduced in 1922. The following selection is a discussion of the theory associated with this concept.

The Hypothesis of Cultural Lag[*]

This rapidity of change in modern times raises the very important question of social adjustment. Problems of social adjustment are of two sorts. One concerns the adaptation of man to culture or perhaps preferably the adapting of culture to man. The other problem is the question of adjustments, occasioned as a result of these rapid social changes, between the different parts of culture, which no doubt means ultimately the adaptation of culture to man. This second problem of adjustment between the different parts of culture is the immediate subject of our inquiry.

The thesis is that the various parts of modern culture are not changing at the same rate, some parts are changing much more rapidly than others; and since there is a correlation and interdependence of parts, a rapid change in one part of our culture requires readjustments through other changes in the various correlated parts of culture. For instance, industry and education are correlated, hence a change in industry makes adjustments necessary through changes in the educational system. Industry and education are two variables, and if the change in industry occurs first and the adjustment through education follows, industry may be referred to as the independent variable and education as the dependent variable. Where one part of culture changes first, through some discovery or invention, and occasions changes in some part of culture dependent upon it, there frequently is a delay in the changes occasioned in the dependent part of culture. The extent of this lag will vary according to the nature of the cultural material, but may exist for a considerable number of years, during which time there may be said to be a maladjustment. It is desirable to reduce the period of maladjustment, to make the cultural adjustments as quickly as possible.

The foregoing account sets forth a problem that occurs when

* From *Social Change* by William Fielding Ogburn. Copyright 1922 by B. W. Huebsch, 1950 by William Fielding Ogburn. Reprinted by permission of The Viking Press, Inc., New York.

there is a rapid change in a culture of interdependent parts and when the rates of change in the parts are unequal. The discussion will be presented according to the following outlines. First the hypothesis will be presented, then examined and tested by a rather full consideration of the facts of a single instance, to be followed by several illustrations. Next the nature and cause of the phenomenon of cultural maladjustment in general will be analyzed. The extent of such cultural lags will be estimated, and finally the significance for society will be set forth.

A first simple statement of the hypothesis we wish to investigate now follows. A large part of our environment consists of the material conditions of life and a large part of our social heritage is our material culture. These material things consist of houses, factories, machines, raw materials, manufactured products, foodstuffs and other material objects. In using these material things we employ certain methods. Some of these methods are as simple as the technique of handling a tool. But a good many of the ways of using the material objects of culture involve rather larger usages and adjustments, such as customs, beliefs, philosophies, laws, governments. One important function of government, for instance, is the adjustment of the population to the material conditions of life, although there are other governmental functions. Sumner has called many of these processes of adjustments, mores. The cultural adjustments to material conditions, however, include a larger body of processes than the mores; certainly they include the folkways and social institutions. These ways of adjustment may be called, for purposes of this particular analysis, the adaptive culture. The adaptive culture is therefore that portion of the nonmaterial culture which is adjusted or adapted to the material conditions. Some parts of the nonmaterial culture are thoroughly adaptive culture such as certain rules involved in handling technical appliances, and some parts are only indirectly or partially so, as for instance, religion. The family makes some adjustments to fit changed material conditions, while some of its functions remain constant. The family therefore, under the terminology used here is a part of the nonmaterial culture that is only partly adaptive. When the material conditions change, changes are occasioned in the adaptive culture. But these changes in the adaptive culture do not synchronize exactly with the change in the material culture.

There is a lag which may last for varying lengths of time, sometimes indeed, for many years.

An illustration will serve to make the hypothesis more clearly understood. One class of material objects to which we adjust ourselves is the forests. The material conditions of forestry have changed a good deal in the United States during the past century. At one time the forests were quite plentiful for the needs of the small population. There was plenty of wood easily accessible for fuel, building and manufacture. The forests were sufficiently extensive to prevent in many large areas the washing of the soil, and the streams were clear. In fact, at one time, the forests seemed to be too plentiful, from the point of view of the needs of the people. Food and agricultural products were at one time the first need of the people and the clearing of land of trees and stumps was a common undertaking of the community in the days of the early settlers. In some places, the quickest procedure was to kill and burn the trees and plant between the stumps. When the material conditions were like these, the method of adjustment to the forests was characterized by a policy which has been called exploitation. Exploitation in regard to the forests was indeed a part of the mores of the time, and describes a part of the adaptive culture in relation to forests.

As time went on, however, the population grew, manufacturing became highly developed, and the need for forests increased. But the forests were being destroyed. This was particularly true in the Appalachian, Great Lakes and Gulf regions. The policy of exploitation continued. Then rather suddenly it began to be realized in certain centres of thought that if the policy of cutting timber continued at the same rate and in the same manner the forests would in a short time be gone and very soon indeed they would be inadequate to supply the needs of the population. It was realized that the custom in regard to using the forests must be changed and a policy of conservation was advocated. The new policy of conservation means not only a restriction in the amount of cutting down of trees, but it means a more scientific method of cutting, and also reforestation. Forests may be cut in such a way, by selecting trees according to their size, age and location, as to yield a large quantity of timber and yet not diminish the forest area. Also by the proper distribution of cutting plots in a particular area, the cutting can be so timed that by the time the last plot is cut the young trees on the plot first cut will be grown. Some areas when cut leave a land which is well adapted to farming, whereas such sections as mountainous regions when denuded of forests are poorly suited to agriculture. There of course are many other methods of conservation of forests. The science of forestry is, indeed, fairly highly developed in principle, though not in practice in the United States. A new adaptive culture, one of conservation, is therefore suited to the changed material conditions.

That the conservation of forests in the United States should have been earlier is quite generally admitted. We may say, therefore, that the old policy of exploitation has hung over longer than it should before the institution of the new policy. In other words, the material conditions in regard to our forests have changed but the old customs of the use of forests which once fitted the material conditions very well have hung over into a period of changed conditions. These old customs are not only not satisfactorily adapted, but are really socially harmful. These customs of course have a utility, since they meet certain human needs; but methods of greater utility are needed. There seems to be a lag in the mores in regard to forestry after the material conditions have changed.

The foregoing discussion of forestry illustrates the hypothesis which it is proposed to discuss. It is desirable to state more clearly and fully the points involved in the analysis. The first point concerns the degree of adjustment or correlation between the material conditions and the adaptive nonmaterial culture. The degree of this adjustment may be only more or less perfect or satisfactory; but we do adjust ourselves to the material conditions through some form of culture; that is, we live, we get along, through this adjustment. The particular culture which is adjusted to the material conditions may be very complex, and, indeed, quite a number of widely different parts of culture may be adjusted to a fairly homogeneous material condition. Of a particular cultural form, such as the family or government, relationship to a particular material culture is only one of its purposes or functions. Not all functions of family organization, as, for instance, the affectional function, are primarily adaptive to material conditions.

Another point to observe is that the changes in the material culture precede changes in the adaptive culture. This statement is not in the form of a universal dictum. Conceivably, forms of adaptation might be worked out prior to a change in the material situation and the adaptation might be applied practically at the same time as the change in the material conditions. But such a situation presumes a very high degree of planning, prediction and control. The collection of data, it is thought, will show that at the present time there are a very large number of cases where the material conditions change and the changes in the adaptive culture follow later. There are certain general theoretical reasons why this is so; but it is not desirable to discuss these until later. For the present, the analysis will only concern those cases where changes in the adaptive culture do not precede changes in the material culture. Furthermore, it is not implied that changes may not occur in nonmaterial culture while the material culture remains the same. Art or education, for instance, may undergo many changes with a constant material culture. Still another point in the analysis is that the old, unchanged, adaptive culture is not adjusted to the new, changed, material conditions. It may be true that the old adaptive culture is never wholly unadjusted to the new conditions. There may be some degree of adjustment. But the thesis is that the unchanged adaptive culture was more harmoniously related to the old than to the new material conditions and that a new adaptive culture will be better suited to the new material conditions than was the old adaptive culture. Adjustment is therefore a relative term, and perhaps only in a few cases would there be a situation which might be called perfect adjustment or perfect lack of adjustment.

It is desirable, however, not to make the analysis too general until there has been a more careful consideration of particular instances. We now propose, therefore, to test the hypothesis by the facts in a definite case of social change. In attempting to verify the hypothesis in a particular case by measurement, the following series of steps will be followed. The old material conditions will be described, that part of the adaptive culture under consideration will be described, and the degree of adjustment between these two parts of culture shown. Then the changed material conditions and the changed adaptive culture will be defined and the degree of adaptation shown. It is necessary also to show that the unchanged adaptive culture is not as harmoniously adjusted to the new conditions as to the old and not as harmoniously adjusted to the new conditions as is a changed adaptive culture.

ROBERT E. PARK

Robert E. Park (1864-1944) was born in Pennsylvania and educated at the University of Michigan, from which he was graduated in 1887. During the early years of his career he was a newspaper man, serving in various reportorial and editorial capacities and learning much that was to be reflected in his sociological papers. He also served for a period as secretary to Booker T. Washington, president of the Tuskegee Institute in Alabama. He took his Ph.D. degree at Heidelberg in 1904 with a dissertation entitled *Masse und Publikum.* For the greater part of his life he was a member of the department of sociology at the University of Chicago, a department that included, in addition to Park, Albion Small, William I. Thomas, William Fielding Ogburn, Ellsworth Faris, Ernest W. Burgess, Louis Wirth, Herbert Blumer, and Everett C. Hughes and which at that time was almost without question the greatest department of sociology in the world. It was at Chicago that Park inspired and supervised the most distinguished series of doctoral dissertations in American sociology. In 1925 he was elected fifteenth president of the American Sociological Society.

Park's own contributions were made primarily to three areas of sociological interest—human ecology, race relations, and collective behavior, the last of which is represented in the selection that follows. His books include, in addition to the Heidelberg dissertation mentioned above, *Old World Traits Transplanted* (with Herbert A. Miller, 1921), *The Immigrant Press and Its Control* (1922), and *The City* (1925). In 1921 he and Ernest W. Burgess published their *Introduction to the Science of Sociology,* one of the most influential of all the textbooks in the field. His miscellaneous papers have recently been edited in two volumes by Everett C. Hughes.

Human Nature and Collective Behavior *

Recent attempts to apply to the study of human conduct the methods of investigation first employed in the study of animal behavior have profoundly influenced the point of view not merely of psychology, but of social psychology and of sociology. Psychology, in becoming objective—that is to say, behavioristic—has emphasized what it calls overt response. Incidentally, consciousness either has been dismissed from any consideration whatever or has been relegated to the position of an incident in a cycle of events which begins with the physiological reflexes and terminates in an act; what Thurstone calls "the psychological act."

What the students of animal behavior actually have done in their laboratories is to put animals under test conditions and then incite them to appropriate action. The mouse, in a maze, tries to find its way out. The lowly earthworm, which, as reported in a local newspaper, a Harvard professor sought to educate, was incited by hunger and the proximity of food to find the easiest and the least painful way of getting it. Under these circumstances the animal responded in every case, not to a single stimulus, but to a situation; and the response was not that of a single reflex or instinct, but that of the organism as a whole. In other words, the response which the situation called forth was not a reaction, if we may be permitted to make a distinction, but an act. A reaction presupposes the existence of a reflex, habit, conditioned reflex, or pattern, in which the response to a stimulus is predetermined. But an act implies, relatively speaking, new adjustment, coordination, and integration of the existing physiological mechanism.

The thing which distinguishes an organism from a mere aggregation of individuals, or of parts, is the capacity for concerted action—the disposition of the parts, under certain conditions, to act as a unit. The structure of an organism, inherited or acquired,

* From the *American Journal of Sociology,* XXXII, No. 5 (March, 1927), 733-741. Reprinted by permission of The University of Chicago Press.

serves to facilitate this concerted action. This is as true of a social as of a biological organism. The fundamental differences between organisms, the character which permits us to arrange them in a progressive series, are the different degrees to which the different parts of which they are composed have been integrated and organized for the purpose of corporate action. What constitutes the organism, then, as distinguished from the mere assemblage of its parts, is, according to Child, an action pattern, which controls and coordinates the reaction of the parts so as to give to the behavior of the organism the character which I have described as an act. . . .

On the whole, the social group behaves like an organism, and the differences between groups may be described in terms of the action pattern which determines the behavior of each. The fundamental difference between a city and a village, from the point of view of sociology, is not the mere size of the aggregates or the number of individuals of which they are composed, but the degree to which these different aggregates have been integrated and organized for concerted action. This suggests that in a study of the social group, as of the biological organism, the point of departure is, properly, not structure, but activity. The thing that gives a community the character of a society is not its structure, but its capacity for concerted action.

The capacity for corporate action is, to be sure, facilitated by structure, but is not dependent upon it. The crowd becomes a society, not by the mere fact that a group of persons are gathered together at a given moment and in a particular spot, but by the fact that this aggregation of individuals is capable of action. Action may take place in the crowd with a minimum of organization or with no organization at all, except what has been called by Le Bon "psychological organization."

Action is first; but the effect of action is to create an action pattern. This action pattern, as may be observed in the crowd, is frequently extremely fragile and ephemeral, and may exist without any clearly defined organization. Permanence of the action pattern, however, is dependent upon the existence of structure, upon a division of labor, and upon some degree of specialization in the individuals who compose the group. When the role of the individuals in the action of the group has become fixed in habit, and particularly when the role of different individuals and their special functions have become recognized in custom and tradition, the social organization gains a new stability and permanence which permits it to be transmitted to succeeding generations. In this way the life of the community and of society may be prolonged beyond the lives of the individuals who compose it.

Institutions and social structures of every sort may be regarded as products of collective action. War, famine, revolution, the struggle against an external enemy and against internal disorganization—any of the ordinary exigencies of communal and collective life which call for collective action—may set a social pattern which repetition fixes in habits, and which eventually become institutionalized in customs and traditions.

Looked at from the point of the individual organism or the individual member of a community, this functioning of the social group and this evolution of society and of institutions presents itself as a response, an accommodation, and eventually a biological adaptation of the individual to habitat; a physical environment and a social milieu. In this habitat the individual becomes, in the course of time, a person, and perhaps a citizen.

The same forces which cooperate to create the characteristic social organization and the accepted moral order of a given society or social group determine at the same time, to a greater or lesser extent, the character of the individuals who compose that society. The individual inherits from his forbears and from a long series of his animal ancestors the potentialities which are realized in specific characters in the course of his association—particularly during childhood and adolescence—with his fellows. The extent to which these potentialities are actually realized and the specific forms which they eventually take is determined, not merely by the general conditions which every society and every social milieu imposes upon its members, but rather more by the extent to which, in any given society, a division of labor has been achieved. It is the division of labor, quite as much as anything else, which determines the degree to which the individual is dependent upon, and incorporated in, the social organization of which he is a member.

Adam Smith long ago recognized that the most striking differences between individuals are due to the division of labor. It is not that these differences were not implicit in the individuals themselves, existing there as potentialities, but it is the division of labor and the discipline imposed by society upon its members that has developed them. . . .

It is not, however, a division of labor, but the fact of social control that characterizes human society. It is not, in other words, the unconscious competition and cooperation of individual men and women within the limits of a human habitat that has impressed upon human nature and human society their most distinctive traits. It is rather the conscious participation in a common purpose and a common life, rendered possible by the fact of speech and by the existence of a fund of common symbols and meanings. The lower animals have neither words nor symbols; nothing, for them, has what we may describe as meaning. The lower animals have, in the words of Durkheim, no "collective representations." They do not organize processions and carry banners; they sing, and sometimes, we are told, even dance, but they do not celebrate; they acquire habits which are sometimes transmitted as a kind of social tradition, but they have no customs, and for them nothing is either sacred or lawful. Above all, the animals are natural and naive, and not concerned, as human beings are, about their reputations and their conduct. They are not tortured by moral scruples. "They do not," as Walt Whitman has put it, "sweat and whine about their condition. They do not lie awake in the dark and weep for their sins." And "over the whole earth there is not one that is respectable or unhappy."

But it is just this sort of behavior—which makes Walt Whitman, as he says, "sick," so that he thinks he could turn and live with the animals, "they are so placid and self-contained"—that is most characteristic of human nature and human behavior. For man is a creature such that when he lives at all, he lives in his imagination, and, through his imagination, in the minds of other men, who share with him not merely their possessions, but their hopes and their dreams. By suggestion, by imitation, by expressions of sympathy and antipathy, men invade one another's lives and participate one with another in their efforts to direct, control, and give expression to their own conflicting impulses.

In human society every act of every individual tends to become a gesture, since what one does is always an indication of what one intends to do. The consequence is that the individual in society lives a more or less public existence, in which all his acts are anticipated, checked, inhibited, or modified by the gestures and the intentions of his fellows. It is in this social conflict, in which every individual lives more or less in the mind of every other individual, that human nature and the individual may acquire their most characteristic and human traits.

It is probably no mere historical accident, as I have said elsewhere, that the word "person," in its first meaning, is a mask. It is rather a recognition of the fact that everyone is always and everywhere, more or less consciously, playing a role. We are parents and children, masters and servants, teachers and students, clients and professional men, Gentiles and Jews. It is in these roles that we know each other; it is in these roles that we know ourselves.

One thing that distinguishes man from the lower animals is the fact that he has a conception of himself, and once he has defined his role he strives to live up to it. He not only acts, but he dresses the part, assumes quite spontaneously all the manners and attitudes that he conceives as proper to it. Often enough it happens that he is not fitted to the role which he chooses to play. In any case, it is an effort for any of us to maintain the attitudes which we assume; all the more difficult when the world refuses to take us at our own estimates of ourselves. Being actors, we are consciously or unconsciously seeking recognition, and failure to win it is, at the very least, a depressing, often a heart-breaking, experience. This is one of the reasons why we all eventually conform to the accepted models and conceive ourselves in some one or other of the conventional patterns.

The consequence of this, however, is that we inevitably lead a dual existence. We have a private and a public life. In seeking to live up to the role which we have assumed, and which society has imposed upon us, we find ourselves in a constant conflict with ourselves. Instead of acting simply and naturally, as a child, responding to each natural impulse as it arises, we seek to conform to accepted models, and conceive ourselves in some one of the conventional and socially accepted patterns. In our efforts to conform, we restrain our immediate and spontaneous impulses, and act, not as we are impelled to act, but rather as seems appropriate and proper to the occasion.

Under these circumstances our manners, our polite speeches and gestures, our conventional and proper behavior, assume the character of a mask. Our very faces are living masks, which reflect, to be sure, the changing emotions of our inner lives, but which more and more tend to conform to the type we are seeking to impersonate. Not only every race, but every nationality has its characteristic "face," its conventional mask. As Emerson points out in his *English Traits,* "every religious sect has its physiognomy. The Methodists have acquired a face, the Quakers a face, the nuns a face. An Englishman will point out a dissenter by his manner. Trades and professions carve their own lines on faces and forms."

In a sense, and in so far as this mask represents the conception which we have formed of ourselves, the role which we are striving to live up to, this mask is our "truer self," the self we should like to be. So, at any rate, our mask becomes at last an integral part of our personality; becomes second nature. We come into the world as individuals, achieve character, and become persons.

Human behavior, so far as it can be distinguished from that of the lower animals, is conscious and conventional; socially controlled, in short. Behavior that is controlled in this way we may call conduct; that is to say, behavior morally sanctioned and subjectively conditioned. This subjectivity, so characteristic of human nature, is at once a condition and a product of collective life. So far as it is subjective it cannot be adequately described as the stricter sect of behaviorists insist it should be, in physiological terms; but so far as it is social it cannot be described in terms of individual behavior, and for this reason psychology, so far as it deals with persons and personality, inevitably becomes social psychology. The motives which compel men to commit suicide, to write poetry, and to go to war are frequently the outcome of long and painful conflict. The acts in which they terminate have, therefore, an antecedent history, and it is necessary to know this history to understand the acts. This is true of most overt acts, as it is of individual opinion, religious creeds, and political doctrines.

Opinions, creeds, and doctrines become intelligible to us only when we know their history; when we know, in other words, the experiences out of which they have sprung. The reason why history and biography exist is not merely to record overt acts, but to make them intelligible.

Not only is it true that we all participate directly or indirectly in making up the minds and determining the overt acts of our fellows, but the craving for this participation in a common life—the desire for sympathy, recognition, understanding, for example—is one of the most fundamental traits of human nature. Just as history is, to a very large extent, the record of the struggles of nations and peoples for prestige and status in an international society, so the humbler, more garrulous, and provincial chronicle of the local newspaper is largely a record of the conflicts of individual men and women in seeking to find a place and a position in some tribe, clan, neighborhood, or household.

It is because human actions must be interpreted in order to make them intelligible that documents—human documents—are more important for the study of human nature than statistics or formal facts. The documents are valuable, therefore, not merely because they describe events, but because they throw light upon motives; that is to say, upon the subjective aspects of events and acts in which human nature manifests itself. Not merely events, but institutions as well become intelligible when we know their histories, and particularly when we know the individual experiences of men and women in which they had their origin and on which they finally rest.

The most significant document, of course, is the one that is most expressive and revealing, and this, on the whole, has been the life-history, using that term in the sense in which Thomas and Znaniecki have defined it in their monumental study, *The Polish Peasant in Europe and America.*

If it is not practical or desirable to confine our investigations of human nature to the overt response, as the behaviorists define that term, the attempt to study human nature objectively has, at any rate, done sociology and social psychology a good turn in so far as it has directed attention to the psychological act rather than to the physiological reaction as a unit of investigation and analysis. For society, as well as mental life, has come into existence not merely in the efforts of individuals to act, but in their efforts to act collectively.

From this point of view the moral struggles of individual men and women and the political conflicts of nations turn out to be merely incidents in the processes by which society and social groups integrate and organize the individual units of which they are composed and mobilize them for collective action. Furthermore, just as the individual person may in some sense be conceived as the product of individual acts, so social institutions may be regarded as the product of collective actions. Just as custom in the group may be regarded as the objective aspect of habit in the individual, so morality in the individual may be construed as the subjective aspect of organization and morale in the group.

FLORIAN ZNANIECKI

Florian Znaniecki (1882-1958) was born in Swiatnik, Poland, and took his baccalaureate degree at the University of Warsaw. His graduate studies were at the University of Geneva, the University of Zurich, the University of Paris, and the University of Cracow, from the last of which he received his doctorate in 1909. He began his career as a poet, turned next to philosophy, and finally found his proper *métier* in sociology. He came to the United States first in 1917 as a lecturer in Polish institutions at the University of Chicago. From 1920 to 1939 he was Professor of Sociology at the University of Poznan, having founded both that department and the Polish Sociological Institute. He taught at Columbia University as visiting professor from 1931-1933 and again in 1939. In September of the latter year, having narrowly escaped the Nazi engulfment of Poland, he returned to the United States and spent the last ten years of his teaching career at the University of Illinois. He was president of the American Sociological Society in 1954.

It is unfortunate that about half of Znaniecki's books were written in Polish and the other half in English. Either half would suffice to give him world renown in sociology and yet the Polish books are inaccessible to all but a small minority of American and English readers. The American works include *Cultural Reality* (1919), *The Polish Peasant in Europe and America* (5 volumes, with W. I. Thomas, 1918-1921), *The Laws of Social Psychology* (1925), *The Method of Sociology* (1934), *Social Actions* (1936), *The Social Role of the Man of Knowledge* (1940), *Cultural Sciences* (1952), and *Modern Nationalities* (1952).

Znaniecki was a systematic thinker in the field of sociology. His approach is illustrated in the following excerpt from *The Method of Sociology*.

From *The Method of Sociology*[*]

Sociology as Theory of "Societies" or "Communities"

Sociology, from the time it consciously began to be constituted as a separate theoretic discipline, distinct from political science, took a peculiar position with regard to the choice and determination of its object matter, which persisted up to the end of the nineteenth century and partly survives even yet among sociologists of a naturalistic bent. While the particular data in which it was primarily interested belong to the domain of culture, it conceived them as components of natural systems. This conception, already outlined in the seventeenth century, became fully developed in the middle of the nineteenth with Comte, Spencer and their followers. Sociology was meant to study "societies." A "society" was conceived as essentially a natural closed system of bio-psychological human individuals. There were other more or less similar systems in nature: aggregations of unicellular organisms, multicellular organisms with differentiated organs and functions, associations of multicellular organisms—homogeneous, like herds and flocks of animals, and heterogeneous, like plant communities. As every sociologist knows, the seeming analogy indicated by Comte between a "society" and a multicellular differentiated organism has been widely exploited by Spencer, Schäffle, Lilienfeld, Worms, Novicov, and many others.

Three principles were used, in various proportions and combinations, to circumscribe this natural system. First, a "society" had to occupy more or less exclusively a geographical territory; secondly, it was expected to possess a certain degree of racial homogeneity. These two were purely naturalistic principles: geographic isolation and racial composition of a human "society" could be ascertained by the same methods of external observation as the isolation and composition of a plant or a colony of polyps.

But the third principle made a breach in the consistency of the naturalistic standpoint through which an enormous mass of cultural data was introduced into this system. A collectivity of hu-

* Reprinted by permission of Rinehart and Company, Inc.

man beings of a certain racial stock (pure or mixed) inhabiting a certain territory constituted a "society" only if they belonged as members to a social group—horde, family, tribe, gens, village, city, state—or at least to a conglomeration of interconnected groups. Now, whatever might be said of "animal societies," human groups are cultural products; membership in a group, and even the mere existence of a social group, however rudimentary its organization, cannot be ascertained without the use of the humanistic coefficient. The gens, the tribe, the state, even the family and the horde have their being only in the experience and activity of their members, who have constructed them and now maintain them.

Sociology did not deny it. On the contrary, its intention was to study not only social groups as cultural products of the human beings included in a collectivity, but all the cultural systems existing within the sphere of experience and activity of these beings, made and maintained by them. "Society" in the sense of Comte included the entire cultural life of the men belonging to it: language, art, religion, philosophy, science, technique, economic organization. Rooted in nature by their bodies, men were immersed in culture by their consciousness. And the culture of a society was common to its members; society, a mere collectivity of individuals from the natural point of view, was on its culture side a superindividual entity, a *community* unified by sharing the same culture. All the cultural systems studied separately by special sciences were most closely intertwined in the cultural life of a "society," formed, in fact, a static and dynamic unity.

The successors of Comte preserved these essential presuppositions with but slight variation. Some ascribed more, others less importance to psychic as against material factors in the formation and existence of societies; some acceded to Comte's idea that the individual as a conscious being was entirely a part of society, and had no conscious life apart from what he shared with his society by sharing its culture; whereas others treated him as a psychological entity secondarily connected with "society" by communication and cooperation. Among the particular kinds of data constituting the culture of a "society," some were thought more, others less fundamental. While Comte had given predominance to intellectual factors, most sociologists emphasized, as St. Simon had already done, the importance of economic or technical phenomena; some, influenced partly by older doctrines, partly by the philosophy of Hegel, saw in the state system the supreme and determining phenomenon of "society."

It is not our intention to subject this sociological conception to systematic criticism at this point, for it has been already judged by history. It has failed to produce a single valid and generally accepted scientific generalization concerning "societies": not one law which could be applied to the explanation and conditional prediction of the changes of "societies": no consistent classification of "societies," not even a general description of any particular class of "societies" which could be guaranteed to take into account all the essential characters common to that class and to no other. We do not mean, indeed, that sociologists working on this theory have not achieved any true, important, and exact scientific results. On the contrary, we believe that their works are greatly undervalued by the present generation of sociologists and that much useful knowledge is contained in them. But none of this knowledge concerns their main object matter, "society": it bears upon what their authors thought minor matters, such as the structural characters and changes of specific groups or institutions, or particular socio-psychological processes.

The whole theory centered around the most striking fallacy. It identified two radically different and incommensurable concepts: "society" as a natural system of which the elements are individual animals of the species *Homo Sapiens,* and "society" as a combination of systems of which the elements are cultural values, like language, religion, technique, economic and political organizations, etc. That this obvious logical discrepancy did not attract the notice of those otherwise deep thinkers who created the great socio-philosophical "systems" of the past must be ascribed probably to the monistic current which prevailed in the scientific philosophy of the last century and carried these thinkers along.

But though the fundamental error was not discovered at once nor made explicit, even after it produced the usual result of scientific unproductivity, nevertheless the very progress of positive inductive research in neighboring fields has gradually corrected it by simply depriving that type of sociology of nearly all of what it conceived to be its proper object matter, and dividing it—at least, as much of it as could be scientifically treated—among other disciplines.

On the one hand, indeed, all the positive and soluble problems bearing upon the natural aspect of human collectivities have been during the last sixty or seventy years appropriated by purely natural sciences, viz., human geography and physical anthropology, which are much better equipped than sociology for dealing with them efficiently. The separation of their fields from that of sociology is perhaps still imperfectly achieved because some geographers and somatic anthropologists show a tendency to "explain" cultural phenomena, while many sociologists are interested in geographic and racial questions. Yet, if we compare in this respect Gobineau with Ripley, or Demolins with Brunhes, we may confidently look forward to the time when the line of demarcation between anthropology and anthropo-geography on the one hand, and sociology and other sciences of culture on the other hand, will be drawn clearly and unmistakably.

Of course, there are innumerable vital problems concerning the relationship between natural and cultural systems, and these must be treated notwithstanding the division of the respective sciences. But it does not follow by any means that, as some defenders of the old conception of sociology as an intermediary between natural and cultural sciences wish to conclude, these problems should, or even could, be the special privilege of one scientific discipline. Far from it. These problems are so multiple and varied that it is absolutely impossible to reduce them to a common denominator. Every particular science handles different ones in the course of its research, and must deal with them on its own ground and with its own methods. The anthropogeographic problems of mutual relationship between certain natural conditions and the formation of large cities are different and require different methods from those faced by a student of technology when, in investigating the development of a certain type of pottery, he tries to determine how much and in what way this development is dependent upon the geographical distribution of potter's clay. No general science of the connection between nature and culture could solve the problems which beset the linguist when investigating changes of pronunciation, the anthropologist studying the connection between racial mixtures, marriage and the caste system, and the religionist trying to determine what, if any, mutual dependence there is between certain forms of mysticism and certain physiological processes induced by the massing of numerous human bodies in closed buildings.

Thus, while the investigation of the natural aspect of human collectivities is gradually but completely passing from the hands of sociologists into the better qualified ones of geographers and anthropologists, a parallel process has lately been affecting the other, cultural side, of the nineteenth century "societies." The self-imposed task of sociology with regard to cultural communities has proved beyond its powers and, indeed, beyond the powers of any one science. For it meant nothing less than the comparative study of cultural communities, viewed in the total wealth and complexity of their civilizations, using the results of the historical and ethnographical studies which have been trying to describe in all relevant details the civilizations of particular communities, their techniques, their prevalent social and economic systems, their religion, language, literature, science, art and piay. Sociology, from Comte on, has attempted to draw generalizations concerning all cultural communities, or at least all those belonging to a certain type.

Here again the actual development of scientific research has dealt a deathblow to such an undertaking, both by showing the impossibility of realizing it, and by substituting instead a different task, which is being fulfilled by a number of special sciences. In ethnography and the history of culture, as long as sweeping synthetic statements of a half-literary type concerning the civilization of particular peoples and nations prevailed over patient, thorough and critical descriptions of facts, comparative generalizations seemed not only possible, but easy. This was particularly true with regard to "primitive societies," whose civilizations appeared very simple in the light of the older ethnographical works (which, by the way, had still lower standards of thoroughness than those already developed at that time in history). But the more actual knowledge of concrete cultural communities increased in wealth and exactness, the more difficult it proved to organize into a synthetic rational picture everything known about the civilization of any particular community, however apparently simple, and the more doubtful appeared most of the similarities on which sociologists (chiefly those of the evolutionary school) used to rely. The conclusion is inevitable that the total cultural life of any human community is much too rich and chaotic, contains too many heterogeneous cultural systems influencing one another in the most various and incalculable ways and is too ceaselessly and unexpectedly changing, to make valid scientific synthesis ever possible—which obviously precludes any comparative science of cultural communities.

There have been, indeed, some relatively limited and relatively stable combinations of various cultural systems recently discovered in the course of historical, prehistorical, and particularly ethnological research. These are the "cultural complexes" of the now predominant school of ethnology. Such a cultural complex does, indeed, contain definite technical, social, religious, aesthetic, economic systems interrelated in such a way as to make them usually appear together in the cultural life of human communities. But such a cultural complex is not coextensive with the civilization of any community, for every civilization we know contains several cultural complexes overlapping; and the ways they overlap, mix and influence one another are again most varied and incalculable. Moreover, there is no rational necessity, no static laws binding the various systems of a cultural complex together, connecting, e.g., a particular religious system with a certain technical system. Nor is there any causal necessity, any universal dynamic law determining the origin and development of complexes and their expansion over certain cultural areas. The existence of any particular cultural complex and its acceptance, complete or partial, by certain cultural communities are simply historical facts which happened once and will never happen again. This is the main reason why modern ethnology is historical as opposed to the earlier evolutionary ethnology, which assumed that the various cultural systems coexisting in a human community were necessarily dependent on one another, and that there were universal laws ruling everywhere the passage from one type of civilization to another. Historical ethnology has thus taken whatever wind there was out of the sails of sociology as a general theory of cultural communities—and it proved to be a weak breeze, merely allowing a careful sailing along the shore of historical facts, not a trade wind capable of driving the vessel of cultural science across the wide ocean of universal determinism.

There are still, however, attempts to revive this conception of sociology as a science of cultural communities. The chief argument in its favor is drawn from the obvious fact that the total cultural life of a community—a tribe, a nation, even a village, or a town—even though it does not constitute a higher kind of organic unity as the old sociologists believed, still is more than a mere sum of heterogeneous data, since its technique, economics, political organization, mores, religion, science, art, literature are closely intertwined and exercise a mutual influence. If there are special cultural sciences, each separately dealing with one of these domains of culture apart from its connection with all the other domains in the cultural life of human communities, should there not be a science investigating their interrelationships? Its task may be difficult, but perhaps its failure heretofore is merely due to the application of wrong methods of research.

But while the premises of this argument are perfectly true, the conclusion is wrong. The mere fact of mutual influence exercised by the various cultural systems upon one another is not enough to justify the existence of a distinct science studying this influence, for this task is already being performed by the several special sciences. All the technical, political, religious, scientific influences to which, say, economic systems are subjected in cultural communities must be investigated by the economists; the religionist has to take into account the modifications which a religion undergoes in consequence of economic, political and scientific processes going on in its cultural milieu, and so on. Something may, indeed, be left over after the various cultural systems composing the civilization of a human community have been taken into account. The people who share a certain set of interconnected systems (and among these systems there are usually also certain social groups —territorial, genetic or telic) may be more or less conscious of this fact, and more or less willing to influence one another for the benefit of their common civilization and to influence this civilization for their mutual benefit. This consciousness and willingness, in so far as they exist, constitute a social bond uniting these people over and above any formal social bonds which are due to the existence of regulated social relations and organized social groups. The reality of this bond is manifested in such familiar phenomena as public opinion, collective control of personalities and groups by their social milieu, development of new cultural ideals and attempts at their realization apart from organized group action. If the term "community" is limited to the humanistic reality embracing these phenomena, there is no doubt but that a "community" in this sense can be scientifically studied, and that sociology is the science to study it as one of the specifically social data. It is a matter for discussion whether such a community is a social group or not, whether it is identical with the "public," whether it should be connected—as MacIver is doing—with territorial groups and nations.

Of one thing we may be sure, however, and that is that new efforts will be made continually to revive the old synthetic conception of sociology, for a powerful intellectual and moral interest is here in play. Every thinking man wishes to obtain some understanding of the totality of the civilization to which he belongs, compare it with other civilizations, interpret their history, discover if possible some guiding lines in the apparent chaos of the whole historical evolution of mankind. These interests are as undying and as justifiable in their way as the old metaphysical interest in interpreting the world of nature as some kind of ordered and rational whole. And there is an old and well-established discipline which satisfies them: it is the *philosophy of history*. We do not mean to deny its rights nor to belittle its importance. All we object to is having sociology, which aims to be a positive inductive science, exact and objective, so far misunderstand its possibilities and impossibilities as to undertake practically the same task. It was in part sociology's own fault that Paul Barth twenty years ago was able to republish the second edition of his voluminous work trying to demonstrate with much first-hand evidence that sociology, such as it had heretofore been, was the same as philosophy of history. Of course, this view was one-sided and behind the times, for it failed to realize the significance of the new movements expressed chiefly in monographic research; but it may be considered symptomatic of the persistence of traditional ideals.

Sociology as a General Theory of Cultural Data

The tendency to become a science of culture in general, as against the special sciences like economics, linguistics and theory of religion, has expressed itself in still another sociological current, of a more recent origin. This current started in the two schools of Tarde and Durkheim which, with all their well-known opposition, have yet much in common, and it has since spread very widely, sometimes moving with the older current, sometimes resulting in important new variations. The common theoretic purpose of both Tarde and Durkheim, their followers and associates, was not to reach a general theory of "societies" (although the concept of "society" remained as a general heuristic foundation of research, particularly with Durkheim), but rather a general theory of *cultural phenomena viewed as social phenomena*. The idea that every cultural phenomenon—technical, economic, religious, intellectual, linguistic—is essentially social, was founded in Tarde's view on the fact that its historical existence as something common to many people appeared due to interaction between human individuals, whose various forms Tarde summed up in his leading concept of "imitation," supplemented by that of "opposition." For Durkheim, however, the social character of the same cultural phenomena resulted from their being accepted by social groups as their values, and imposed upon the individual by the group to which he belongs. Under either assumption, sociology became the science which, by studying this common social foundation of all cultural phenomena, became the fundamental science of all culture, of which other special sciences were meant to be variations or even mere subdivisions.

But, however interesting and even apparently convincing this conception of cultural phenomena as social phenomena might have been, the striking fact is that during the fifty years or thereabouts which have gone by since the first promulgation of the works of Tarde and of Durkheim, sociologists alone have become aware of the need of basing scientific research in the various fields of culture upon sociology, with the exception of the few, very few, religionists, economists and linguists who have become converted Durkheimians. This suggests either that all students of culture have been and still remain incomprehensibly blind to the logical relationship between their science and sociology; or else that, whatever sociology has to say to them, though by no means irrelevant—there are few specialists nowadays who entirely ignore sociological problems—is nevertheless not absolutely essential to the pursuit of their proper studies. The first solution of the puzzle is unthinkable, particularly since during these fifty years great progress has been made in most of the special sciences of culture, not under the leadership of sociology and often without much assistance from it. Thus, we must presume that the second solution is the true one.

And, indeed, if we do take into account a cultural system like a factory, a bank, a work of literature, a system of religious dogmas and rites, a physical or mathematical theory, even though it is obvious that individual interaction, as emphasized by Tarde, was indispensable for its construction and remains indispensable for its maintenance; and even though it is usually accepted (as the school of Durkheim insists) by some group which sanctions its existence and in a sense vouches for its validity: nevertheless the system as such is *nonsocial* in its composition and structure in the sense that the individuals who work to construct it and maintain it are not its elements, nor is the group which supports it its structural basis. The factory, the bank, the religion, the work of literature, or the physical theory may remain exactly the same after all the individuals who participated in its maintenance leave or die and give place to others. The factory as a technical system does not necessarily change in its composition or structure by passing, say, from the control of a group of private capitalists to that of the state, nor a religion after a new nation has been converted to it, nor a physical theory in consequence of its being finally recognized in scientific circles, after having been for a while violently combated. There are cases, of course, when after such a change of participating individuals or supporting groups modifications of the system do follow, but these are directly due to the introduction of new technical instruments or processes, new religious dogmas or myths, new scientific concepts, for which the new men were perhaps responsible, but which might also have occurred while the system was still maintained by its former supporters.

This relative independence of the composition and structure of cultural systems from their social background makes a type of investigation possible which ignores this background entirely, and such is the type that predominates in all special sciences of culture. A language may be and often is studied without any other knowledge of the people who use it than that they do speak it and understand it. A factory can be described exclusively in terms of materials, machines, methods, products, with no mention of the social life of the men who run it except that these men furnish the active forces needed to do so. A physical theory can be fully understood even if nothing is known about the personal life of the scientist who created it, his social relationship with his original opponents, or the organization of the scientific societies or congresses where it was finally approved.

When we do try to explain either the origins of a system or its later modifications, we must indeed take social factors into consideration even as other kinds of factors, natural or cultural. But it does not follow from the fact that social factors contributed to the composition and structure of Islam, of Shakespeare's *Hamlet*, of the Ford automobile factory, or of Einstein's theory that these systems are social, any more than the indubitable influence of geographic conditions in shaping the ritual of Islam makes it a geographic system, or the fact that money is needed for physical experiments makes them financial undertakings.

Now, while we doubt all possibility of a positive science of natural "societies" or cultural communities, we are far from denying that a general positive science of cultural phenomena—or, more exactly, of cultural systems—is possible. There are even, we believe, particularly in older philosophic literature, certain germs of it which can be developed into a science. If such a general theory of culture is founded, then indeed all the special sciences will be dependent upon it, just as nowadays botany and zoology are branches of general biology. But it can be founded only by a slow process of induction in which the specific structural characters and changes of the systems constituting each particular domain of culture—technics, religion, art, economics—are investigated and compared with those of other domains. It is a tremendous task needing the cooperation of many specialists perfectly acquainted with their respective domains and at the same time able to rise above the limitations of their specialities.

Sociology as a Special Science

Having rejected the two main older conceptions according to which sociology should deal with all culture, either as a science of cultural "societies" or as a science of cultural phenomena in general—or rather, having simply accepted the unmistakable verdict the history of science has passed upon these conceptions—it still remains to show what the standards are that sociological research must apply in selecting its own data from the unlimited wealth and complexity of the empirical world. As a matter of fact, these standards need not be created. They are already implied in the successful, first-hand, positive investigation which has been carried on during the last forty or fifty years and whose results are embodied in thousands of monographs and systematic works. Most of this investigation bears the name of sociology in America, whereas in other countries, though the content is similar, it is often differently called; but the names are a minor matter. The essential point is that these investigations bear only on a certain portion of the material the older sociological schools claim as their own; but this is a portion which even in those older schools was the object of particular interest and—what is more important—this material is not dealt with at all or only inefficiently by the established special sciences of culture, with one or two exceptions which will be pointed out later.

Attempts have already been made to formulate explicitly these implicit standards of selection of sociological data under the same assumption as ours, viz., that sociology is a special cultural science with an empirical field of its own; and if we try to improve on them by giving our own definition it is only because most of them seem still somewhat influenced by the older schools. This refers particularly to the conception of Simmel, according to whom all cultural phenomena have a social "form," though their "content" is not social but religious, economic, linguistic. This conception, though it has had great influence on the present German methodology (see Vierkandt) is misleading. For this "social form" of cultural phenomena does not manifest itself either in the composition or in the structure of cultural systems. At the same time, as Simmel and others have shown, it is something which can be empirically ascertained and studied apart from the systems of which it is supposed to be the "form." Therefore, it is obviously not a mere "form," but a specific class of empirical data accompanying various cultural systems in much the same way as theoretic reflection accompanies most of them in higher civilizations and religious beliefs and practices in earlier stages of culture. The actual object matter of the sociological research of Simmel was thus different from what he believed it to be.

PITIRIM A. SOROKIN

Pitirim Alexandrovitch Sorokin (1889-) has perhaps the most comprehensive grasp of the history of social thought, in all languages, of any scholar writing in the twentieth century. Born in Russia, he survived a childhood of incredible hardship and attended first a provincial teachers college, then the Psycho-Neurological Institute in St. Petersburg, and finally the University of St. Petersburg, from which he received the degree of Magistrant of Criminal Law in 1915, the doctorate in sociology in 1922, and an honorary doctorate in 1950.

Sorokin was active in the Russian Revolution and spent time in jail under both the Czarist and the Bolshevik regimes. He had a brief period in authority as secretary to Kerensky during the provisional government and was a member of the Russian Constitutional Assembly. He was condemned to death in 1922 by the Communist Government and finally banished from the country, finding sanctuary at first in Czechoslovakia, whose first president, Thomas G. Masaryk, was also a sociologist. In 1923 Sorokin came to the United States, taught at the University of Minnesota from 1924 to 1930, and became in the latter year the first chairman of the department at Harvard University, where he remained until his retirement in 1957. He is a member of many learned and scientific societies, both in the United States and abroad, and was president of the International Congress of Sociology in 1937.

Throughout the years Sorokin has produced books and articles in almost unbelievable profusion. The most important of these works, in the English language, are *Social Mobility* (1927), *Contemporary Sociological Theories* (1928), *Social and Cultural Dynamics* (4 volumes, 1937-1941), and *Society, Culture and Personality* (1947). In 1957 he published a revised and condensed version of his four-volume *magnum opus* and it is from this version that the following excerpts are taken.

From *Social and Cultural Dynamics*[*]

Familistic, Contractual, and Compulsory Types of Social Relationships

The above modalities, or types of social relationships, in the organized systems of interaction also rarely exist in an isolated form, but ordinarily are combined with one another, thus producing a few types of social groups or systems of interaction, which occur frequently and are met in any human universe. Of these "combined" types, three appear to me particularly important from many standpoints. They are met in almost any human universe, past, present, and probably future; primitive and modern; Oriental and Occidental. They are the Familistic, the Contractual, and the Compulsory types.

A. *The Familistic Type.* If we select from the above modalities of social relationships in the interaction system the following ones: (1) *universal totalitarian or all-embracing in extensity,* (2) *high in intensity,* (3) *purely solidary in direction,* (4) *durable* —then a combination of all the four modalities gives us what I style the familistic system of interaction or social relationship. Such is its "chemical formula."

A concrete example of this is given by the relationship between a loving mother and her baby; between the mutually devoted members of the family; between true friends, in the Aristotelian sense of real friendship. In these systems of interaction almost the whole circle of life activities of the parties is involved in the process of interaction, and certainly all the most important life relationships. In this sense, their whole lives are thrown together and organically united into one "we." There is almost nothing of the "it does not concern me," "it is none of my business," "mind your own affairs" attitude. On the contrary, what concerns one party concerns the other: joy and sorrow; failure and success; sickness and recovery; food, clothing, shelter; com-

* Reprinted by permission of the author and of Porter Sargent, Publisher.

fort, mental peace, beliefs, convictions, tastes of one party—all these concern most vitally the other, and meet concurrence, care, approval, aid, and sympathy.

It is as though they are bound by so short a rope that one party cannot make a step without pulling the other. Not only is the interaction all-embracingly extensive and highly intensive, but it is solidary par excellence. This solidarity comes out in millions of forms and continuously. It is as close as, sometimes even closer than, the mutual well-being of the various parts of one organism. The sorrow, joy, misfortune, success, of one becomes that of the other party. Their lives are fused together; their personalities are merged into one "we." The individuals here need one another, seek one another, and are bound into one unity, neither by compulsion, nor by considerations of profit, nor by contract; but spontaneously, for the sake of "being together," for the sake of the other party itself, regardless of pleasure, profit, compulsion, or contract.

Coercion is necessary here not to keep them together but to keep them apart. Likewise the bond is not a contract or a covenant. Most mothers want to be with their children spontaneously, organically, regardless of any contract or duty. The same is true of real friends. If a man is a "friend" of another man by mere contract, this means he is a pseudo friend. The real friend is, as Aristotle says rightly, "one who intends and does what is good (or what he believes to be good) to another for that other's sake; or one who wishes his friend to be and to live for that friend's own sake." Such a relationship among friends may give and usually results in some utility or pleasure for the parties, but neither one of these factors is the reason for the existence of such a tie; on the contrary, it is a mere result or by-product. Side by side with pleasure and utility, there is also sorrow and sacrifice in such a relationship, because any sorrow of one party becomes that of the other; the oneness of the parties leads each of them to offer or to render—again spontaneously—to the other any service or any sacrifice that is needed.

The contractual principle and psychology are heterogeneous to the familistic. In a collective oneness of the "we" of the familistic group, there is no place for a contractualism with its "so much, no more and no less." Any "no more and no less" is superfluous for a unity of the "we," where each individual, like an organ in a body, is a part of the whole, and as such spontaneously does and is expected to do his best, up to the ultimate sacrifice of his life for the "we" or its parts. "Sacrifice" here is felt as a privilege of free gift of a part to the whole. And the more is given, the more sublime is the "gladness" that flows from it.

As a consequence of that, no detailed *external* delineation of the duties and rights, of the "how much" and "under which circumstances," and other specifications and limitations of an *external* nature imposed by society are necessary for that kind of relationship. They become superfluous too.

The next point to be mentioned in regard to these relationships is the specific coexistence of *internal freedom of individuals with the external appearance of its limitation.* Considered outwardly, from a behavioristic standpoint, the familistic relationship may often appear as a great limitation of the freedom of the parties. From the standpoint of a contractual "flapper," the fact that the mother stays with the children, instead of going places and having parties, passes many a sleepless night instead of comfortably resting, spends her money buying necessities instead of purchasing a new dress for herself; for such a "flapper" all this is a "frightful" slavery or serfdom, a great limitation of freedom. However, when one puts himself in the position of the familistic party, most of these "limitations of freedom" of an individual are not such at all. The mother or the father does not feel that "slaving" for the children is a limitation of freedom; on the contrary, they are glad to do it and prefer it to the freedom of the flapper. In brief, the familistic relationship permits us to reconcile duty and discipline with freedom; sacrifice with liberty.

Such in the ideal form is the nature of the familistic relationship or social bond. I style it familistic because most often, and in the purest form, it is met in the relationship between the members of the good and harmonious family. In a more diluted form it exists, of course, in many other nonfamilistic groups: between devoted and close friends; between the members of a religious organization; even between the members of the State, and of many other groups, as will be shown further. On the other hand, the term familistic must not lead to the conclusion that all or even the majority of the social relationships among members of the family are familistic. We shall see that it is not so, especially in application to the modern family, where, besides the familistic, the contractual form composes a considerable part of its total system of relationship. Such is the first fundamental form of social relationship and of the social bond in the organized groups.

B. *The Contractual Type.* In the terms of the modalities, its "chemical formula" is as follows.

(1) *It is limited definitely in the extensity* of the life activities involved in the interaction.

(2) *As to the intensity,* it may be high or low, depending upon the nature of the "contracted sector" of activities, but this sector is always limited; therefore the high intensity is limited by this sector and never extends over the whole life circle.

(3) It is limited in its duration; even when it is durable, the duration is again specified by the contract.

(4) Within the contract sector it is *solidary* (in a contract which the parties freely enter into and which fairly distributes their rights and duties). But this solidarity is in a sense egotistic, directed to getting either mutually some pleasure or service or profit or utility from the other party, or even to getting "as much as possible for as little as possible." It is egotistic-bargaining solidarity of rationalistically computed profit. The other party is important, not so much as an associate, and is not sought for itself, but as an agency or instrumentality which may render some service, enjoyment, utility, or profit. Besides the limited sector of the contracted interaction, the parties may remain either total strangers to one another in their "private life," or even be inimical and antagonistic to one another. Such, in brief, is the formula of the contractual relationship in the terms of the above modalities. On this skeleton framework we can now paint the living picture of contractual relationship. It is a well-known picture. "I agree to do so and so for you, and you agree to do so and so for me. If you do not discharge your obligation, I am freed from mine and, besides, you will have to bear some unpleasant consequences of your breaking the contract." The parties may agree according to the classic Roman formula: *"Do ut does, facie ut facies, do ut facies, facie ut does"* ("Give to be

given, serve to be served, give to be served, serve to be given.") Here parties do not merge into one "we," but each feels and acts as an independent party not concerned with any interests but its own. In this sense, the contractual group is more nominalistic and singularistic and less universalistic than the familistic group. Respectively, the place of sacrifice or dissolving of the individual interests in the collective "we" in contractual relationship is taken by the bond of mutual *bargaining.*

This means that the explicit or implicit attitude of the contracting parties toward each other is a *sensible egotism,* moderate or extreme, reasonable, or unreasonable.

As a result of such a negotism, *the real contractual relationship cannot be blank, unlimited, or undefined meticulously.* As each party is pursuing in it its own interests, there cannot be, as a rule, a faith, a confidence, or a trust that one party will not try to take advantage of the other if their covenant is not specified and definitely agreed upon. More than that: there is often even no confidence that the other party will not try to twist the contract to the disadvantage of his partner. Therefore, a fixed or written contract, witnesses, and the notary to certify to its authenticity are a usual part of such an agreement. Since a definite distrust in regard to the sincerity and honesty of the other party is inherent in it, experts or experienced lawyers are hired to make the agreement clear and to leave no loophole through which the interests of a given party may be harmed by the other. Contractual relationship is the lawyers' paradise, their "bread and butter," while the familistic relationships do not need them, or a public notary, or even a judge.

Therefore, the members of the contractual group *always remain to a considerable degree strangers and outsiders in regard to one another.* They are contracted, or bound together, only in that specific respect which is covered by the contract. In all other respects, they do not concern one another; do not know one another; and do not want to be known. One calls his plumber, carpenter, or painter; agrees about the job to be done and the price to be paid for it—so far the parties cease to be complete strangers. But in all other aspects of which the life relationships are made up, they remain strangers.

It follows from the above that, compared with the familistic relationships, the contractual relationships bind the party not only by fewer bonds (only by those which constitute the contract), but these bonds are, as a rule, also shorter, so far as their duration in time is concerned. Most contracts have a definite time limit—a day, a week, a month, a year, and so on.

In contrast to that, most of the familistic relationships are more durable; the real familistic relationships are for life, even beyond it.

Finally, it follows that *the contractual relationship is inseparable from a great degree of freedom of each party from the other.* Since to enter or not enter the contract (in real contractual relationships—not in pseudo-contractual, which are but a variety of the compulsory relationships) depends upon the choice of an individual; since the conditions upon which he enters depend upon him also, he is free to a great degree, at least outwardly. And since in the real contracts his precontractual position is such that he can afford to choose, the individual in a contractual group is indeed given a large opportunity for display of his singularistic freedom.

Again, in various forms and proportions, *the contractual relationships compose a considerable part of the network of the social relationships of many and various social groups, beginning with the "employers and the employees," "buyers and sellers," "owners and tenants," and ending with many a religious, political, state, occupational, educational, artistic, scientific, and even family groups and associations.* So it was in the past and so it is in the present.

C. *The Compulsory Type.* Its main trait is that it is *antagonistic* in its nature. Being such, it gives many varieties. It may be most intensive, seeking extermination of the party, and less intensive, seeking to inflict some pain, damage, or fines upon it. Again, its area can cover the whole circle of life or only a small sector. Respectively, there may be, like the familistic relationship, an all-embracing compulsory relationship, and one very limited, confined to one narrow sector of the interacting activities. The living picture of the compulsory relationship can be drawn up as follows.

When one of the interacting parties imposes upon the other certain forms of conduct, certain duties and functions—*contrary to the desire and inclination of that party,* and subjectively and objectively not for its welfare—and forces their realization exclusively by application of various forms of physical and psychophysical coercion, the social interrelation is compulsory in its nature. The bond which unites the parties and hinders its rupture is this coercion. It may have various forms, from a purely physical compulsion, infliction of various physical harms, tortures, and pains, up to the more complex psychosocial coercion, assuming now the form of depriving the party of necessities, like food, shelter, freedom of movement, and so on; now the form of threat to inflict injury upon other persons dear to the party: wife, husband, children, friends, and so forth.

The relationships of the master and slave or serf; of the executioner and the executed; of the conqueror and the conquered; of the despotic government and the governed; of the extortionist and the victim; of the ravisher and the ravished, are rich in this type of relationship. As a specific case come the pseudo-familistic and the pseudo-contractual relationships. By pseudo-familistic is meant a relationship where the stronger party takes over the similitude of the familistic relationship—its terminology, its "clothing," as "this is done with fatherly feelings," "for your own good," and so on—while factually the interests and the welfare of the weaker party under coercion are not considered at all, and the compulsion or pains imposed do not serve its welfare in any way. By the pseudo-contractual is meant a relationship where the weaker party enters into the contract seemingly by its own will, but in fact does not have any choice, and the "free agreement" is but a simulacrum of a really free decision.

In contradistinction to the familistic and contractual relationships, the compulsory relationships are marked by the following traits.

(1) They are internally *antagonistic.*

(2) *It does not give any freedom to the coerced party, while to the coercing party it gives a freedom* (in the sense of doing what one pleases) *sometimes much greater than that given by the contractual relationships to both parties.*

(3) Respectively, in the *pure compulsory* relationship, the parties remain to each other total strangers and outsiders, much

more so than in any of the preceding relationships. And not only a stranger and outsider, but often a negative value, worse than a mere stranger. A slave to a cruel master is but a mere instrument, something even more "unhuman" than his cattle; at the best, he is but a species of animal. On the other hand, the coercing party remains also a stranger to the coerced. It is felt and perceived not as a human personality capable of understanding, feeling, being united by a psychosocial *rapport;* it is perceived merely as an instrument of oppression—cruel, inhuman, perverse, unjust, a kind of "whip" which only hurts, tortures, and oppresses. There is no bridge of real mutual understanding between the parties as human beings and personalities; there is no mutual fusion and no "we" feeling except the purely external, mechanical, like that between a cruel driver and his horse. The inner world of each party is mutually closed to the other; often there is not even a desire to open it.

D. *Mixed Forms*. These three forms seem to embrace almost all the pure forms of social relationship. The numerous concrete forms represent mostly their combination. Through a combination of various modifications of each of these three forms, it is possible to obtain most of the forms of social relationship given in the interaction of individuals and groups. As a matter of fact, the totality of interrelations within practically all the social groups represents usually a combination of these main forms: they are partly familistic, partly contractual, and partly compulsory. But the proportion of each type in the totality of the network of social relationships of various groups is not the same. It varies from group to group; and, in the course of time, changes even within the same group.

(1) If we select various social groups, we can easily see that some of them at all times have had *one of these types more predominant than the others*. If we take such groups as *the family, the Church, the association of real friends,* we find they almost always had an abundant portion of the familistic relationship in their relationship system. The ratio of this "familism" certainly varies from family to family; but as a rule it is considerable and in most cases is the dominant form of relationship. The others, the compulsory and the contractual relationships, are certainly present but, with few exceptions, they are hardly the main forms.

Likewise, the *religious groups* have nearly always been built along the pattern of the familistic group. This is shown clearly in the terminology of such a group. "Our Father" (God), "we are children, sons and daughters of God," "God the Father," "God the Son," "Mother of God," "Mother Church," "Holy Father," "Sisters in Christ," "Brethren," "the Spouse of Christ," and so on.

The same is true of real friends. Here again, as indicated, the relationship by definition is familistic and always assumes this type. This is shown again by such terms and "rites of passage" as mixing of blood, as drinking *Bruderschaft,* and the like.

If now we take such groups as the compulsory military group—the army as such (with the exception of groups like early medieval "companions in arms," which were modeled along the familistic pattern)—there compulsory relationships are always present to a considerable degree, especially where the army is large and recruited from all kinds of people. Likewise, in the state network of social relationships, especially in a despotic, dictatorial, or tyrannic State, a great portion of relationship is compulsory, as is manifest in the mechanism of the coercion of the State: its police, its army, its jails, its courts, its punishments, and other coercive forces.

Finally, when we turn to the commercial and trade organizations, they always had, to a considerable degree, a developed system of contractual relationship. Trade is ordinarily a "bargaining," the exchange of something for something.

These examples give an idea that some of the organized groups by their very nature are "destined" to have one of the main types more preponderant than the others and that there are several types of social groups which at all times have tended to build their network of social relationships predominantly either out of the familistic, or the contractual, or the compulsory relationships.

(2) *Warning: Do not confuse the existing nature of the relationship with how it originated or was established.* One must not mix these two different things. A given interaction and relationship may originate in a contractual form—for instance, the relationship between married parties or the relationship of the *fidelitas* in the Middle Ages. But in the course of time it may turn into either the familistic or compulsory type. The marriage

contract even nowadays often turns into a real and pure familistic relationship between the husband and wife, parents and children. A business contract and subsequent meetings of the parties often lead to an establishment of true friendship between the contracting parties. Even many relationships compulsory in their origin turn into the familistic (for instance, in the past, in many marriages imposed upon one or both parties by others) or contractual form. On the other hand, a diluted familistic relationship, in the course of time, sometimes degenerates either into a contractual or even a compulsory one; or a contractual relationship degenerates into a compulsory one. In other words, one thing is *the way in which the relationship originated* (contractually or compulsorily or familistically); and quite another thing is *what it is in its nature* (familistic or contractual or compulsory). A certain form of origin does not always mean that its nature is the same as the form of origin and vice versa.

The above concise but sufficiently precise characterization of the process of social interactions, of the modalities, of the types of social systems of interaction, and then of the familistic, contractual, and compulsory relationships with the respective systems of interactions, is sufficient to permit us to pass to a study of the fluctuation of the proportion and the quality of each of these relationships in the main social systems of the European population, from the beginning of the Middle Ages up to the present time.

The Crisis of Our Age

The organism of the Western society and culture seems to be undergoing one of the deepest and most significant crises of its life. The crisis is far greater than the ordinary; its depth is unfathomable, its end not yet in sight, and the whole of the Western society is involved in it. It is the crisis of a Sensate culture, now in its overripe stage, the culture that has dominated the Western World during the last five centuries. It is also the crisis of a contractual (capitalistic) society associated with it. In this sense we are experiencing one of the sharpest turns in the historical road, a turn as great as any of the other few made by the Graeco-Roman and Western cultures in passing from Ideational to Sensate, and from Sensate to Ideational, phases.

The diagnosis of the crisis of our age which is given in this chapter was written in 1934. Gigantic catastrophes that have occurred since that year are not included here; however, they strikingly confirm and develop the diagnosis.

We have seen during the course of the present work quite definite signs of such a turn. Not a single compartment of our cultural, or of the mind of contemporary man, shows itself to be free from the unmistakable symptoms. We have observed, also, that these signs, this "handwriting on the wall," are particularly clear as we approach the end of the nineteenth and advance into the twentieth century. The curves of painting, sculpture, music, and literature; of movement of discoveries and inventions; of the "First Principles" of science, philosophy, religion, ethics, and law; up to those of wars and revolutions—all make a violent turn as we approach our time. Shall we wonder, therefore, that if many do not apprehend clearly what is happening, they have at least a vague feeling that the issue is not merely that of "prosperity," or "democracy," or "capitalism," or the like, but involves the whole contemporary (Sensate) culture, society, and man? If they do not understand it by intellectual analysis, they feel sharply the painful claws of the events, whether they be kings or housewives.

Shall we wonder, also, at the endless multitude of incessant major and minor crises that have been rolling over us, like ocean waves, during recent decades? Today in one form, tomorrow in another. Now here, now there. Crises political, agricultural, commercial, and industrial! Crises of production and distribution. Crises moral, juridical, religious, scientific, and artistic. Crises of property, of the State, of the family, of industrial enterprise, of the republic and monarchy, autocracy and democracy, dictatorship and self-government, capitalism and socialism, fascism and communism, nationalism and internationalism, pacifism and militarism, conservatism and radicalism. Crises of truth, of beauty, of justice, of righteousness. Crises of the whole system of values of our culture. Each in a rich variety of forms and with varying degrees of power, but endlessly rolling, its roar reverberating in every daily newspaper. Each of the crises has battered our nerves and minds, each has shaken the very foundations of our culture and society, and each has left behind a legion of derelicts and victims. And alas! the end is not yet in view. Each of these crises has been, as it were, a movement in a great terrifying symphony, and each has been remarkable for its magnitude and intensity. Each movement has been played, during the last three decades, by enormous human orchestras, with millions of choruses, stage performers, and actors. In 1911 the four-hundred-million-piece Chinese orchestra began one of its first festivals. This still goes on, and the mountain of its contributor victims grows higher and higher from year to year.

In 1914 a new brass band of many nations with hundreds of participants started its deadening "*Marche Militaire:* 1914-1918." The effects of this performance were appalling. The stage—the soil of this planet—was soaked with blood. Most of our values were poisoned by gas; others were blown to pieces by artillery. The very foundations of our society and culture cracked. . . .

Before this festival had ended, the Russian orchestra of some 160,000,000 virtuosi set forth its own variation entitled "Communist Revolution." The first blow of its percussion instruments overthrew the social and cultural system of the old Russia. Subsequent movements have shaken the whole human world. The performance has been so brilliant that millions of onlookers have acquired a profound distaste for the old-fashioned music of the capitalist system and gone mad with the communist modernism. In Russia millions of listeners and participants have died in the process. Other millions have sunk to the bottom of human misery, and, weary and half dead, have been longing for the end of their hopeless and joyless existence. Still other millions have been thrown into the social gutters, left moaning their desperate calls for help, and finding neither response nor assistance. The festival still continues magnificently, with ever new tricks and surprises. Having saturated the soil of Russia, the red fertilizing blood began to flow across its boundary, into the soil of the onlookers of this "marvelous experiment."

Dozens of other companies—Turkey and Hungary, Austria and Germany, Bulgaria and Rumania, Spain and Portugal, Italy and Poland, Abyssinia and Manchukuo, the Central and South American states, Japan and Arabia, Palestine and Egypt, Syria and Afghanistan—have also been giving their crisis festivals. Some of them, like the Central and South American orchestras, have turned it into a daily entertainment; others, like Abyssinia and Manchukuo, played it to their own death. Meanwhile, the vast continent of India, too, has taken definite steps to stage its gala concert. For several years the immense India orchestra has already been rehearsing. At the first rehearsals the symphony was played *pianissimo*. Then it was replaced by the *moderato* of nonviolent resistance, more and more often intercepted by a sharp staccato of machine guns and drums, bombs, and the blows of police sticks. There is hardly any doubt that soon we shall hear the *fortissimo* of this thundering festival.

If we turn our ears to Europe, we can hear, without the need of any short-wave radio, as many crisis festivals as we like. One day various fascists occupy the stage; another, communists; then the Hitlerites; then the Popular Front—red shirts and black shirts and brown shirts and silver shirts, and blue shirts and green shirts. At one moment the Spanish crisis is on the front page; at another, the French or Austrian; and all accompanied by news of the shakiness of the English pound, or the American dollar, or the French franc, or the German mark. Then come "cordial cooperation and mutual understanding" between Chinese and Japanese; or blessed salvation of Abyssinia from itself; or a Soviet demonstration of "pacifism" and a plea for the "sacredness of the contracts" on the part of a government that broke all contracts; or other forms of similar "international solidarity and good will." They give for a moment excellent publicity to that otherwise forgotten homeopathic family physician, the League of Nations, or call forth one of the endless international conferences of the "shepherds of the people" to "adjust the maladjustment," after which there usually spring up a dozen new maladjustments where before there was only one.

Up to 1929 the blessed Land of the Pilgrims was free from the crisis vogue. We preferred to listen to the crisis concerts of the other countries while at home we enjoyed mainly the *andante cantabile* of "sweet prosperity." Since the end of 1929 our taste seems to have changed. Prosperity has fallen at least temporarily into disfavor. The crisis music has also captured our fancy. From any radio we hear now almost exclusively either the "classical" or "crooning" versions of the crisis of industry and agriculture, of employment and unemployment, of education and morals, of stock market crashes, of bank failures; the *adagio lamentoso* of dissipated luxury; the *marche funèbre* and *in memoriam* of faded hopes; the *requiem* to evaporated fortunes; the *allegro non troppo* of the murmurs of dissatisfaction; the *crescendo* of the criticism of the existing order; and occasional *scherzos* of hunger marchers, "sit-down strikers," and clashes between police and radicals. With a lag of a few years we also have acquired the taste for the new music.

These are but a few of the variations on the main theme of today's symphony of history. The total number of all the variations is immense. Not only the economic and political systems, but every important aspect of the life, organization, and culture of the Western society is included in the crisis. Its body and mind are sick and there is hardly a spot on its body which is not sore, nor any nervous fiber which functions soundly.

We are seemingly between two epochs: the dying Sensate culture of our magnificent yesterday, and the coming Ideational or Idealistic culture of the creative tomorrow. We are living, thinking, acting at the end of a brilliant six-hundred-year-long Sensate day. The oblique rays of the sun still illumine the glory of the passing epoch. But the light is fading, and in the deepening shadows it becomes more and more difficult to see clearly and to orient ourselves safely in the confusions of the twilight. The night of the transitory period begins to loom before us and the coming generations, perhaps with their nightmares, frightening shadows, and heart-rending horrors. Beyond it, however, the dawn of a new great Ideational or Idealistic culture is probably waiting to greet the men of the future.

Thus history, so far, has been proceeding along the schedule of the *Dynamics*. The great crisis of Sensate culture is here in all its stark reality. Before our very eyes this culture is committing suicide. If it does not die in our lifetime, it can hardly recover from the exhaustion of its creative forces and from the wounds of self-destruction. Half-alive and half-dead, it may linger in its agony for decades; but its spring and summer are definitely over.

Under these conditions the great task of our generation and the next consists, not in a hopeless resuscitation of what is already hollow, but in a solution of two different problems: first, of making the *dies irae, dies illa* of the transition as painless as possible; second, of laying down constructive plans for the future society and culture. Any farsighted plan for a new sociocultural order must go beyond the "old regime of Sensate culture" towards the new regime of either Ideational or Idealistic culture. Without such a fundamental change no really constructive and creative society is possible in the future.

Such, it seems to me, is the position we are at on the road of history. The evidence of all the preceding chapters points in this direction. And we find our conclusion in an irreconcilable contradiction with the other current diagnoses.

First of all, it stands in sharp contradiction to all the theories of a "moderate," "sensible," and "orderly" progress. Not realizing that their progress cult is already out of date, a throng of intellectuals, humanitarians, pacifistic and progressive parlor socialists, liberal ministers, professors, politicians, and a legion of intellectual Rotarians and Kiwanians of all kinds still profess this credo. They look at the historical process as at a good little boy who steadily advances from the first grade to graduation and progressively becomes bigger and better. They depict "the next stage" as a paradise where milk rivers flow between shores of ice cream, where all arms are remade into golf clubs, radio receivers, and electric toasters, and where "international cooperation," "mutual understanding," and "good will" reign supreme. No war, no crime, no insanity, no bloodshed, no foolishness, no trouble; there the happy existence of the contented and highly progressive ladies and gentlemen (both being blessed with birth control). All the labor is performed by mechanical appliances. Everybody's dinner consists of asparagus, fried chicken, ice cream, and pie a la mode, with cocktails before and liqueurs after the meal. Everybody will have full opportunity to educate himself through reading every best seller and all the Book of the Month Club selections; through listening to the radio addresses of the latest "authorities"; through glancing over the "Literary" and "Reader's" and "Scientific" digests; and, finally, through movies, dance halls, and television.

Instead of this paradise, alas! my thesis offers a rather gloomy time of blood, cruelty, and misery, with "humanity uprooted," with the sweet humanitarian dreams thrown to the winds, and

—what is more important—with the main and eternal values trodden down. Even the culture of tomorrow, as I see it, is in no way going to resemble this cloud-cuckoo land of the after-dinner imagination. Created in its present specific form in the second half of the nineteenth century, this utopia has been one of the fascinating soap bubbles with which contented Victorian Europe liked to amuse itself. This Europe being on the wane, its bubbles are bursting. Anybody who likes this utopia is welcome to its hearty enjoyment. On my part I hear distinctly the *requiem* that the symphony of history is playing in its memory.

My theory is no less contradictory to all the ideologies of a violent and revolutionary progress *à la sans-culotte, à la* Karl Marx-Lenin-Stalin, or *à l'anarchie*. After all, the difference between the theories of moderate and violent progress is small: it amounts to a mere difference in the temperament of the devotees and the technique of progress-promotion. Both parties are equally over-Sensate and both believe in a Sensate advance, but the moderates do not wish to rush its realization. They dislike bloodshed, loss of their savings, and having their parlors invaded by ruthless and crazy mobs. The extremists, on the contrary, want to hurry along progress by all means, at any cost, and regardless of whether or not others wish to enter their paradise. They have little or nothing to lose. Therefore, they are not afraid of being ruined, or of shedding blood, or of any other of the riotous occurrences of revolutionary progress making.

These revolutionary schemes are but utopias of a disintegrated mind, of demoralized man, and come as the by-product of the disintegrated culture of the transitionary period. As we have seen in the chapters on disturbances, periods of the disintegration of social and cultural systems are regularly marked by the emergence of such schemes, and by revolts of the masses of humanity with *un*integrated minds led by groups of intellectuals with a *dis*integrated mentality. The emergence and growth of the power of these unintegrated and disintegrated minds are two of the decisive characteristics of the fading day of the passing epoch. These mobs and their leaders are the vultures that appear when the social and cultural body is decomposing. Their eternal historical function is to pull it to pieces, and thus, though involuntarily, to clear the ground for a new life. Creation is not given to them. Both their "constructive" plans and they themselves are flesh of the flesh of the last phase of the disintegrating culture, with all the unpleasant traits of such a phase and without the virtues of the Sensate culture at its climax.

At the best, only a few of the traits of the coming integrated culture and society may possibly find, in distorted form, an echo in their schemes. With this exception, their utopian culture and society are as different from the society and culture to come as the familistic society differs from the compulsory, and the Ideational from a disintegrated Sensate culture.

Finally, *my thesis has little in common with the age-old theories of the life cycle of cultures and societies with its stages of childhood, maturity, senility, and decay.*

These summary remarks show that our theory and diagnosis are not a variety of any of the above conceptions, of any moderately linear, revolutionarily progressive, or cyclical-decay-and-decline ideologies. The theory developed here stands by itself, unrelated to any of the dominant social philosophies of the present. It does not need their support nor approval, because its feet are stronger than theirs and stand upon a much firmer foundation.

For the champions of the overstuffed, after-dinner utopia the theory may appear pessimistic. In a sense it is. But from a deeper standpoint it is highly optimistic. It is optimistic because it shows sociocultural forces to be infinitely richer in creative power than does the inflexible ideal of these utopians. It is richer than any theory based on the Sensate, or Ideational, or Mixed form of culture taken alone, because it embraces all these, and gives *suum cuique*. And it is also optimistic, because it does not predict either the certain death or decay of the Western culture and society. If it points to the decline of the present Sensate phase and the probability of a grim transition, at the same time it indicates the possibility of the rise of a new magnificent Ideational or Idealistic culture, society, and man. Such a standpoint raises no fear of the temporary decline, nor even regrets it. Any value at the time of its decline deserves gratitude and compassion but not admiration. Still less does it deserve the efforts to keep it alive when a new value—as great and as good, perhaps—is coming.

Mankind should be grateful to the Sensate culture for its

wonderful achievements. But now when it is in agony; when its product is poison gas rather than fresh air; when through its achievements it has given into man's hands terrific power over nature and the social and cultural world, without providing himself with self-control, with power over his emotions and passions, sensate appetites and lusts—now, in the hands of such a man, with all its achievements of science and technology, it is becoming increasingly dangerous to mankind itself and to all its values.

The most urgent need of our time is the man who can control himself and his lusts, who is compassionate to all his fellow men, who can see and seek for the eternal values of culture and society, and who deeply feels his unique responsibility in this universe. If the conquest of the forces of nature is the main function of the Sensate culture, the taming of man, his "humanization," his ennoblement as the participant in the Divine Absolute, has always been the function mainly of the Ideational or Idealistic culture. The Sensate culture did its best in the way of degrading man to the level of a mere reflex mechanism, a mere organ motivated by sex, a mere semimechanical, semiphysiological organism, devoid of any divine spark, of any absolute value, of anything noble and sacred. Such a debasement now becomes increasingly dangerous for the Sensate man himself. Hence the urgency of the shift from Sensatism to Ideationalism or Idealism, from the subjugation and control of nature by man to the control of man by himself.

This control is impossible without a system of absolute or universal and perennial values. Such values are irreconcilable with the Sensate mentality and culture which by their nature are relative, utilitarian, hedonistic, and expedient only. Hence the logical necessity and practical urgency of the shift to a new Ideational or Idealistic culture. Such a man can be trusted with the power created by the Sensate culture. Even with the present power and technique, such a man could build a society and culture with less poverty and misery, free from individual and group hatred, more noble, more just, more human, and more godly, than the present phase of our Sensate society.

ROBERT M. MacIVER

Robert Morrison MacIver (1882-   ) was born in Stornoway, Scotland, and educated at Edinburgh (M.A. 1903; D.Phil. 1915) and Oxford (B.A. 1907). He taught both political science and sociology at Aberdeen from 1907 to 1915 and at Toronto from 1915 to 1927. In the latter year he came to Barnard College and in 1929 he became Lieber Professor of Political Philosophy and Sociology at Columbia University, a post he retained until his retirement with the title of Emeritus in 1950. His energies, however, seem inexhaustible. Since his retirement he has directed a comprehensive study of academic freedom in the United States and in 1957 he became director of a Juvenile Delinquency Evaluation Unit for the City of New York. He served in 1940 as the thirtieth president of the American Sociological Society and he holds honorary degrees from Edinburgh, Columbia, Harvard, Yale, Princeton, The New School for Social Research, and The Jewish Theological Seminary of America.

MacIver is the author of a long series of books in both political science and sociology, including, among others, *Community: A Sociological Study* (1917), *Labor in the Changing World* (1919), *Elements of Social Science* (1921), *The Modern State* (1926), *The Relation of Sociology to Social Work* (1931), *Society: Its Structure and Changes* (1931; rev. 1937 and, with Charles H. Page, 1949), *Social Causation* (1942), *The Web of Government* (1947), and *Academic Freedom in Our Time* (1955).

Beginning his career as a political scientist, MacIver came to an early and insightful recognition that behind the order to which government gives formal expression there is another, more ultimate order, which is the order of society itself. His major contributions to sociology exhibit the nature of this order in a thoroughgoing and systematic fashion. *The Web of Government,* from which the following selections are taken, is probably the most profound examination of the sociology of government in the literature.

From *The Web of Government**

GOVERNMENT AND LAW

Without law there is no order, and without order men are lost, not knowing where they go, not knowing what they do. A system of ordered relationships is a primary condition of human life at every level. More than anything else it is what society means. Even an outlaw group, a pirate ship, a robber gang, a band of brigands, has its own code of law, without which it could not exist. The picture of the "lawless savage," running wild in the woods, is wholly fictitious. The "savage" is never lawless, he clings to his own laws more tenaciously, more blindly, than does the civilized man. Only the completely *déraciné,* the man torn from his social environment, or the extreme sophisticate, or the tyrant who emerges in a time of confusion, can be described approximately as lawless. The law of the "savage" is not our law, and there is no law between him and the outsider—a situation that still exists, in times of war, for civilized peoples. The world has been, and up to the present has remained, a collocation of areas of lawfulness, communities with no law binding the one to the other.

To the primitive his law is sacred. It is unchallengeable. For him the law is not something made by chief or legislator or judge. It is timelessly ordained. He can no more disown it than he can disown his tribe. No chief can interfere with it, or he becomes lawless himself. It does not indeed follow that the primitive never disobeys his law, only that he rarely doubts and practically never disbelieves its rightfulness. A man may firmly believe in God, and still break under temptation what he believes to be God's commandments. The primitive finds ways of evading the law and under strong impulsion will directly violate it. But it is still the law of his life. It is not like our civilized law, a specialized

* From *The Web of Government.* Copyright, 1947, by Robert M. MacIver. Reprinted by permission of The Macmillan Company.

body of *legal* rules. It is one with custom, it is the way of the folk, hallowed by tradition, breathing the very spirit of the folk. It is unwritten law, and that sometimes raises troubles, for on particular points the interpreters may differ. It has little or no legal form, and that sometimes causes difficulties, for, as has been said of the law of the Cheyenne Indians, its conclusions do not fall "into easily accessible patterns to draw minor trouble-festers to a head, and so to get them settled. This shows again and again in smoldering irritations over points of fact." But it is the firmament of order in society.

To the primitive his folk-law is not something men can make and remake. It is as much given to him as the earth he lives on. He scarcely recognizes it for what it is, a cultural product that changes imperceptibly with the changing culture. But of course Thomas Hobbes was right when he explained that law in human society is not like the law that rules the communities of ants or of bees. It is not in that sense "natural," not biologically determined but socially constructed, a folk-creation. Hence there is still the need for social sanctions. The errant member of the flock must be disciplined, or his example will weaken respect for the law. Sometimes the folk itself is the sufficient guardian of its ways. The disrepute it attaches to the offender, the ostracism with which it penalizes more serious transgressions, or the direct punishment it inflicts when strongly aroused—as when the people turned against the offender Achan and "all Israel stoned him with stones"—these reactions serve in place of the machinery of law. But, as we have seen, there is always leadership, even for the seemingly spontaneous responses of the folk. The habit of personal government that developed in every family circle would be enough, apart from other considerations, to stimulate the establishment of personal government over the larger community. At first the chief might merely settle disputes, but in doing so he was unconsciously changing and making law. The government thus set up, the chief or the council of elders, came easily to be regarded as the guardian of the folkways. It was in effect an executive and judicial authority, rather than a legislative one. Its direct law-making activity was at most minor, incidental, and sporadic. Occasionally, at a more advanced stage, the heroic figure of a "law-maker" appears, like Lycurgus or Solon or

Hammurabi or Moses. But the Great Legislator is usually represented as being either a codifier of the laws or a prophet who receives them from God.

Even after government is established it remains more the guarantor than the maker of the law. The structure of order in any society is a rather elaborate affair. It is the result of long-time adjustments between man and man and between man and environment. What we call the simpler societies have folkways that are remarkably subtle and complex, as for example in their kinship relationships. Only as the anthropologist comes to know the actual life of the people does he gain any conception of the finer balances of the system. In passing we may observe that the order of a modern society is so highly patterned and so ramifying that it can scarcely be grasped in its totality. Within it the personal aims and activities of millions are held in one orbit, like the countless stars of a galaxy. Within it many and changeful groups pursue their special and conflicting interests, still held together by the embracing order. These interests are circumscribed by the law of the state, they are kept in place and within limit by that kind of law, *legal* law, the law that the courts interpret and apply. But there is a vast number of conventions and customs and understandings, of every kind and range, that regulate the more intimate working of the system. No government makes these, no court applies them, no political executive enforces them. There is a margin at which enforcement operates, there are frontiers of conformity set by the effective law. But this kind of law, voluminous as it is in the law books, neither comprehends nor regulates the vast intrinsic traffic of society.

In a modern society we distinguish between custom and law, and recognize that custom and other nonlegal principles control a great sector of human behavior. In simple societies there is no clear-cut distinction between custom and law. The specific legal code, with its specific machinery of enforcement, has not yet developed. Consequently such government as existed was not regarded as making rules for the community, but only as administering its affairs, settling disputes, and guarding the folkways against the dangerous violator. Where, however, communities expanded in population and resources, where they extended their boundaries, through war or otherwise, and took under their dominion other groups or communities, where by reason of such conditions the tempo of social change was accelerated, and especially where serious conflicts and maladjustments arose between the more demarcated economic categories or social classes of the larger society, there the old established folkways no longer gave the needed guidance. Government took on the job of *legislation.* Often the strife between privileged classes and oppressed or exploited classes caused intolerable unrest and dissension. To allay it a whole new system of laws was necessary. This was the task to which the famous lawgivers of the ancient world devoted themselves. In Athens, for example, when strife became acute between the oligarchic families or Eupatridae and the discontented population, Draco came forward with a system of ruthless penal laws that failed to achieve their purpose. Solon followed and abolished many of the privileges of the Eupatridae, setting up at the same time an entirely new apparatus of government. Later Cleisthenes appeared and sought to unify a still divided people by establishing a remarkably democratic constitution, giving to the citizen body as a whole the most complete right to control the entire policy of the state.

But neither the most famous lawgiver nor the most powerful despot abrogated the general pattern of law-ways already existent among their peoples. The great lawgiver was mostly concerned with reforming the constitution, the broad framework of government, the respective shares of different groups in the making of policy, the powers and privileges possessed by different classes of the community. The main body of laws and law usages remained and, where necessary, was readjusted to the new order. The despot scarcely tampered with the laws at all. The typical dynast of China or of Egypt or of Babylonia disposed freely of men and of things, but he did little to change the code. Even if he personally violated the laws he still did not alter them. There was an established order, in part set out in the terms of law but in much larger part expressed in folkways. The folkways derived their authority not from the monarch but from the folk—or from God. They were invested with sanctity. The ruler, no matter how despotic he might be, had no power over them. He might "protect" them but he could not overthrow them. Emperor or rajah or sultan lived, like their peoples, under the aegis of the sacred law.

Every society, at every stage of civilization, rests on a firmament of law that is vastly greater and much more intricate than any ever devised by any government, one that is too great and too intricate to be completely overturned even by the most revolutionary of governments. We must recognize this elementary fact if we are to understand the nature of government and the authority of government. This firmament of law is composed of various interfused elements, the composition varying with the kind of society. There are societies in which it is almost wholly folk-sustained customary law, with practically no element of legal law, that is, of law interpreted and enforced by courts or judges. There are others in which the social firmament has a considerable element of common law, law accepted and enforced by courts but not enacted by governments. Then as we pass to more complex societies we find an increasing amount of statute law, law made expressly by governments, combined with the element of common law, while this more precise framework is filled in its myriad interstices with the pervasive element of custom.

Not only in primitive society but also in the ancient civilizations and in the medieval world it was accepted doctrine that the ruler was subject to the laws, not above them, and that the body of laws was something scarcely touched by the fiat of authority. The law is the law of the community, not the law of the ruler. Sometimes the law was regarded as expressive of the will of God, as among the Hebrews; sometimes it was regarded as emanating from the whole people. When princes and emperors came to be more assertive in lawmaking, the prevailing conception was that they did so as agents of the people and that their authority was derived from the people. This was throughout the doctrine of the Roman jurists. There is a famous passage in the *Digest of Ulpian,* a jurist of the late second century A.D., that if taken in isolation seems to contradict this doctrine. *Quod principi placuit, legis habet vigorem*—what the prince wills has the force of law. But Ulpian explains immediately thereafter that this maxim holds because the people has conferred by constitutional law (lex regia) this power upon the prince. Consequently, as the emperors of

Rome themselves acknowledged, the prince was bound by the laws and derived his authority from the laws.

The same doctrine held throughout the Middle Ages. It was differently oriented to correspond with the different social structure. The medieval king or emperor did not make laws or decrees of his mere pleasure, but with the consent of his council. His council was supposed to stand for the community. His authority was always presumed to be derived from the community, and, as Bracton put it, the law was the bridle of authority. Furthermore, the notion of natural law as the abiding model of human law prevailed in the thought of the times. And of course there was the constant admonition to the ruler that he was subject to the law of God. In the Middle Ages there was no lack of accepted ethical and religious standards to which political authority was "in principle" subject. It is true that the approach of practice to principle was often remote. Perhaps there has been no great period of history wherein ethical prescriptions were so clearly formulated and so universally espoused while yet the behavior of those in power seemed in effect regardless of them. "The king stands below the law of nature," "the prince cannot change the law of nature," "any act that violates the law of nature is null and void"—such expressions recur in the writings of medieval thinkers but they neither deterred princes from their ambitions nor protected the people from arbitrary power. Abstract rights could give small comfort against concrete wrongs.

It is true also that while the community was represented as being the source of authority and itself ultimately supreme the community was here understood in the light of a caste ideology. The consent of the people meant in effect the approval of the powerful, the nobles, the "good men and true" who stood close to the king, at most the substantial commoners who paid the taxes.

Even with these qualifications government in the Middle Ages was far more the creature than the creator of the prevailing system of law and order. The custom of the community everywhere prevailed. Sometimes it was rudely disturbed by war but always it resumed its sway. Acts of violence and of lawlessness, oppression and libertinage in high places, did not crack the ordered cohesion of everyday life. The patterns of communal order changed slowly, almost imperceptibly. The grounds of authority were remarkably firm. Above all we must remember that, however much kings and emperors may have been occupied with stratagems and spoils, they were not particularly concerned with making and with changing the law. As McIlwain says, "to the medieval mind 'government' is mainly an act of interpretation, and our so-called 'executive' and 'legislative' departments of it are subordinate to what we should term the 'judicial.' For Bodin, and for almost all since his day, the king is primarily a lawgiver; for Alvarus and all of his time, every king is primarily a judge."

With the Renaissance we find the rise of another doctrine concerning the relation of government and law, a doctrine that in its fulfillment denied the older conception of the basis of order in society and at times shook and even cracked the whole firmament of law. This was the doctrine that set the ruler above the law and made his single will the very source of law. As we pointed out in Chapter Three, political thinkers of the sixteenth century in Western Europe, and particularly in France, were engaged in buttressing the authority of the king, since their age was weary of the old wars of feudal barons within the disunited realm and of the new and more embittered wars of religious sects that threatened to destroy whatever unity the realm still possessed. The solution was to elevate the monarch to a commanding height above all other men and leaders of men and to invest him with complete supremacy over them all. So the doctrine of sovereignty was redevised and greatly amplified and elaborated. The king, formerly the defender of the community-made law, now became the supreme lord who gave its law to the community. Hitherto the king had owed, in the thought of learned and ignorant alike, his authority to the law; now the law owed its authority to him. He was, in the language of Jean Bodin and his school, *legibus solutus,* unbound by the laws. This expression, *legibus solutus,* is found in earlier medieval thinkers, and also in the law book (the *Corpus Juris*) of Imperial Rome, but whatever it meant in these passages, its literal interpretation was certainly quite incompatible with the prevailing concepts of the Middle Ages.

We should here observe that the new emphasis on sovereignty, which on the whole prevailed through the sixteenth and seventeenth centuries in Western Europe, was itself in part inspired by the new dangers that threatened the old firmament of law. Medieval religion, one and indivisible, worried only by minor heresies that touched none of its foundations, gave a kind of anchorage to the loose political structure of feudalism. It strongly corroborated the class structure. Now a time had come when deep schisms were driven into this unity, and these schisms cut across the lines of communities and of peoples. With the schisms went a loosening of the hold of religion itself and more immediately of the authoritative guardians of religion. The wars of religion were in effect civil wars. Men felt the need for new authority and a new unity. The new unity they found was the greater state, coming gradually to be viewed as the nation-state. The new authority was the authority of the sovereign.

But there was a serious flaw in the new doctrine, and it was manifest from the first. The sovereign was one, indivisible, omnicompetent. What then of the claims of religion? There were many who on this ground resisted the new exaltation of the king. Among them was the great Jesuit leader, Suarez, who vindicated the autonomy of the spiritual realm against the state, asserting again the higher authority of the former and the right of men to wage war against tyrannical rulers. Where there were no religious divisions within the greater state the problem could be somehow met. The king could still be by God appointed, invested with the divine right of kings, entering into a concordat with the church and acting as defender of the faith. But how could the adherents of one faith accept as sovereign over their religious brotherhood a ruler of another faith? How could they accept the principle of the treaty of Augsburg, that the religion of the prince held for the territory over which he ruled? The religion of every group proclaimed that it was better to obey God than man. Only three years after Bodin's work on *The Republic* there appeared also in France the famous Huguenot treatise, *Vindiciae contra tyrannos,* the author of which asserted that the sovereign becomes a tyrant, whom it is the duty of the magistrates to resist, if his commands run counter to true religion and the law of God. From the time of the Reformation the number of religious sects was on the increase. In some countries the ruler was Roman Catholic, in others he was Protestant. Everywhere there were religious groups that suffered persecution for their faith. The age had not yet discovered that the ruler need not meddle with the religion of his subjects or that it was unnecessary to make a particular religion a condition of civic rights or that, when citizens were divided by religious differences, the firmament of order was not weakened but on the contrary much strengthened if each group was free to worship in its own way or to worship its own God. The new myth of sovereignty blocked, instead of promoting, the solution of this sharpening issue.

Meanwhile, although the states of Western Europe—France, England, and Spain—consolidated the monarchy, making the throne strong against the crumbling claims of the feudal hierarchy, their internal order was threatened again and again by religious strife. Bodin's trust in the law of nature gave no comfort to oppressed minorities, subject to the omnicompetent sovereignty of ruthless kings. He himself believed in tolerance and detested religious fanaticism. But his doctrine of sovereignty merely gave to a fanatical age a new doctrinal sword. The religious group that had the monarchy on its side was only too ready to attribute to the secular arm the defence of the faith. In this there was no difference between the reformist Luther or Melanchthon, the Presbyterian Calvin or Beza or Knox, the Anglican bishops who in their *Convocation Book* declared that any rebellion against king or magistrate, for any cause whatsoever, is "a sin very detestable against God," and the Catholic Bossuet. When, as happened often enough, the situation was reversed and their own faith was persecuted, the same groups were apt to invoke the law of God against the tyrant, and to declare, with many scriptural supports, that "to obey man in any thing against God is unlawful and in plain disobedience." So wrote, for example, Christopher Goodman in his work *How Superior Powers Ought to Be Obeyed*. So said Calvin and Knox regarding monarchs who professed other faiths than their own.

The Massacre of St. Bartholomew, the "English Terror" organized by Thomas Cromwell under Henry the Eighth, the persecution of Protestants under "Bloody Mary," and the numerous "wars of religion" highlighted the omnicompetence of sovereignty. Revolts of the middle economic classes, especially in England, began to increase the confusion that hitherto had centered in the religious issue. The old bases of authority were menaced, the firmament of order was threatened. A new kind of society was developing within the greater state, a society no longer, like feudal society, uni-centered in its faith nor uniform in its economic pattern. It was the dawn of modern multi-group society. The authoritarian order, whether the feudal type or the new type of royal absolutism, was no longer appropriate, could not much longer be maintained. But the doctrine of the new order was not yet developed. The idea of "toleration," as a concession to nonconformist faiths, was wholly inadequate. Men felt the need for a new basis of order but old traditions yielded slowly. Even when the breakdown of royal absolutism was quite evident, first in England, when already powerful sectarian groups refused to be "coordinated" under a state religion, when a monarch was beheaded in final defiance of the divine right of kings, when a puritan squire became the first and only dictator of England, when insurgent groups were still presenting manifestoes and "agreements of the people" that were remarkably radical for that age, Thomas Hobbes was preparing for publication a new defence of absolutism, the *Leviathan.*

The most complete exposition of a social myth often comes when the myth itself is waning. It was so with the *Leviathan.* Bodin still tempered his doctrine of sovereignty by his partial trust in the great law of nature. He was half an agnostic whereas Hobbes was wholly a sceptic. The law of nature does not regulate in any sense the behavior of men who are moved mainly by vanity, mistrust of their fellows, and "a perpetual and restless desire for power after power, that ceaseth only in death." The sovereign has the prerogative to regulate religion as well as everything else, and the only consolation Hobbes offers the devout believer who professes a different faith is the somewhat inconsistent one that "belief and unbelief never follow men's commands." The only thing that holds men together in society is the erection of a power able "to overawe them all." And the only rationality men display is their implicit willingness (the "social contract") to surrender their plaguy rights and liberties in order to avoid the miseries they bring, the life of the "state of nature" which is "solitary, poor, nasty, brutish, and short."

Regarding man as wholly unsociable by nature, declaring that the ancient notion of man being "a creature born fit for society" is "certainly false," Hobbes ignored all the social bonds that spread out from the life of the family, all the traditions and indoctrinations that hold groups of men together, all the customs and innumerable adjustments that reveal the socializing tendencies of human nature. He was right only in asserting that beyond these there was need for the more embracing allegiance to a common government. But because he ignored these other things he relied solely on the absolute dominion of "one man or assembly of men." For Hobbes the only alternatives were total surrender of all rights to one sovereign power or—chaos, the state of nature which is the war of all against all.

The Western world was moving through processes of social change that made Hobbes' solution of the problem of order obsolete. It rejected the logic of his stark alternatives, total surrender or chaos. After much struggle and strife the principle gradually came to be accepted that civic allegiance did not require religious conformity. Diversity of belief and opinion and mode of thought inevitably developed in the more advanced countries, and there men came to understand that the social order was more, not less, secure if no sovereign power attempted to regulate or "coordinate" this diversity. They learned, in some measure at least, that a community is held together by many bonds, that many of these are not political, and that the liberty of men to pursue their different allegiances can attach them the more strongly to the greater unity that sustains their differences. *Legal* law is only the outer framework of the great firmament of order in society. . . .

THE MULTI-GROUP SOCIETY

Our main argument to this point is that the relation of man to the many groups and forms of organization to which he is more nearly or more distantly, more deeply or more superficially, attached is not solved by making one of these, whether the state or any other, the sole or inclusive object of his devotion, the one social focus of his being. There are other forms of order than the simple uni-centered order. There is the order of the balance and interadjustment of many elements. The conception of the all-inclusive all-regulating state is as it were a pre-Copernican conception of the social system. It appeals to the primitive sense of symmetry. As we explore more deeply the social universe we must discard it and frame a conception more adequate to social reality. In this exploration we learn, among other things, to understand better the nature of the multi-group society of modern man.

With this theme we shall deal here very briefly. We start from the fact that men have many different kinds of interest, that some of these are universal, in the sense that they are pursued by all men everywhere—all seek alike the satisfaction of certain elementary needs—while some are particular, making appeal to some men and not to others. Now since organization conveys power men learn to join with others so as to pursue their interests more effectively, each for each as well as each for all. Some of these interests are purely distributive, as are most economic interests. These we may speak of as like interests. The benefits of organization then accrue to each separately, so that the proceeds become private dividends, privately enjoyed by each. Other interests are *common,* in such wise that what each receives does not divide the product of the collectivity or lessen the benefits available to all the rest. To this class belong our cultural interests, the advance of knowledge, the exploration of art, of thought, of literature, of religion, and so forth. While the individual explorer or creator may receive particular awards, honors, or emoluments, the things that he explores or creates are potentially for all men. The wells of knowledge and of inspiration are not less full for the number who drink of them. When a man makes shoes it is for private use. When he makes a work of art or literature it is generally available, in one way or another, for the enjoyment of those who care for it.

Thus we can distinguish two types of organization, according to the nature of their product, leaving aside those that are intermediate or that in some manner combine both functions. Let us consider particularly the character of the second type. The cultural interests of men are exceedingly diverse and they exist on every level from the highest to the lowest. Many men have many minds. Children subjected to the same conditions and to the same influences react in very different ways. The attitudes of every group differ from the attitudes of every other. There is much incompatibility of outlook, of opinion and belief, of interpretation, of enjoyment, of the whole realization of life. Different men find very different sustenance within the fields of culture. In the seeking of this sustenance they are most themselves, most alive, most creative. Whether the sustenance be refined or vulgar, ample or meager, it is always that through which man seeks fulfillment. Everything else on earth is for the spirit that is in man nothing but apparatus or mechanism.

To satisfy this need men weave manifold relationships with their fellows. These extend from the give-and-take of love or comradeship through informal neighborly groupings for recreation, gossip, and so forth, up to the world-wide religious brotherhoods. There are two conclusive reasons why the numerous organizations thus engendered cannot be coordinated, over any range of territory great or small, under the aegis of the state. One is that the various organizations of the same cultural species are not only dissimilar in viewpoint, in method, in system of values, but actually antipathetic, alien, or hostile to one another in these respects. The differences are not reconcilable, nor are they so unimportant that they could be omitted from some universal charter or creed that would seek to embrace the different faiths within a single organizational fold. There are schools and styles in every form of art, in every field of cultural expression. The followers of any one abjure the other schools and styles. They take delight in their own, in the difference itself. Religions may alike proclaim the brotherhood of man or the fatherhood of God, but each has its own conception of the fatherhood. To coordinate them all into one would be to destroy their characteristic qualities, to drain them of their vitality. Coordination could be imposed only by sheer compulsion, and there is essential truth, even if the statement be too strongly worded, in the comment of the absolutist Hobbes, "Belief and unbelief never follow men's commands." Here we reach the second reason why neither the state nor any other form of organization can be all-embracing. Every way of life and every way of thought is nourished from within. It is the conviction that counts, the habit of mind, the devotion to a cause, the impulse to artistic expression, the congeniality of the group. It cannot be controlled from without, it cannot be directed by an indifferent or alien power. The creative force of all culture lies in its own spontaneity. It is killed by compulsion, reduced to a lifeless mechanism. Only the arrogance of the tyrant or of the dogmatist denies this truth. The dogmatist, secure in his own faith, would refuse other men the right to theirs, blindly seeking to destroy in them the same spirit of devotion from which he nourished his own being.

This truth was appreciated by T. H. Green, Hegelian though he was. In his *Lectures on the Principles of Political Obligation* he put forward the thesis that the state should not command the doing of things the value of which depends on the spirit in which they are performed and not on the mere externals of performance. This thesis is relevant to the whole area of cultural pursuits, though of course there arise marginal issues. We may put forward as a corollary of this thesis the further point that wherever actions are of such a kind that the performance of them by one group in one manner or style does not impede the performance of them by other groups in a diverse or contradictory manner or style such actions should not be on intrinsic grounds subject to coordination by the state or any other collectivity. When we say "on intrinsic grounds" we mean that, for example, no one should be forbidden to worship in his own way because the ruling powers entertain a religious objection to that form of worship. If however the worship involved, say, head-hunting or any other interference with the liberties of other men or any infringement of a criminal law that itself was not motivated by religious considerations but only by regard for public safety, then the performance would be subject to ban or control on extrinsic grounds. Our formula applies to the whole business of the expression of opinion, to the great realms of art and of thought in every form. One man is not precluded from advancing his opinion because another man has a contrary opinion. One man is not prevented from worshiping his own God because another man worships a different kind of God. Thus the objective conditions of public order do not demand uniformity in the cultural realm.

There is some contrast here between the cultural realm and the realm presided over by the organizations that fall predominantly within our second type. Economic activities, for example, cannot be left to the free arbitrament of individuals and groups without serious interference with public order. Thus an employer cannot lower the wages of his employees below the prevailing rate without seriously affecting the business of other employers who may have more concern for the welfare of their workers. He cannot extend the hours of labor without doing harm to his fellow employers as well as to his employees. He cannot "run his own business in his own way" as though it were a private imperium islanded from the rest of the world. No more can a man rightly claim to use his property in any way that seems good to him. His property not only is the fruit of the cooperative labor of many men but also it is the potential if not the actual source of the livelihood of others. If he neglects it, lets it run to waste or ruin, or actually destroys it he is injuring his fellows. He does the same thing if, say, he buys a patent from an inventor so as to prevent its exploitation, for the sake of his own greater profit. But there is no end of such examples. The economic order is a vast network of interdependence.

It might be claimed that a like statement could be made concerning the cultural order. A man cannot ventilate his opinions, cannot write a popular novel, cannot even worship his God without having some influence somehow on others. But there is a crucial difference. One man influences another in this manner because the other is freely responsive to that influence. We may adjudge the influence good or bad. We may condemn and oppose it. That also is our right. Opinions and creeds are for ever in conflict. Every man must find and respond to his own. There is no other way save compulsion, and we have already shown how alien and perilous that is. Moreover, with respect to economic relations the effect of one man's action on that of another is external and even automatic. The effect is measurable. We have a common standard, an objective index. Economic advantage, economic prosperity, has the same meaning for all men, even though some are more devoted to it than others. Thus the main objections that apply to the control of opinion are not relevant here. There is in fact only one relevant limit to specific economic controls, and that is precisely the consideration how far such controls conduce to the general economic welfare, how far they are efficient, how far they may go without restraining the spirit of initiative and enterprise, the spring of energy, vision, and responsibility, without which organization degenerates into the wasteful routine of bureaucracy.

Let us return, however, to our first conclusion, that the many cultural organizations of society have not and cannot have any one focus, cannot without losing their identity and their function be amalgamated and absorbed as mere departments of the state. Now we face the question of the interadjustment of all these organizations, and of the groups who maintain them, within the ordered yet free life of the community. Here is the essential problem of our multi-group society.

In every range and at every stage of social life this problem exists. In the simplest societies it is embryonic, and it reaches its full proportions only in the ambit of the modern nation. In the world of Western civilization it first became acute when various religious groups broke away from the universalism of the mediaeval church. The assumption that every community, every state, must have a single religion had a tremendous hold over the minds of most men. Only the sheer impossibility of maintaining this assumption at length persuaded them that they could live decently together, as members of one community, with those who professed a different faith. Centuries of persecution, war, and civil strife were needed to achieve this result. Manifestations of the old intolerance persist in the more liberal states while new forms of it, not associated with a religious principle, have appeared in some other states and shown a virulence not surpassed by the most extreme instances of earlier times. The full requirement of cultural liberty has rarely, if ever, been realized. In democratic countries it is now *politically* established. These countries have advanced far since the days when the king of one of them announced that he would "make the extirpation of the heretics his principal business." Gradually they passed from persecution to toleration and from toleration to the position that a man's religion is no concern of the state. The Edict of Nantes in 1598 was the first acknowledgment of a Roman Catholic government that "heretics" should be accorded civil rights, but even as late as 1776 the greatest of French radicals could assert that it was "impossible for men to live at peace with those they believe to be damned." In Protestant countries Roman Catholics were at length "tolerated," but it was only in 1819 that even England admitted them to citizenship. As for Jews, they have suffered longer and more grievously from persecution and the denial of civil rights than those who professed any other religion.

The principle set out in the First Amendment of the United States Constitution, that no law shall be enacted respecting an establishment of religion, has in effect been accepted by most democratic countries as well as by some others that cannot be placed in that category. But the problem of the multi-group society is not solved merely by the formal recognition of equality before the law. Such equality can exist while nevertheless minority groups or groups in an inferior economic or social position may be subject to such discrimination that they are practically excluded from participation in the life of the community. An outstanding example is the situation of the Negroes in the United States, particularly in the South. Other groups suffer discrimination to different degrees. The Jewish people are exposed to it but so in a measure are various ethnic groups, especially those of Eastern European countries, while yet stronger disabilities are applied against the Chinese, the Japanese, and the people of India. If we add to these groups the American Indians, the Filipinos, the Mexicans and other Latin-Americans we get the picture of a country constitutionally dedicated to the equality of men that nevertheless exhibits a complex pattern of rifts and fissures ramifying across the life of the community.

In different countries the problem takes different shapes. While in the United States minority groups are dispersed throughout the population, in some other countries they have a territorial locus, as in the Balkan area. Sometimes ethnic differences are associated with differences of religion. Often the disadvantaged groups occupy an inferior economic status. Not infrequently there is political as well as social and economic discrimination. This situation is found in its extreme form in colonial possessions, where the usual relation of majority and minority is reversed in favor of a dominant alien group.

Under all conditions the discrimination of group against group is detrimental to the wellbeing of the community. Those who are discriminated against are balked in their social impulses, are prevented from developing their capacities, become warped or frustrated, secretly or openly nurse a spirit of animosity against the dominant group. Energies that otherwise might have been devoted to constructive service are diverted and consumed in the friction of fruitless conflict. The dominant group, fearing the loss of its privileges, takes its stand on a traditional conservatism and loses the power of adapting itself to the changing times. The dominated, unless they are sunk in the worse apathy of sullen impotence, respond to subversive doctrines that do not look beyond the overthrow of the authority they resent. Each side conceives a false image of the other, denying their common humanity, and the community is torn asunder.

There is no way out of this impasse, apart from revolution, except the gradual readjustment of group relations in the direction of equality of opportunity—not merely of legal equality. Since this readjustment requires the abandonment of habits and traditions, the breaking of taboos, the reconstruction of the distorted images cherished by each group of the other, and the recognition that the narrower interests and fears and prides that stimulate discrimination and prejudice are adverse to the common good and often empty or vain, its achievement can be effected only through the arduous and generally slow processes of social education. The sense of community, dissipated by the pervading specialization of interests, needs to be reinforced. The common values of the embracing culture need to be reasserted and again made vital. The provision of equality of opportunity will not of itself bring about any such result. It will serve chiefly by removing a source of division that stands obdurately in the way of social cohesion. Only when this obstacle is removed can the positive values of the multi-group society be cultivated—if we have the wisdom to seek and to find them.

The sense of the need of community, if not the sense of community, is still alive and seeks embodiment. It is witnessed to by men's devotion to the nation and by their attachment to some local community they feel—or once felt—to be their home. But these bonds do not satisfy the need, do not sufficiently provide the experience of effective solidarity. The nation is too wide and too diverse. The local community is too heterogeneous, if it is large, or too limited, if it is small. Often the attachment to it is nostalgic or merely sentimental. So the unit gropes for a more satisfying unity, seeking to recover the spirit of cooperative living that animated the uni-group society. Sometimes men seek to recover it by methods that would reimpose the old order on the new. They would restore the myth of the uni-group society; they would make the all-inclusive state the sufficient focus of our moral and spiritual being; they would even, as totalitarians, ruthlessly coordinate out of existence our cultural heterogeneity. But there is no road back. The course of civilization is as irreversible as time itself. We have left behind the one-room social habitation of our ancestors. We have built ourselves a house of many mansions. Somehow we must learn to make it ours.

KARL MANNHEIM

Karl Mannheim (1893-1947) was born in Budapest and died in London. His professional career included, among other universities, Frankfort and London. His intellectual career took an interesting course, beginning, as it did, with Marxism, moving then to pragmatism, and issuing finally in an interest in Christian theology. Along with Scheler, Mannheim is one of the principal protagonists of a relatively new division of sociology called the sociology of knowledge.

Although Mannheim was greatly influenced by the Marxian tradition and even, as has been said, made it *salonfähig* or socially acceptable, his own views departed from it in important respects. For Marx, it will be remembered, social organization and cultural achievement have their base in modes of production, and it is these modes, as economic factors, which serve ultimately to explain the processes of social change. Mannheim popularized the Marxian conception contained in the sentence that "It is not the consciousness of men that determines their being, but their being that determines their consciousness," but he modified it to lay special emphasis upon the factor of class. Ideas have their origin in the matrix of society and are affected, if not indeed determined, by the class position of their originators. Thought is thus class-bound except in the case of the *freischwebende Intelligenz,* the class-free intelligentsia.

Two other concepts of Mannheim merit a comment—"ideology" and "utopia." Ideological thinking is that thinking which aims to justify and preserve the *status quo*. Utopian thinking, on the contrary, is directed toward change. Both of these types of thinking receive extended discussion in the excerpt that follows from *Ideology and Utopia,* translated from the German by Louis Wirth and Edward A. Shils. Mannheim's other works now in English include *Essays on the Sociology of Knowledge; Essays on Sociology and Social Psychology; Freedom, Power and Democratic Planning; Man and Society;* and *Essays on the Sociology of Culture.*

The Sociology of Knowledge*

The Sociological Concept of Thought

This book is concerned with the problem of how men actually think. The aim of these studies is to investigate not how thinking appears in textbooks on logic, but how it really functions in public life and in politics as an instrument of collective action.

Philosophers have too long concerned themselves with their own thinking. When they wrote of thought, they had in mind primarily their own history, the history of philosophy, or quite special fields of knowledge such as mathematics or physics. This type of thinking is applicable only under quite special circumstances, and what can be learned by analysing it is not directly transferable to other spheres of life. Even when it is applicable, it refers only to a specific dimension of existence which does not suffice for living human beings who are seeking to comprehend and to mould their world.

Meanwhile, acting men have, for better or for worse, proceeded to develop a variety of methods for the experiential and intellectual penetration of the world in which they live, which have never been analysed with the same precision as the so-called exact modes of knowing. When, however, any human activity continues over a long period without being subjected to intellectual control or criticism, it tends to get out of hand.

Hence it is to be regarded as one of the anomalies of our time that those methods of thought by means of which we arrive at our most crucial decisions, and through which we seek to diagnose and guide our political and social destiny, have remained unrecognized and therefore inaccessible to intellectual control and self-criticism. This anomaly becomes all the more monstrous when we call to mind that in modern times much more depends on the correct thinking through of a situation than was the case

* From *Ideology and Utopia* by Karl Mannheim. Reprinted by permission of Harcourt, Brace and Company, Inc., New York, and Routledge and Kegan Paul, Ltd., London.

in earlier societies. The significance of social knowledge grows proportionately with the increasing necessity of regulatory intervention in the social process. This so-called pre-scientific inexact mode of thought, however (which, paradoxically, the logicians and philosophers also use when they have to make practical decisions), is not to be understood solely by the use of logical analysis. It constitutes a complex which cannot be readily detached either from the psychological roots of the emotional and vital impulses which underlie it or from the situation in which it arises and which it seeks to solve.

It is the most essential task of this book to work out a suitable method for the description and analysis of this type of thought and its changes, and to formulate those problems connected with it which will both do justice to its unique character and prepare the way for its critical understanding. The method which we will seek to present is that of the sociology of knowledge.

The principal thesis of the sociology of knowledge is that there are modes of thought which cannot be adequately understood as long as their social origins are obscured. It is indeed true that only the individual is capable of thinking. There is no such metaphysical entity as a group mind which thinks over and above the heads of individuals, or whose ideas the individual merely reproduces. Nevertheless it would be false to deduce from this that all the ideas and sentiments which motivate an individual have their origin in him alone, and can be adequately explained solely on the basis of his own life experience.

Just as it would be incorrect to attempt to derive a language merely from observing a single individual, who speaks not a language of his own but rather that of his contemporaries and predecessors who have prepared the path for him, so it is incorrect to explain the totality of an outlook only with reference to its genesis in the mind of the individual. Only in a quite limited sense does the single individual create out of himself the mode of speech and of thought we attribute to him. He speaks the language of his group; he thinks in the manner in which his group thinks. He finds at his disposal only certain words and their meanings. These not only determine to a large extent the avenues of approach to the surrounding world, but they also show at the same time from which angle and in which context of activity objects have hitherto been perceptible and accessible to the group or the individual.

The first point which we now have to emphasize is that the approach of the sociology of knowledge intentionally does not start with the single individual and his thinking in order then to proceed directly in the manner of the philosopher to the abstract heights of "thought as such." Rather, the sociology of knowledge seeks to comprehend thought in the concrete setting of an historical-social situation out of which individually differentiated thought only very gradually emerges. Thus, it is not men in general who think, or even isolated individuals who do the thinking, but men in certain groups who have developed a particular style of thought in an endless series of responses to certain typical situations characterizing their common position.

Strictly speaking it is incorrect to say that the single individual thinks. Rather it is more correct to insist that he participates in thinking further what other men have thought before him. He finds himself in an inherited situation with patterns of thought which are appropriate to this situation and attempts to elaborate further the inherited modes of response or to substitute others for them in order to deal more adequately with the new challenges which have arisen out of the shifts and changes in his situation. Every individual is therefore in a twofold sense predetermined by the fact of growing up in a society: on the one hand he finds a ready-made situation and on the other he finds in that situation preformed patterns of thought and of conduct.

The second feature characterizing the method of the sociology of knowledge is that it does not sever the concretely existing modes of thought from the context of collective action through which we first discover the world in an intellectual sense. Men living in groups do not merely coexist physically as discrete individuals. They do not confront the objects of the world from the abstract levels of a contemplating mind as such, nor do they do so exclusively as solitary beings. On the contrary they act with and against one another in diversely organized groups, and while doing so they think with and against one another. These persons, bound together into groups, strive in accordance with the character and position of the groups to which they belong to change the surrounding world of nature and society or attempt to maintain it in a given condition. It is the direction of this will to change or to maintain, of this collective activity, which produces the guiding thread for the emergence of their problems, their concepts, and their forms of thought. In accord with the particular context of collective activity in which they participate, men always tend to see the world which surrounds them differently. Just as pure logical analysis has severed individual thought from its group situation, so it also separated thought from action. It did this on the tacit assumption that those inherent connections which always exist in reality between thought on the one hand, and group and activity on the other, are either insignificant for "correct" thinking or can be detached from these foundations without any resultant difficulties. But the fact that one ignores something by no means puts an end to its existence. Nor can anyone who has not first given himself whole-heartedly to the exact observation of the wealth of forms in which men really think decide *a priori* whether this severance from the social situation and context of activity is always realizable. Nor indeed can it be determined offhand that such a complete dichotomy is fully desirable precisely in the interest of objective factual knowledge.

It may be that, in certain spheres of knowledge, it is the impulse to act which first makes the objects of the world accessible to the acting subject, and it may be further that it is this factor which determines the selection of those elements of reality which enter into thought. And it is not inconceivable that if this volitional factor were entirely excluded (in so far as such a thing is possible), the concrete content would completely disappear from the concepts, and the organizing principle which first makes possible an intelligent statement of the problem would be lost.

But this is not to say that in those domains where attachment to the group and orientation towards action seem to be an essential element in the situation, every possibility of intellectual, critical self-control is futile. Perhaps it is precisely when the hitherto concealed dependence of thought on group existence and its rootedness in action becomes visible that it really becomes possible for the first time, through becoming aware of them, to attain a new mode of control over previously uncontrolled factors in thought.

This brings us to the central problem of the book. These remarks should make it clear that a preoccupation with these problems and their solution will furnish a foundation for the social sciences and answer the question as to the possibility of the scientific guidance of political life. It is, of course, true that in the social sciences, as elsewhere, the ultimate criterion of truth or falsity is to be found in the investigation of the object, and the sociology of knowledge is no substitute for this. But the examination of the object is not an isolated act; it takes place in a context which is coloured by values and collective-unconscious, volitional impulses. In the social sciences it is this intellectual interest, oriented in a matrix of collective activity, which provides not only the general questions, but the concrete hypotheses for research and the thought-models for the ordering of experience. Only as we succeed in bringing into the area of conscious and explicit observation the various points of departure and of approach to the facts which are current in scientific as well as popular discussion, can we hope, in the course of time, to control the unconscious motivations and presuppositions which, in the last analysis, have brought these modes of thought into existence. A new type of objectivity in the social sciences is attainable not through the exclusion of evaluations but through the critical awareness and control of them.

GEORGE A. LUNDBERG

George A. Lundberg (1895-   ), thirty-third president of the American Sociological Society (1943), was born in North Dakota. After taking his high school subjects by correspondence, he went to the university of his native state for his B.A. degree, which he received in 1920. His Master's degree (1922) was from the University of Wisconsin and his Doctor's (1925) from the University of Minnesota, where he wrote his dissertation on the history of poor-relief legislation. He also took work at the University of London in 1919 and at Columbia University in 1927. He has taught at the University of Washington, the University of Pittsburgh, Columbia University, and Bennington College. Since 1945 he has been Walker Ames Professor of Sociology at the University of Washington, where he also served as chairman of the department until 1953. From 1941 to 1945 he was editor of *Sociometry*. Lundberg's most important book, *Foundations of Sociology,* was published in 1939. Other works include *Social Research* (1929; rev. 1942) and *Can Science Save Us?* (1947). With others he has written *Trends in American Sociology* (1929), *Leisure* (1934), and *Sociology* (1954). In addition he has been a prolific contributor to the sociological journals.

Lundberg's thesis is simple, clear, and Comtean. With vigor and enthusiasm he has insisted that sociology is a natural science and that in order to become a successful science as well it must adopt the methods of the natural sciences. The answer to the question posed by the title of his little book—*Can Science Save Us?*—is an emphatic affirmative. Indeed, he goes further. Not only can science save us; it is the only thing that can. Positivism, operationalism, behaviorism, and a quantitative methodology are all congenial doctrines with Lundberg and he has frequently been at war with their opponents. He is one of the ablest of polemicists in the field of sociology.

The excerpt that follows, from *Foundations of Sociology,* illustrates his views both of science and of sociology.

From *Foundations of Sociology**

THE POSTULATES OF SCIENCE AND THEIR IMPLICATIONS FOR SOCIOLOGY

A. SCIENCE AS A TECHNIC OF ADJUSTMENT

Human sociology deals with the communicable adjustment technics which human groups have developed in their long struggle to come to terms with each other and with the rest of their environment. Science is, in the fields where it has been tried, the most conspicuously successful of these technics. As a human adjustment technic, science is primarily a *sociological* subject. Hence, if we start out with a brief consideration of this technic, we are not going outside our subject, but into a very vital aspect of it. Furthermore, since we wish to attempt to use this technic in the study of human group behavior itself, it is not only permissible but necessary to consider first the implications of that approach.

All inquiry begins with an experienced tension or imbalance of some sort in the inquiring organism. "Tension" and "imbalance" are words used to describe the result of an imperfect adjustment. "Adjustment" is in turn a word used to describe the situation under which the activities of an organism come to rest or equilibrium. The latter we define, as in physics, as the state of maximum probability in any organism or other system. We shall also refer to this state of maximum probability as the "normal" in any societal situation.

When certain tensions are formulated verbally they tend to take the form of a question. The tentative, experimental answer to this question is called a hunch, a guess, a hypothesis, or a postulate. A tentative answer of this kind serves as a basis for the orderly assembling of data which will establish more firmly, modify, or refute the hypothesis. A hypothesis which is cor-

* Reprinted by permission of The Macmillan Company.

roborated by repeated observations made by all qualified observers is thereupon called a principle or a law. Hunches, hypotheses, and guesses are produced, of course, by the responses of the organism to some situation, i.e., through data of experience, just as are the more adequately supported generalizations called principles or laws. "Hunches" differ from "principles" only in that the former rest upon more subjective (i.e., private, unverified), transitory, and quantitatively inadequate data. These characteristics frequently have misled men to believe that "hunches" are somehow generated spontaneously in the "mind" —a view which is here repudiated in favor of the position stated above.

In its maturest form the content of science consists of a body of verified propositions so related that under given rules (logic) the system is self-consistent and compatible with empirical observation. The more universally applicable these propositions are, i.e., the greater the variety of phenomena covered by the propositions, the more adequate is our knowledge of the field which they cover. Thus, nearly all empirically observed behavior of bodies from the point of view of their movement in space and time are "covered" by the general "principles" of physics. That is, events as "different" (from some points of view) as a man falling from a twentieth story window, a bullet fired into the air from a rifle, or drops of water in a rain storm, are all "explained" by the same basic principle.

No two cases of any of these events are ever identical in all respects nor are the natural conditions under which they occur ever the same. Yet by a process of ignoring all this variety and concentrating our attention on some single characteristic or aspect of the event (abstracting), we can make general statements that are equally true for all falling men, all rain drops, and all projectiles. This standardization of widely different events is achieved either through actual laboratory controls or through symbolic, usually statistical, devices. Thus are myriads of unique events of the most heterogeneous nature described, classified, summarized, and "explained" by showing that they are only special cases of a general rule or law already "understood" and in terms of which we have become accustomed to make adjustments to these events. We say that anything is "explained" or "understood" when we have reduced a situation to elements and correlations with which we are so familiar that we accept them as a matter of course so that our curiosity rests. By "element" we mean any component which we do not consider it necessary or possible further to analyze. Understanding a situation means, from the operational point of view, discovering familiar elements and correlations between them.

As a result of his familiarity with the principles which govern (describe, explain) most of the events in the so-called "physical" universe, man adjusts today to these events with relative emotional equanimity. That is, his curiosity and other adjustments come to rest relatively easily and without the fears, doubts, angers, and magical practices which accompanied his adjustment to these events in prescientific times. The absence of reliable principles brings forth a vast amount of trial-and-error blundering and emotional squirmings in social adjustments as compared to our relatively systematic adjustments to the "physical" world. Scientific knowledge operates, therefore, as a sort of mental hygiene in the fields where it is applied. If the morning paper reports an earthquake, an eclipse, a storm, or a flood, these events are immediately referred to their proper place in the framework of science, in which their explanation, i.e., their relationship to other events, has already been worked out. Hence each new event of this character calls for very little, if any, "mental" or "emotional" strain upon the organism so far as our intellectual adjustment to it as an event is concerned.

Political and social upheavals, on the other hand, such as wars, revolutions, and crime are to most people a matter of shock and much personal recrimination and other emotionalism. Yet these societal events are "natural" in the same sense that "physical" events are "natural." "Natural" and "physical" are of course merely words by which we describe a relatively objective (corroborated) type of adjustment to the phenomena so designated. Unfortunately, it is at present very generally assumed that these terms represent not merely a type of adjustment technic on our part, but that such terms as "physical" and "natural" are inherent characterizations of *some* phenomena in the universe but not of others. The other type or types of data are variously and vaguely designated as "social," "cultural," "mental," and "spiritual."

These terms, instead of being regarded as describing those situations to which we make at present a relatively subjective and emotional type of adjustment, are likewise *attributed to data as inherent characteristics.* The result of this semantic confusion has been a most mischievous separation of fields of knowledge into the "natural" and "physical" on the one hand as against the "social" and "cultural" (mental, nonmaterial, spiritual) on the other. As a consequence, it has been assumed that the methods of studying the former field are not applicable to the latter. The generally admitted lag in the progress of the "social" as contrasted with the "physical" sciences has been a further result.

The history of science consists largely of the account of the gradual expansion of realms of the "natural" and the "physical" at the expense of the "mental" and the "spiritual." One by one "spiritual" phenomena have become "physical." This is not the place to review that history. It is readily available elsewhere and its implications for the point here under discussion are reasonably clear. The evolution of the concept of the "soul" is especially relevant, because its final stage of transition or translation by way of the "mind" into purely "physical" concepts is still under way. The resistance which this transition is encountering in some quarters is especially instructive because it illustrates the widespread linguistic confusion as to the nature of verbal symbols.

B. THE POSTULATES OF SCIENCE

To prevent constant digression and misunderstandings from arising, it is necessary in this connection to call attention explicitly to the postulates and their corollaries upon which this volume proceeds. This will seem to some to be a needless repetition and elaboration of the obvious. To others the postulates will seem unjustified. The implications of these assumptions will be set forth in this and subsequent chapters. Only as much of the reasoning will be given here as is necessary to make clear the assumptions themselves. The ultimate justification for the point of view adopted must wait upon the results it yields in clarifying thinking, in stimulating cumulatively productive research, and finally in providing that groundwork of knowledge on which alone effective practical adjustments can be made.

The basic postulates regarding the nature of "reality" and "knowledge" upon which all science proceeds may be briefly stated as follows:

1. All data or experience with which man can become concerned consist of *the responses of the organisms-in-environment.* This includes the postulate of an external world and variations both in it and the responders to it.

2. Symbols, usually verbal, are invented to represent these responses.

3. These symbols are the immediate data of all communicable knowledge and therefore of all science.

4. All propositions or postulates regarding the more ultimate "realities" must always consist of inference, generalizations, or abstractions from these symbols and the responses which they represent.

5. These extrapolations are in turn represented symbolically, and we respond to them as we respond to other phenomena which evoke behavior.

C. COROLLARIES AND IMPLICATIONS FOR SOCIOLOGY

Some of the corollaries and implications of these postulates, especially as they affect present methods in the social sciences, need to be emphasized and elaborated briefly.

1. The Inferential Nature of Knowledge and "Reality"

In the first place according to these postulates, all statements about the nature of the universe or any part of it are necessarily a verbalization of somebody's responses to *that which* evoked these responses. The nature of that which evoked them must always be an inference from the immediate datum, namely, our symbolized sensory experience. All assertions about the *ultimate* "reality," "nature," "essence," or "being" of "things," or "objects" are therefore unverifiable hypotheses, and hence outside the sphere of science. Conversely, we assume that man and culture are definitely part of the cosmos. The *cosmos* is a word by which we designate the sum total of all the influences that precipitate responses in man. We assume further, that all phenomena of man and culture, in common with all nonhuman phenomena, are entirely contained within the cosmos and entirely dependent upon the energy transformations within that cosmos. We start with symbolized human responses as the immediate datum. As a metaphysical necessity we grant *that which* in the universe outside of the responding mechanism precipitates the response. After this is done, science is not concerned with the particular metaphysical hypotheses anyone may prefer to hold about the more ultimate nature of *that which* arouses responses.

2. Words as Objective Phenomena

It follows from the above that for scientific purposes all attempted distinctions, hypotheses, or assumptions regarding differences in the *ultimate* "nature" of so-called "physical" as contrasted with "social" data, between "material" and "immaterial," "mental," "spiritual," or "cultural" phenomena are ruled out. No relevant data (e.g., behavior designated by such words as "spiritual," etc.) are ruled out if they are manifest in human behavior of *any observable kind*. At present we shall attempt to deal only with the more objective of these behaviors. But since objectivity is here regarded *not as a characteristic of things but as those ways of responding which can be corroborated by others,* it follows that the framework of science affords place for all known or knowable data. Of course, the less developed our objectifying technics are for certain experiences (i.e., the "subjective" and "spiritual") the greater is the task of communicating them so that they can be verified (the test of objectivity). Indeed, this process of objectifying them may involve analysis, reclassification, and designation by new and strange symbols. Many terms at present employed probably will be abandoned entirely as devoid of content when the behavior phenomena to which they once referred have been more adequately described by other terms. As science has advanced, this has been true of all prescientific terms and categories. In this connection we encounter one of the chief obstacles to the translation of subjective experience into objective data, i.e., communicating the former and rendering them verifiable. Let us take only one illustration.

In the opinion of the best chemists as recently as 150 years ago, *phlogiston* was a necessary element in the explanation of combustion. The theory was that in all materials that burn there is present phlogiston, a substance without color, odor, taste, or weight. Even Priestley, to whom the discovery of oxygen is usually credited, continued to maintain during his lifetime the existence of phlogiston and the part it was supposed to play in combustion. By experiments involving much careful and accurate weighing, Lavoisier was able to demonstrate finally the unnecessary character of the hypothetical entity, phlogiston. Nevertheless, the older chemists of the day, thoroughly habituated to thinking about fire in terms of phlogiston continued to "feel" that the new explanation "left something out." It did leave something out, namely, a *word* to which the chemists of the day had become thoroughly habituated, and which was therefore as "real" to them as the word "wood" or whatever other words are used to symbolize the factors assumed to be present in a given fire. However, we do not contend that by abandoning phlogiston, modern chemists refuse to recognize a vital or relevant element in the explanation of fire.

Today, however, a considerable number of students of societal phenomena are still firmly convinced that the phenomena with which they have to deal cannot be adequately described or explained without, for example, a category called "mind," which carries with it a whole vocabulary of subsidiary terms (thought, experience, feeling, judgment, choice, will, value, emotion, etc., etc.). "We forget that these nouns are merely substitutes for verbs and go hunting for the things denoted by the nouns; but there are no such things; there are only the activities that we started with." By this oversight, also, we avoid the necessity of defining operationally the behavior units into which the phenomena of any field must be divided for scientific purposes. Any attempt to deal in other words with the behavior which these words are used to represent meets with the most determined resistance on the ground that "*something* has been left out." And what has been left out? Why, "will," "feeling," "ends," "motives," "values," etc. These are the phlogiston of the social sciences. Argument or demonstration that the behavior represented by these words is accorded full recognition within the present framework of the "physical" sciences are to some apparently as futile as were the arguments against phlogiston to Priestley. He *just knew* that any system which left out the word phlogiston was *ipso facto* fallacious. I have no doubt that a considerable part of the present content of the social sciences will turn out to be pure phlogiston. That fact will be discovered as soon as someone attempts operational definitions of the vocabulary which at present confounds these sciences. Yet, it is on the basis of such words that we undertake to set up a separate universe to which the methods of inquiry recognized in the other ("physical") universe are held not to apply. The Germans properly designate this former field as that of the "Geisteswissenschaften." The distinction between "science" and "social science" is, in fact, quite generally accepted as a matter of course. The present work continues, as a matter of necessity, to use the terminology here criticized because it is our purpose to communicate with the present generation. Also it is necessary to bring about the desired transition through the substitution of a new content for some of the old terms rather than abandoning them outright. Useless or undesirable words should be allowed to die as their content is taken over by new and more adequate terms. . . .

The following illustration from contemporary sociological literature further illustrates the tendency to regard familiar words as essential components of situations: "There is an essential difference, from the standpoint of causation, between a paper flying before the wind and a man flying from a pursuing crowd. The paper knows no fear and the wind no hate, but without fear and hate the man would not fly nor the crowd pursue. If we try to reduce fear to its bodily concomitants we merely substitute the concomitants for the reality experienced as fear. *We denude the world of meanings for the sake of a theory itself a false meaning which deprives us of all of the rest.*"

Note the essential nature of the words *hate* and *fear* in this analysis. Even their translation into terms of their behavior referents is alleged to "denude the world of meanings." Now if anyone wishes to interpret the flying of a paper before the wind in terms of hate and fear, as has doubtless frequently been done in ages past, I know of no way of refuting the analysis for it is determined by the terms, the framework, and the meanings adopted. *These categories* are not given in the phenomenon. Neither are the categories I should use in scientific description so given. In fact, I have no objection to the words "fear" and "hate" if they are defined in terms of physico-chemical, biolinguistic, or sociological behavior subject to objective verification. I have no doubt, either, that descriptions in these terms would vary widely in different cases of flying objects. For this reason, I do not declare MacIver's analysis of the man and the crowd as *false*. I merely point out that possibly I could analyze the situation in a frame of reference not involving the words "fear" or "hate" but in operationally defined terms of such character that all qualified observers would independently make the same analysis and predict the behavior under the given circumstances. Such a demonstration would not, of course, constitute an adequate substitute explanation to some people any more than Lavoisier's interpretation of fire was satisfactory to Priestley. Indeed, that interpretation is still meaningless to those not familiar with the framework and terminology of chemistry and physics. On the other hand, the principle of parsimony requires that we seek to bring into the same framework the explanations of all flying objects. In an animistic culture the imputation of fear to all flying objects (under the above circumstances) fulfills this requirement. Gradually, however, this explanation was abandoned for all inorganic phenomena, and more recently for the lower animals. The fear-hate categories are not generally used in describing or "explaining" the approach of the amoeba to its food although even the amoeba approaches food that can move away in a different way than it approaches food which has no power of locomotion.

The idea that the same general laws may be applicable to both "physical" and societal behavior may seem fantastic and inconceivable to many people. It is literally inconceivable to those who do not possess the symbolic technology in terms of which alone it can be conceived. For this reason, it may be that the next great developments in the social sciences will come not from professed social scientists but from people trained in other fields. The contributions of men like Comte, Ward, and Pareto, all of them technically trained in other sciences and in mathematics, is significant in this connection. In present day psychology, likewise, the major contributions are being made by men trained in engineering, physiology, and other "physical" sciences. This does not mean the contribution of social scientists will be worthless. They have performed and will perform valuable services in pointing out data, problems, and difficulties in their field. With much data already available, scientists with more adequate technical equipment will probably make the most important contributions to systematic sociology for some time to come. In the meantime, the general scientific and technical equipment of social scientists is, of course, rapidly improving.

The doctrine that man is the one unique object in the universe whose behavior cannot be explained within the framework found adequate for all others is, of course, a very ancient and respectable one. We merely make the contrary assumption in this work. From the latter point of view a paper flying before the wind is interpreted as the behavior of an object of *specified characteristics* reacting to a stimulus of *specified characteristics* within a specified field of force. Within this framework we describe the man and the crowd, the paper and the wind. The characteristics of these elements (and they may be specified to any degree desired) would never be the same in any two cases of wind and paper or of men and crowds. But it is the faith of science that sufficiently general principles can be found to cover all these situations, and that through these principles reliable predictions can be made of the probability of specific events. . . .

4. *The Visibility and Objectivity of Societal Phenomena*

Within our universe of discourse, then, all data are known to us only through human responses and we infer both the existence and the characteristics of any phenomena from these responses. A taboo, a custom, an "idea," or a belief is, therefore, as a datum, as "tangible," "real," observable, measurable, and otherwise susceptible of scientific study as is a stone, a table, or a horse. The contrary assumption flows from the fact that the responses aroused through certain senses, notably of touch and sight, being responses for which the most highly developed objective symbols have been invented, are therefore assumed to possess a "tangibility" which events that have not yet been thus symbolized do not have. Now the words "tangibility," "reality," etc., may be used profitably to describe a degree of objectification of our responses to some data while such terms as "tangible," "spiritual," "nonmaterial," describe a lesser degree of objectivity of responses.

But these terms cannot be used to indicate intrinsic characteristics of data in the present frame of reference. The alleged greater "tangibility" of certain "physical" events resides not in the events, but in our more highly objectified methods of responding to them. *That response* which we call custom, affection, pain, anger, the welfare of our grandchildren, the Future Life, or what not, consists of reactions of sense receptors to stimuli from outside or inside the organism as truly as our experience of a stone or a tree.

This point is fundamental and must be taken quite literally if we really contemplate bringing societary phenomena within the framework of natural science. We must be able to show that symbols such as honor, duty, loyalty, etc., and the behavior which they represent are as observable and objective data as are baseball, the seasonal flight of birds, or the jump of an electric spark. "Baseball," "flight," and "spark" are words by which one person communicates to another certain of his responses to whatever phenomena precipitate these responses. Honor, duty, and loyalty are another group of such words designating people's responses to other phenomena. The capacity of a word or any other stimulus to evoke a given response depends upon our conditioning, at some time in our existence as an organism, to respond in a given way in a given stimulus-response situation. All of these words stand for behavior of some sort. To the extent that numbers of individuals use the same word to designate similar behavior phenomena (i.e., to the extent that numbers of individuals behave in a given way in a given situation) it is conventional to designate the phenomena to which they respond as objective. Phenomena are objective in science to the extent that this criterion of agreement, corroboration, or verifiability is satisfied.

Failure to grasp this relativistic meaning of objectivity is perhaps the basic reason for fundamental misunderstandings in the social sciences. The common objection to the position advanced in this book, usually designated as behavioristic or positivistic, is that it cannot, it is said, take account of what men feel or think. In elaboration of this statement Cooley's "bold statement that the solid facts of social life are the facts of the imagination" is quoted. "My friend is best defined," it is said, "as what I imagine he will do and say to me on occasion"—a surprisingly behavioristic statement. The point is further illustrated by the statement that "when John and Tom meet there are six persons present. There is John's real self (known only to his Maker) [sic], John's idea of himself, and John's idea of Tom, and, of course, three corresponding Toms. Cooley goes on to say that there are really twelve or more, including John's idea of Tom's idea of John's idea of Tom. In these 'echoes of echoes of echoes' of personality we have an *a fortiori* consideration of the importance of *the subjective aspect of conduct.*"

If it is assumed that any social scientist, behaviorist or other, proposes to ignore any or all of the above data, it is not surprising that the thought has caused considerable agitation. No supporter of such a view is ever cited by the critics, and I have never in the course of a considerable survey of the literature encountered an exponent of the position. The better known authorities, including the most extreme behaviorists, have specifically disavowed any such view. Not only have the behaviorists apparently failed to communicate what their position is, but they have succeeded in arousing in their critics nightmares of vast proportions. The obvious fact is that communication has broken down on this subject. Whether the fault lies at the sending or the receiving end is not immediately relevant. The important thing is to clarify the position if possible, since the possibility of objective study of phenomena of the kind illustrated above is obviously basic to a science of sociology.

I hold that "echoes" and "shadows" are just as truly physical phenomena subject to objective scientific study as are the phenomena which shadows and echoes reflect. The charge that we propose to ignore the phenomena of "imagination," "thought," or "consciousness" is as unwarranted as would be a similar charge that physicists deny the phenomena of shadows and echoes. The physicist demands verifiable sensory evidence of echoes and shadows exactly as he does of original noises that echo or of objects that cast shadows. The sociologist must similarly demand sensory evidences of the imaginings, thoughts, and other phenomena of "consciousness." When he has such evidences he is as much interested in the phenomena of what men think and feel as in any other data. Imaginings, thoughts, and feelings manifest themselves if at all through symbolic or other neuromuscular behavior. As such they are as proper subject for scientific study as are all other phenomena. This holds for all so-called introspective phenomena as well as for phenomena assumed to originate outside of the observer. (Actually, of course, all *responses* are "subjective" or "introspective" in the sense that the response occurs before it is communicated.)

The assumed inaccessibility of the data of consciousness to objective study arises from the undeveloped state of the technic for such study. No behaviorist questions the scientific validity of a physician taking his own temperature, pulse count, or recording by any method subject to verification, his observation of the behavior of any part of his organism in relation to stimuli of whatever kind, societal or "physical." It is a problem of developing an objective terminology and instruments with which to observe and describe experience which is now very inadequately communicable or subject to verification. "The possibility of one man's observing another's mental processes, like the possibility of observing another's digestion becomes a question of developing laboratory technique." This technic need not contemplate substituting our experience for his directly. Like all other knowledge it is usually inferred from objective signs. In short, it is only a matter of what degree of objectivity we shall require before we can use them as a basis for scientific generalizations. Of course, we are using and should continue in the meantime to use these data for all they are worth in their present form.

The same reasoning holds for the common assumption that a strictly behavioristic description of societal behavior denies "the relevance of anticipated social ends as a partial determinant of social action." Anticipated ends, in the sense of "conscious" prevision, whenever they become stimuli to action, exist as words or other symbols to which the organism responds as it does to other stimuli. The same is true of memories, "values," "meanings," "ideals," "ideas," and all the rest of the phenomena which are alleged to be unapproachable by the accepted methods of science. Again, the error lies in assuming that the telic character or purposiveness which we like to attribute to societal behavior is an intrinsic character of the behavior rather than our way of describing it. All phenomena *may* be described in teleological, theological, or magical terms. We have merely abandoned the practice of ascribing "malice" to the tree which falls "in order to" block our path, or of attributing "planning" to the amoeba in approaching its food.

Physicists have likewise lost interest in the question of whether an echo or a shadow is "objective," "real," or "exists." The investigation and description of an "echo of an echo of an echo" proceeds according to the same principles as the investigation and description of any other noise. When we adopt this attitude toward the "intangibles" which so bedevil and frustrate contemporary sociological theory, we shall presently find that certain metaphysical questions of "existence," "reality," "subjectivity," and "tangibility" can take their place with the question of how many angels can stand on the point of a needle and other profound issues that agitated learned men of other ages.

Full inquiry into the conditions affecting the observed behavior is required in any case. If it is desired to designate a certain type of conditions common among human beings by the term "malice," there is no objection to doing so. It is the use of the word as a substitute for the investigation of the conditions that is here under criticism. As convenient classifications of types of data there is, likewise, no objection to designating some as "physical" and "material" and others as "cultural," "social," or even "spiritual," provided we do not make assumptions that these classifications affect the method by which we know the phenomena in question, i.e., through sensory responses of some kind. It is true that both an iron fence and a taboo will keep men from touching an object or going to a certain place. It is also true that the taboo will have this effect only upon the behavior of men conditioned to a certain culture, while the fence may have the same effect on all men. Therefore, by men in general, greater objectivity is ascribed properly to the fence. But *to the men conditioned by the given culture,* the taboo has the same degree of objectivity, the test of objectivity in either case being the observed behavior of the men. From this behavior of the men, the existence, meaning, objectivity, and other characteristics of both fence and taboo is inferred. Obviously, the fact that we ascribe equal degrees of objectivity to two things for given groups of men does not mean that we claim they are the "same," "alike," or "similar" in any or all *other* respects. The fact to keep in mind is that all existence, data, reality, or being is relative to some observer and, of course, to his frame of reference. Obviously, to some of the lower animals with different sensory apparatus and background of experiences, many data sensed by all men do not exist and *vice versa*. Likewise, different men sense different things. Things which all or nearly all men respond to in very much the same way, i.e., an iron fence, we call relatively objective, physical, material, tangible, etc. Things to which only relatively few, or only one, respond in the same way without special cultural conditioning are termed subjective, intangible, spiritual, etc. We are not contending that the data called intangible and spiritual today may not be properly so described. We merely point out wherein their intangibility resides, so that, if we develop response technics which permit the checking and corroboration of the responses to things today called intangible, they would then be tangible. Whether this can ever be done to some "subjective" data remains to be seen. In any case we are more likely to make progress in this quest if we assume as a working hypothesis that it can be done. We have no choice but to proceed on that hypothesis if we wish to bring these data within the domain of science.

HOWARD BECKER

Howard Becker (1899-) was born in New York City and educated at Northwestern University after a youth of considerable hardship which involved manual labor at the age of fourteen and admission to college by special examination. He took his Ph.D. degree at the University of Chicago, after a year at the University of Cologne, and served as an instructor in sociology both at Chicago and at the University of Pennsylvania before going to Smith College in 1931. In 1937 he became professor of sociology at the University of Wisconsin, where he has remained, serving as chairman of the department from 1951 to 1955. He became President of the American Sociological Society in 1959.

Becker has made important contributions to at least four different areas of sociology. His work with Harry Elmer Barnes on the history of social thought—*Social Thought from Lore to Science* (2 volumes, 1938; rev. 1952)—is almost without question the best treatment of its subject in any language. He has written on Germany, particularly on youth movements in that country; on marriage and the family; and extensively on sociological theory. In this last respect mention should be made especially of his useful translation and adaptation of the *Allgemeine Soziologie* of Leopold von Wiese that he did in 1932 under the title of *Systematic Sociology*. He has exerted an influence in addition on many men now active in academic posts who took their graduate work with him at the University of Wisconsin.

The excerpt that follows is a small sample of Becker's writing and thinking. It illustrates some of the differences between the sacred and the secular, a distinction he has been interested in developing in recent years.

*The Sacred and the Secular**

The Comprehensiveness of Sacred and Secular

Sacred and secular values and value systems represent a quite abstract level of formulation, although they inductively derive from very substantial bodies of empirical evidence. In the later part of this chapter, dealing with some of the history of sacred-secular constructs, the close interplay of induction-deduction is made reasonably clear; the constructs progressively emerged when certain perplexities arose, and were not set up in advance. But here the writer anticipates unduly; it seems best to continue with substantive presentation.

Reluctance and readiness to accept or initiate social change provide the construction lines of what may be called a sacred-secular scale or continuum. Any society or part thereof that imparts to or elicits from its members evaluations that can be altered, if at all, only in the face of definite emotionalized reluctance is a sacred society—a shorthand term for a society bearing a cultural system making for the reluctance indicated. Conversely, any society or part thereof that imparts to or elicits from its members evaluations leading to well-marked readiness to change is a secular society in a similar shorthand sense. Problems relating to social and cultural change (see Chap. 9, by Alvin Boskoff, in the present volume), therefore, are built into the sacred-secular scale, as are also what in some ways are their counterparts, problems of social control.

Given such considerations, and the empirical evidence relating to them, sacred values must be treated as comprising far more than the religious, divine, spiritual, and so on. Any conduct whatsoever may be viewed as hinging on sacred considerations when it is accompanied by characteristic reluctance to change values and/or their related needs. Putting it differently, unwill-

* Reprinted by permission of the author and Henry Holt and Company. From *Modern Sociological Theory,* edited by Howard Becker and Alvin W. Boskoff. Copyright 1957.

ingness or inability or both—linked with distress or similar signs of tension—to alter any aspect of one's "way of life" is sacred evaluation. The person who makes such evaluation has certain needs so interwoven with certain values that he feels and acts in an "upset" manner when change in those needs and values is even suggested, let alone demanded.

Culture Is Crucial

Whether sacred or secular, all values are culturally defined in some manner and degree. What is sacred to any people in eating, mating, fighting, and worshiping is what they have been taught in some fashion or another to hold sacred. In discernibly different but similar ways, the same is true of secular values, for although the secular is not merely the reverse of the sacred, it is still safe to say that readiness for and liking of change must be learned. Ability or willingness to change are, like their opposites, acquired capacities. The learning of secular conduct is clearly, from what has been said above, much more than the acquisition of avowedly or unavowedly nonreligious, profane, or skeptical needs and values. These are all secular, of course, but the designation reaches far beyond them. Any sort of conduct may be viewed as centering on values designable in secular terms when well-marked needs to seek those values, whatever the changes entailed, are in some way evident. Persons so evaluating have learned to concentrate on certain ends, tangible or intangible as the case may be, in a manner such that they may even be unable to refrain from pursuing them by any means available and regardless of the disapproval, however severely expressed, of their fellows.

Here likewise culture is powerfully at work. No innovation ever is entirely without a "cultural base," and from such a standpoint all innovations are culturally conditioned, but over and above this it is obvious that if they are not to disappear when their introducers die, they must be passed on to others who have come to accept or, in some cases, to welcome them. Stated otherwise, changes in culture must be imparted to at least one succeeding generation if they are to become more than merely private variations or deviations; communication over time is indispensable. Cultural changes must be transmitted, learned, and shared quite as definitely as must cultural continuities. Sacred and secular value-systems, then, are both products and producers of culture, particularly when viewed as embodied in evaluative actions leading subsequent actors to evaluate similarly.

From Reluctance to Readiness

The writer earlier remarked that the major theoretical task now under survey is the constructing of a sacred-secular continuum along which evaluations can be ranged. Such a continuum, if it is formalized as a scale, should have specified end points. The present state of our knowledge makes specification of this kind rather venturesome or even somewhat arbitrary, but it cannot be avoided. Therefore, let us array several types of evaluation along a line leading from estimated maximum reluctance to change old values to estimated maximum readiness to seek new values. (Incidentally, "old" and "new" must be assigned the definitions offered, in whatever ways, by the *subjects* concerned; it makes no difference for present purposes whether the values involved are "really" old or new.) As long as unduly precise connotations are not thereby introduced, the scale in question may be constructed algebraically—that is, from maximum plus to maximum minus, with a zero or transitional point somewhere about the middle.

What Is Holy Must Be Kept Holy

Starting with maximum plus as the strongest empirically manifested reluctance to change, we may give appropriate attention to the frequent embracing of martyrdom for oneself or the inflicting of it on others that men have time out of mind practiced for the sake of preserving religious needs and values. Their orientation toward what they have regarded as supernatural forces or beings has frequently been so compulsive that they have sacrificed themselves or their fellows rather than permit changes in the evaluation of those orientations, or supernatural agencies, or both. Now and then, it may be admitted, there prevails a conception that impious innovators are supernaturally punished, and that hence the pious need not themselves take action. "Vengeance is mine; I will repay, saith the Lord." When this is the case, the heretical deviant merely becomes an outcast or, less frequently, may be allowed to remain a member of the society, albeit at the lower levels. But in spite of this and other exceptions noted later, holy evaluation in one or another form bringing sacrificial extinction with it has so often been evident that there seems considerable warrant for placing it at the maximum-plus pole of the sacred-secular scale.

Indulging in terminological comment: "Holy" is expressly limited, following established precedent, to evaluations bound up with supernaturalism, which is to say with religion as here viewed. Much confusion has resulted and will probably continue to result, from the loose use of "religion" to designate nonsupernaturalistic evaluations of compelling kind—for example "Communism as a religion." Similar confusion comes about when the sacred and the religious are treated as coterminous; religion *per se* is but one aspect of the sacred. A very large amount of sacred conduct has little or nothing to do with the supernaturalistically oriented—which is to say, with the religious. The holy, on the other hand, has long been properly restricted in English to religious manifestations in the narrow and only suitable sense: holy water, holy days, holy wedlock, holy communion, holy orders, the Holy Land, His Holiness the Pope, the Holy Bible, and so on. Attention to the holy as a kind of evaluation inseparably linked with supernaturalism was taken as a matter of course by anthropologists and sociologists until well beyond Tylor's time—in fact, until Durkheim and Sumner (to name only the more prominent) befogged significant distinctions by using all-inclusive and vague categories. Only in the second quarter of the present century, with Otto and other students of comparative religion, was the importance of the holy again recognized. Even now only a few sociological investigators such as Goode seem to have kept abreast of the newer evidence and emphasis; for the most part, anthropologists as well as sociologists seem confused and out of date. Unless religion, which is to say holy evaluation, which is to say conduct oriented toward objects regarded as supernatural, is analytically distinguished from other varieties of the sacred, little predictive worth attaches to it as a category.

Nobody Loves a Traitor

Having at least provisionally placed the holy at the plus extreme of the evaluation scale, it must nevertheless be noted that the basic criterion, action involving martyrdom or its equivalents, is also present in several other kinds of sacredness. The loyalistic, for example, comprising clan allegiance, patriotism, identification with one or another race, class, faction, party, or what not, calls forth everything from "altruistic suicide" to murder—or shall we say "liquidation"? It is easy to bring to mind instance after instance of the terrific power of loyalism; multitudes of men have perished because of their own or their opponents' devotion to groups of one or another kind. So numerous are the instances, in fact, that loyalistic sacredness seems closely to rival and now and again to surpass the holy variety as a contender for the maximum-plus position on the scale.

The historical record is by no means clear, and it may well be that supernaturalism is not the most important source, numerically speaking, of "supreme sacrifice." The obscurity enshrouding much of the past is increased by the fact that the holy and the loyalistic are often difficult if not virtually impossible to separate, not only empirically but also analytically. Just where the line can be appropriately drawn between Hindu religious belief, practice, and feeling as such, on the one hand, and the intermeshing evaluative conduct constituting the structure of Hindu castes, guilds, village councils, and similar loyalty-eliciting groups on the other, baffles the most thoroughly informed students of such matters.

Moreover, there is a substantial amount of evidence showing that it may occasionally be far safer openly to denounce a god than to assert independence of a group, much less to become traitor to it. A researcher, in his work among the Winnebago, found that one skeptic boldly expressed contempt for the holiest of the tribal deities and that, when the deity in question appeared in order to inflict lethal disease as punishment, his impious critic remained immune. The consequence was that the deity, hoping to escape ridicule, begged the man to succumb, but in vain. The same researcher also found that nonobservance or defiance of established social relations carried far more serious consequences than did religious dissent; those unable or unwilling to conform socially faced banishment or death. In short, religious heretics sometimes held their own, but social mavericks never did.

In spite of this and like evidence, however, the writer feels that although the loyalistically sacred, together with several other varieties to be mentioned later, may come very close indeed to the holy in life-or-death power, the holy has probably been stronger in a somewhat greater number of cases. This feeling arises from a considerable amount of reading in the relevant sources, but proof or disproof would require elaborate and costly research.

The Bonds of Intimacy

Thus far we have dealt only with the holy and the loyalistic, but several other kinds of sacredness must be discussed, among them that connected with what have long been called primary groups. Intimate sacredness, represented by ties with playfellows, friends, comrades, mates, and partners, is encountered on every hand. Intimacy, once well and favorably established, is usually regarded as not lightly to be terminated or even altered in slight degree.

Manifestly, the grounds of intimacy, as of all other aspects of the sacred and the secular, differ strikingly from one society to another, but the world over we encounter evidence of the supreme devotion that it calls forth; it also often rivals the holy in the sacrificial zeal it evokes. Cooley's praise of democracy had little realistic reference to the mass political phenomena apparent to other than Pollyanna observers even in his day, but what he had to say about kindly give-and-take, shared responsibility, good faith, willingness to cooperate, and neighborliness was warranted for what he saw among face-to-face and relatively small groupings practicing—however short of perfection—a kind of rural and small town American version of nineteenth-century Protestant Christianity. The core of his sociology was a cheerful exaggeration of the scope and power of the intimately sacred, but he did validly point to its importance.

The Moralistic and Its Qualifications

Proceeding further along the scale, it seems that moralistic sacredness may be assigned the next section of the continuum. This variety has a range more limited than that of the familiar mores, for the latter has been so loosely used, from the very beginning, that it takes in everything from the holy to the fitting and has been applied to some aspects of secular conduct as well. What is here meant by the moralistic covers evaluations referring directly to enjoined or forbidden types of conduct specifically distinguishable from the total personalities of those engaged therein. Concretely, a man may be viewed as having bad morals but not as being a hopelessly bad man; further, his morals can be improved piecemeal, as it were. In contrast, grave breaches of the holy, loyalistic, and intimate put the offender beyond the pale in many societies; condemnation is complete.

In the case of the moralistic, to be sure, the "manners and customs" concerned are often so entrenched that marked indignation is the immediate consequence of even the mere suggestion that they should be changed. Nevertheless, the potential or actual violator is not exterminated, cast out, or wholly ostracized; there is some possibility of making amends. This may be illustrated by the fact that in American society, particularly of almost bygone rural type, violations of sexual morals among the unmarried could be remedied by the "shotgun wedding." With moralistic requirements thus satisfied, the ensuing conduct of the once outraged guardian of the moral code was ordinarily the reverse of violent; the son-in-law acquired by threat was frequently treated as though no major deviation had occurred. Obviously, this example also serves to indicate that on occasion the moralistically sacred carries with it the ultimate sanction of death—but usually as alternative, not as inevitability.

Placing the moralistic at a considerable remove from the maximum-plus end of the scale therefore seems warranted. Again, however, there must be inserted the proviso that the wide variations between one culture and another may bring about *notable shifts* in scale position, not only of the moralistic, but also of other types of sacredness.

Still another qualification must be imposed with regard to the ethical, viewed as the moralistic at a more general level. Ethical sacredness, as is well known, often engenders exalted and passionate devotion. That is to say, abstract ethical precepts may approximate the holy in the zeal they call forth. Further, in form they are often highly rational (in the formal, discursive sense), although in content they are usually, at least with regard to origin, quite as nonrational as the moralistic. Moreover, ethical precepts may be held with such intensity as to lead to rejection of ritual; take the example of the Hebrew prophets who declared that Yahveh desired justice rather than burnt offerings. Ethical demands, in other words, may be closely linked with the transcendent claims of the holy. Consequently, the treatment of the ethical as merely the moralistic at a more abstract level may beg some questions in favor of the present scaling procedure. Let it be understood, then, that there is nothing sacred about this procedure. If it proves predictively useful, well and good; if not, alterations are certainly advisable.

"It Jest Ain't Fittin'!"

Next along the scale comes a kind of evaluation of distinctly lower intensity than any of those thus far considered. This may be called the fittingly sacred; it occupies the hazy band between the moralistic and the merely appropriate. Designations for conduct falling in this band are many; a short list includes proper-improper, "done"—"not done," "good form"—"bad form," mannerly-unmannerly, decent-vulgar, and the like. This list draws on the vast fund of what is viewed as etiquette in the formal sense, but there are equivalents, likewise representing a low intensity of the sacred, for all other forms of the fitting. Few persons would regard the custom, observed in some circles, of not immediately picking up one's change on the bar when a drink has been served as in the realm of etiquette, for example; but it may nevertheless be viewed as eminently fitting even by those not conversant with Emily Post.

One of the most convenient ways of distinguishing the fittingly sacred from closely related varieties is to take account of the conduct attending its violation. Moralistic offenses evoke indignation, whereas failure to observe the fitting elicits little if anything more than contempt. The almost imperceptible shrug of the shoulders, the raised eyebrow or the curled lip, the sudden and noticeably continued silence when the obtrusive newcomer enters the clubroom frequented only by the long established members, are all unspoken but nevertheless definite judgments that the fitting is being disregarded in a culpable way.

Reference has been made to the low intensity of the fitting, yet there may be a high degree of reluctance to change even in what those of us inclined toward informality call "mere manners." Men seldom die for the sake of the fitting, but they may undergo extreme discomfort and sometimes danger. Those of us who have watched Britishers quietly finish their tea-drinking before proceeding to air-raid shelters, even though the noise of bursting bombs was to be heard all through teatime, have gained some notion of the fact that though the fitting is not oriented toward holiness, it represents a reluctance to change that can hardly be viewed as other than sacred.

"Dinner Jackets Would Be Appropriate"

The sacred on the fringe of fadeout has sometimes been placed in the realm of the folkways; but like the mores, the folkways take in too much of both sacred and secular. It here seems best to make use of a more limited term such as the appropriate. There is a minimum of any controls savoring of indignation or contempt, but resort to ridicule is still possible. "Suitable," "customary," "regular," "expected," "normal," "usual," and similar more or less interchangeable words often have a sacred tinge; they indicate that "right" and "wrong" ways of doing things are not matters of indifference, and that there is some reluctance to relinquish, or to see others relinquish, the appropriate ways.

At the same time, those who wittingly or unwittingly perpetrate the inappropriate are not viewed as unworthy, but rather as uninstructed. Their remediable ignorance, indifference, or impatience may be viewed with nothing more than mild and courteously concealed amusement. The man who wears yellow-tan shoes and bright blue socks with a green suit and a pictorial necktie at a garden party will, it is assumed, learn better after a while. In the interval, the temptation to smile in his presence remains only a temptation. Defense of the appropriate, which is to say of the sacred almost at the vanishing point, here amounts to no more than an inadvertent twitch at the corners of the mouth; the shift to the secular is close at hand.

The Pervasiveness of Ceremonial

Discussion of this shift must be delayed, however, until some reference is made to an aspect of sacred conduct evident in all its varieties, from the holy to the merely appropriate, that may be labeled the ceremonially sacred. Its importance is readily perceived when we focus on the holy, for ritual, in the sense of religious ceremonial *per se,* is often the most obvious mark of supernaturalistic orientation. In fact, Jane Harrison and others have pointed out that *dromena*—"things done" rather than "things believed"—may be overwhelmingly more evident in some kinds of religion than are doctrines and creeds. Ritual in the strict sense, as set forms of worship, may be performed when the worshipers have only the vaguest of notions as to what the supernaturalistic forces or beings worshiped may be like. The misty outlines of the supernaturalistic object may fluctuate tremendously, as it were, in accordance with the hazily defined and therefore fluctuating needs of the worshiper, while the ritual varies little if at all. Stock ejaculations in ancient tongues, dimly comprehended but rote-learned formulas, elaborate genuflections, and intricate processions may be accurately repeated again and again by men who have achieved no *explicit* orientation toward a *definite* supernaturalistic object.

Ceremonial as bound up with the holy, which is to say as ritual in the strict sense, is clearly of great importance, but there are many other significant kinds of ceremonial. This fact is usually overlooked, and confusion between ritual and other ceremonial is induced and increased, because we lack terms for distinguishing these other varieties, except for a few such as "commencement" for graduation ceremonial, "commemoration" for anniversary or otherwise time-defined ceremonial, and the like.

TALCOTT PARSONS

Talcott Parsons (1902-   ), the youngest sociologist to be represented in this volume, was born in Colorado and was educated at Amherst College, from which he was graduated in 1924. In 1924-1925 he was a student at the London School of Economics and in 1927 he took his Ph.D. degree at the University of Heidelberg. The German influence is readily apparent both in his approach to the problems of sociology and in his contributions to their solution. He taught economics first, both at Amherst and at Harvard, and became an instructor in sociology at Harvard in 1931, assistant professor in 1936, associate professor in 1939, and professor in 1944. He became chairman of the department of sociology in 1944 and served as chairman of the department of social relations from the time of its organization in 1946 until 1956. He has been a visiting professor at Columbia, Chicago, and Cambridge, and was elected president of the American Sociological Society in 1949.

Parsons won his academic spurs with a translation, in 1930, of Max Weber's *The Protestant Ethic and the Spirit of Capitalism.* In 1937 the first of his major works appeared, *The Structure of Social Action,* in which he claimed to have discovered important theoretical convergences in the work of three outstanding European sociologists—Emile Durkheim, Vilfredo Pareto, and Max Weber. His book *The Social System* appeared in 1951 and he has continued, in other books and in his essays, to develop a comprehensive theoretical system in which to encompass all of what he calls the sciences of action.

The excerpt that follows, from *The Social System,* will afford some notion of the character of the Parsonian enterprise.

From *The Social System*[*]

The Place of Sociological Theory Among the Analytical Sciences of Action

The substantive task of the present volume has been accomplished as far as it will be until the preparation of a revised edition is undertaken. It remains only to point up a very few main considerations which are relevant to the interpretation of what has been attempted, and hence of the relative success which the attempt has achieved, and then to discuss briefly the problem of classification of the sciences of action.

First a few final words may be said about what order of theoretical task has in fact been undertaken. The volume is unequivocally meant as an essay in *systematic* theory. It is not an attempt to formulate a theory of any particular concrete phenomenon, but is the attempt to present a logically articulated conceptual scheme. The title of the book, *The Social System,* is meant to emphasize this systematic reference. Social systems are empirical systems, but it is by virtue of their relevance to an articulated conceptual scheme that such empirical systems are classed together and made subject to a uniform analytical procedure within an explicitly defined frame of reference. Furthermore, the status of the book as an essay in theory *construction* justifies the two facts that, first, it has not attempted systematic codification of available empirical knowledge and, second, it has not tried to present a critical evaluation of the literature of theory itself in the field.

The book is thus an essay *in* systematic theory but the suggestion is quite explicitly repudiated that it attempts in one sense to present a system *of* theory, since it has been consistently maintained that in the present state of knowledge, such a system cannot be formulated. Put a little differently, it is a theory of systems rather than a system of theory. It attempts to represent the best attainable in the present state of knowledge with respect

* Reprinted by permission of the Free Press.

to the theoretical analysis of a carefully defined class of empirical systems. It is fully recognized that this theory is fragmentary and incomplete. But at the same time, the concept of system as a guiding conceptual scheme is of the first importance as an organizing principle and a guide to research. It may thus be said that the concept of a theory of systems is the most strategic tool for working toward the attainment of a system of theory. The general character of this particular theory of systems has been quite sufficiently discussed so that further elucidation is unnecessary. The general relations between structural categories, the general and special imperatives of social systems, the paradigm of motivational process and the "growing points" of research relative to these elements of theory have been repeatedly stated.

The Place of Social Systems in the General Theory of Action

It has further been made quite clear that the theory of social systems is, in the sense of the present work, an integral part of the larger conceptual scheme which we have called the theory of action. As such, it is one of the three main differentiated subsystems of the larger conceptual scheme, the other two being the theory of personality and the theory of culture.

The interdependence of the three has constituted a major theme of the whole present analysis. This has been fully and systematically set forth in *Values, Motives and Systems of Action* as well, and need not be recapitulated in detail here. It should, however, be quite clear to the reader that without a fundamental clarification of the relation of social systems to these other branches of the theory of action, the level of clarity in the analysis of social systems which has been attained in the present work would not have been possible.

By this is meant a clarification going well beyond what is now current in even the best literature of the subject. In this connection the experience of the author in connection with the development of the present volume, which was cited in the preface, may appropriately be recalled. A draft of about three-fourths of what had been planned had already been written when, in connection with the work going on in the general theory of action in collaboration with Professors Shils, Tolman and others in the fall of 1949, certain fundamental new insights concerning the relations between cultural and motivational elements in action generally developed. The work which was done in following up these insights, the results of which are documented in *Values, Motives and Systems of Action,* was not primarily and directly concerned with the theory of the social system as such, but with the general frame of reference of action. Theoretical developments from these starting points touched the fields of personality and of culture just as much as they did that of the social system. Yet the implications of that work for the theory of the social system were so far-reaching that, when work on the present book was resumed, it became necessary to start entirely anew, and it turned out that only a small proportion of the old manuscript, most of it consisting of illustrative material, could be made use of without complete rewriting. In other words, work on the general frame of reference of action necessitated a radical reorganization of thinking about the theory of the social system. Nothing could illustrate more vividly the fact that the theory of the social system is not a wholly independent conceptual scheme.

It will hence be clear to the reader why the implications of this situation have had to be so consistently followed through in the present work. We cannot speak of the structure of the social system in theoretical terms at all without speaking of the institutionalization. If we are to do so sensibly we, of course, must know whereof we speak with respect to what the patterns which are institutionalized in fact are, in some sense also how they can be classified and otherwise analyzed. Similarly we have consistently maintained that the motivational processes of the social system are *always* processes within the personalities of the component individual actors. If the implications of such a statement are to be carried through it is obvious that we must know quite definitely what we are talking about when we speak of a personality system and its motivational processes. We cannot rely on common-sense levels of insight for this purpose; the problems become definitely technical.

It is fundamentally because, for the theory of the social system, the solution of these problems goes back to the general frame of reference of action that the anchorage of the present book in that general frame of reference is of such fundamental importance, and that important developments on the general level have proved to have such profound repercussions on the subject matter of this volume.

If the ultimate unity of the theory of action as a conceptual scheme has been strongly emphasized by these theoretical developments, it is perhaps almost equally important that the mutual *independence* of personality, culture and social systems are subsystems of action has been strongly confirmed. The insight of what is here considered the best tradition of sociological theory, that as a conceptual scheme it cannot legitimately be "reduced" in either direction is thus justified, and its grounds immensely clarified. On the one hand, the treatment of social systems only as "resultants" of the functioning of personalities in the sense common to writers with a "psychological" point of view, is clearly inadequate most fundamentally because it ignores the organization of action about the exigencies of social systems as systems. On the other hand, to treat social systems as only "embodiments" of patterns of culture, as a certain trend of thought common among anthropologists has tended to do, is equally unacceptable to the theory of the social system.

The mere assertion of the theoretical independence of the social system in both these directions has served an important function in the development of social science in that it has enabled sociologists to focus their attention on problems which would not have had justice done to them either in terms of psychology or of cultural anthropology. But, even in the thought of Durkheim, whose insight was probably the deepest in this respect, many aspects of the theoretical relationships involved in the combination of this aspect of independence with the equally important interdependence of these three system concepts, remained unclarified. The present work and that on which it rests in the more general theory of action may be said to have gone considerably farther in the clarification of these relationships. We are now in a position not merely to assert that a combination of independence and interdependence must be recognized, but to state on a certain level precisely in what this consists. We know just what we mean by the institutionalization of patterns of culture, and by the sense in which the structure of the social system is and is not an embodiment of a set of such patterns. We know certain of the most fundamental elements of personality as a system of action and its interrelations with the social system. We know that they *both* go back to the fundamental processes of interaction between actors, that in this one sense personality is just as much a "social" phenomenon as is the social system. We know certain fundamental relations between the institutionalization and the internalization of culture. Above all, perhaps, we know that the fundamental *common sector* of personalities and social systems consists in the value-patterns which define role-expectations. The motivational structures thus organized are units *both* of personality as a system and of the social system in which the actor participates; they are need-dispositions of the personality and they are role-expectations of the social system. This is the key to the "transformation formula" between the two systems of personality and social system. It is maintained that, in spite of the many brilliant insights bearing this relationship, especially in the works of Durkheim and of Freud, in terms which are both precise and highly generalized this set of relationships has never been so clearly understood before. This fundamental relationship between need-dispositions of the personality, role-expectations of the social system and internalized-institutionalized value-patterns of the culture, is the fundamental nodal point of the *organization* of systems of action. It is the point at which both the interdependence and the independence from each other of personality, social system and culture focus. If the nature of this organization is not clearly understood and formulated with theoretical precision, confusion on this fundamental subject will inevitably spread in all three directions and poison the whole theory of action. It is a new level of clarity about this fundamental phenomenon, which more than any other factor has made the present level of analytical refinement of the theory of the social system possible.

The Theory of Action and the Natural Sciences

The clarification of the general theory of action and of the place of the theory of the social system in it, which has just been discussed, makes it possible to say something relatively systematic about the field of action generally.

We may start with the general relation between action and

"nature." It does not need to be emphasized that human action is in the most various ways profoundly influenced by the physical, chemical and biological properties both of the environment and of the organism itself. The question is that of the theoretical relevance and adequacy of the conceptual schemes of what, in this sense, are the "natural sciences" for full analysis of the phenomena of action. There is ample evidence of the inadequacy or inconvenience or both of these conceptual schemes for this purpose and thus of the independent justification of the action frame of reference.

The relevance of the action frame of reference is anchored in three fundamental considerations. The first is that the concern of the sciences of action is with the *relations* on a certain level of the concrete entities, which in their biological relevance are called organisms, to their environments. The conceptual scheme is, that is, wholly and fundamentally relational. The individual "actor" is a name for the same concrete entity as the organism, but seen as a unit in this relational context.

However, only a certain aspect of the concrete relations of the organism-actor to the environment is abstracted as being of interest to the theory of action; this is the aspect we call "action" or "behavior." There is, obviously, as of central concern to the biological sciences, a continual physico-chemical interchange between organism and environment, with reference, for example, to heat, and to the chemical interchange involved in food intake and elimination of waste products and in respiration. This, however, is not action, or behavior, however much it may be empirically *dependent on* action. Action involves not a biochemical conceptual scheme but an "orientational" scheme as this conception has been developed here and elsewhere. Its units are conceived in terms of a specifically relational frame of reference which is *peculiar* to organisms as units, and not one which is common to organisms and all other physico-chemical systems. In this sense behavior is a phenomenon of higher order organization in the world of nature than is the "functioning" of organisms. Or, put somewhat differently, the physico-chemical interchange of organism and environment is change over the boundaries of the organism as itself a *system,* the internal processes and equilibrium of which are of primary interest to the scientist. Physiology, as the most fundamental biological sub-science, is, we may suggest, essentially the science focused on the boundary-maintaining properties of the organism as a physico-chemical system.

But for the theory of action the organism is *not a system, but a unit point of reference.* The focus of interest for the theory of action is not in the internal equilibrating processes of the organism as a system, but in the equilibrating processes involved in its relations to an environment or situation in which other organisms are of crucial significance. It is *this relational system which is the system of action,* not the organism as a system. It is particularly important here to avoid an insidious version of the fallacy of misplaced concreteness which has been particularly common among psychologists. This is the conception that "the organism" is a concrete ontologically real entity and that somehow its internal physico-chemical processes, and their interchange with the environment are the "real thing" whereas behavior is a kind of resultant or epiphenomenon. It is exceedingly difficult for persons who think in this way to become aware that biological theory is abstract in exactly the same sense as any other scientific theory. Therefore, the organism in this sense is no more an ontological reality than is the famous particle of Newtonian physics. Pari passu the organism, as the boundary-maintaining physico-chemical system, *is in absolutely no sense more or less real than the system of action.* Both stand on fundamentally the same footing. Both are systems conceived in terms of a conceptual scheme. Both are subject to empirical verification in the same senses. Underlying much of the psychological bias referred to above within the theory of action has been this biological bias, the tendency to think that only the internal system of the organism is somehow "real" while its relational system is not.

A system of action, then, is a system of the relations of organisms in interdependence with each other and with nonsocial objects in the environment or situation. It is in order to keep this system distinct from the organism as a physico-chemical system that we prefer, instead of referring to the "behavior of the organism," to speak of the "action of the actor," and instead of using the term environment, to speak of the "situation of action." We do not wish to quarrel about words, but we do submit that use of the biological terminology is frequently associated with genuine confusion of the frames of reference.

The second fundamental feature of systems of action is that as relational systems, they are boundary-maintaining systems. We have given ample justification for this statement earlier in this work and elsewhere. It is this property of systems of action which *states* the analytical independence of the frame of reference of action from that of biological theory. If this were not the case, there would be no point in complicating matters by using this additional frame of reference for the analysis of concrete organisms as behaving entities. The lack of empirical success of attempts to "reduce" most action phenomena to biological terms is well known and need not be further discussed here. Suffice it to say that this statement that systems of action are boundary-maintaining systems has the same justification that any fundamental methodological assumption about a scientific conceptual scheme has. It is *not* as such an empirical generalization, but is logically prior to all empirical generalizations which are stated in terms of the theory of action.

Finally, the third fundamental consideration touches the much discussed "subjective point of view," namely, the study of action "from the point of view of the actor." Contrary to the view held by the author in the *Structure of Social Action* it now appears that this postulate is not essential to the frame of reference of action in its most elementary form. It is, however, necessarily involved at the levels of elaboration of systems of action at which culture, that is shared symbolic patterns, becomes involved. It is, that is, a consequence of the fact that action comes to be oriented in terms of symbols which also serve to communicate with other actors.

Another way of looking at the postulate is to consider the implications of the fact that scientific investigation is itself a process of action. Precisely, in terms of our present conceptual scheme, if the object of investigation is a physical object—which includes organisms—there is no process of social interaction between ego and the object. The object, that is, does not *re*act to ego's action in terms analyzable in terms of the theory of action. But if the object is a social object, the process of investigation is itself a process of social interaction, and must be understood in the appropriate terms. Such interaction, however, in terms of the present conceptual scheme clearly involves communication. It is not possible in these terms to interpret alter's behavior in terms of the action frame of reference without communicating with him, without "understanding his motives" in the full sense of the theory of action as we have developed such a conception. This is essentially what is meant by the subjective reference or the subjective point of view of the theory of action.

It is, of course, possible to remain a behavioristic purist and avoid this subjective reference, but only in one of two ways. The first is to repudiate the action frame of reference altogether and attempt to maintain a biological frame of reference. The other is to use the action frame of reference, but to keep the elaboration of the theory of action to pre-symbolic, that is pre-cultural levels. The issue of "behaviorism" then really boils down to that of whether it is possible to handle the more differentiated levels of the frame of reference of action with the precision and care which the scientist attempts to attain. As in other branches of science "the proof of the pudding is in the eating."

The Classification of the Sciences of Action

We may now turn to the problem of the internal division of labor between the sciences of action. We shall consider only those which have a claim to the status of analytical sciences in the sense that, whatever their specialization of interests in relation to classes of empirical phenomena, their primary claim to independent status as sciences rests on their concern with and responsibility for a relatively independent and distinctive conceptual scheme. Such a conceptual scheme need not be a closed system, but we will set up as a criterion that it must not simply be an "application" of a more generalized scheme.

In these terms the theory of action clearly differentiates most broadly into the theory of personality as a system, the theory of social systems and the theory of culture. There are, however, certain problems concerning the implications of this differentiation which need to be taken up.

The theory of personality as a system seems to coincide, with one exception which will be taken up presently, with the field of psychology as a discipline. Perhaps, it would be better to say it coincides with what psychology from our point of view ought to be, and it seems on the whole is tending toward. There are two primary strictures on the suggestion that this formula is descriptive of the present focus of psychology. The first is the persistence of the tendency to regard psychology as essentially a biological science. The problem this raises can, it would seem, be satisfactorily handled by analogy with the physical sciences. There is, of course, no question whatever of the overwhelmingly great importance of the interdependence between the organism as a biological system and the personality as a system of action. But for the reasons we have just reviewed, this interdependence does not justify treating personality as simply an "extension" of the organism. The fruitful analogy is that with the status of biochemistry relative to the biological sciences. There is obviously room for specialization in the field of "psycho-biology," and in fact much of it of the most fruitful kind exists both in "physiological psychology" and in the field of "psychosomatic" medicine. But we must insist that the legitimacy, promise and importance of this field does not justify treating the theory of personality as a branch of biological science, or putting the center of gravity of the theoretical interests of psychology into the biological sciences. This is a problem which the members of the psychological profession must ultimately face more squarely than they have hitherto done.

The second stricture consists simply in the fact that genuinely systematic treatment of personality *as a system* on the action level or any other for that matter, has not as yet been common among even the most eminent theorists in the field. The situation is parallel to that in the social system field, where Pareto stands almost alone in his clear and explicit conception of the social system. Even Freud, though it may be said that the conception of personality as a system was definitely emergent from his work, did not use it as a definite guiding conception, and he never fully disentangled the action aspects of personality from the biological. Furthermore, adequate treatment of personality as a system has had to await clarification of its relations to the social system and to culture. We may hope for rapid advance in this direction from psychologists, but what may be called bio-psychological eclecticism remains more typical of psychologists who are not either behaviorists or biologists than does systematic personality theory.

The exception referred to above, to the appropriateness of the definitions of psychological theory as the theory of personality as a system, concerns the problem of where the study of certain fundamentals of action process which underlie all organization of action in systems belongs, the field that is of what is sometimes called "behavior psychology," which includes the field of "simple learning." The present view is that this belongs more appropriately in psychology than in any other of the theoretical sciences of action. This is essentially because the processes in question are prior to and underlie the organization of action in more complex systems, either personality or social. This is precisely the kind of thing which can be most fruitfully studied on pre-symbolic levels. Usually this implies that the experimental situation is one in which social interaction and its variability are not crucial—as is obviously true of most animal learning study, though such studies of animal imitation as those of Miller and Dollard raise other questions. But even on this level variability on both the social system levels and the cultural level are not likely to be problematical. The focus of interest is in the underlying action process itself.

As an analytical discipline, then, we would here define psychology as the science concerned with the elementary processes of action and their organization in personalities as systems. The status of social psychology raises special problems which can best be taken up after the problem of the theory of the social system has been discussed.

The theory of the social system is, as we have seen, in a certain fundamental sense, directly parallel to that of personality, though the relation of personality to the organism means that the relations of the two systems are only partly symmetrical. It would, therefore, seem logical that there should be an analytical science of social systems which was correlative with psychology as that of personality systems. This is in a broad sense an acceptable view, but there are complications touching the problems of the status of economics and political science which we must take up.

The advances in the theory of the social system which have

been documented in the present work make it possible to clarify further a view of the proper status of sociological theory with which the author has been concerned for a number of years. It was first tentatively stated in the final chapter of the *Structure of Social Action,* and a further revision of it was stated in the paper on *The Position of Sociological Theory* (*Essays,* Chapter I). The focus of this view has been on the importance of institutions and institutionalization as the primary concern of sociology as a science. In the earlier version also the property of "common value-integration" was strongly emphasized.

If a sphere for sociological theory as a distinctive conceptual scheme is to be delineated, it must be either the theory of the social system as a whole, or some special aspect of the theory of the social system rather than the whole of it. First, we may suggest that the former formula might or might not be interpreted to include a "theory of culture." The problem of the status of such a theory will be taken up presently. Let it be said here only that the treatment of the involvement of culture in the social system is not in this sense a "theory of culture" any more than that of the involvement of personality and motivational process has to be psychology in the sense just stated.

The choice between the broader and the narrower views of the scope of sociological theory just stated does not involve this question, but turns essentially on that of the status of economic theory. The broader view would treat economic theory as "applied sociology" while the narrower would not. The narrower is the view taken here. It is consistent with the view that the central concern of sociological theory is with the phenomena of institutionalization.

It has been brought out in Chapter IV above that within the institutionalized framework of a social system where the instrumental division of labor was sufficiently elaborated, there could be a peculiar quantification of control of facilities through the processes of exchange by means of what was called "purchasing power." This peculiar quantification is an emergent phenomenon appearing at certain levels of differentiation of social systems, and coming to be of high significance only within a relatively limited, though very important, class of social systems. It is the processes of equilibration of a system of such exchange-oriented actions which constitute the focus of economic theory as a conceptual scheme.

As a theory of process, economic theory depends on the relevance of the processes of decision-making to the determination of prices and quantities in the system of exchange. Hence within an economy where freedom for decision to operate is sufficiently broad this decision-making process is at least one primary process by which the allocation of resources, i.e., in our terms of facilities, comes about. This economic process may be the resultant of large numbers of discrete decisions by participants in the market. But it may also be a centralized decision process carried out by a government planning body. The functional significance of the economic process for the social system in either case is a matter of its relevance to the allocation of facilities.

The *combination* of study of the functional significance of the process and its analysis in terms of a given conceptual scheme, however, depends on its analysis in terms of the famous "postulate of economic rationality." This can only be interpreted to mean that the science of economics has little *explanatory* relevance to the processes of allocation of resources in a "traditionalistic" economy where only "drift" leads to alteration of the allocation system. At most it can serve only a "criterion" function by measuring the actual allocation against a standard of what in some sense would be an "economically rational allocation."

The postulate of rationality, however, occupies a somewhat curious status in the theory of action. It is a clear implication of the theory of action on both the personality and the social system levels, that "rational action" is a type which presupposes a certain mode of the *organization* of all the elements of action. It is something which is possible within the limits imposed by value-orientation patterns and by the situation, and by a certain mode of integration of motivational elements. On the personality level, that is, rational action is a type which exists within certain limits of the organization of personality. On the social system level, correspondingly, there is scope for rational adjustments within certain limits imposed by the institutionalized role-system.

Three levels of the organization of rational action in action systems may be distinguished. The first of these, the most elementary, is that involving the mobilization of resources for the attainment of a single given goal, by an individual actor or a collectivity. This is essentially what, in the *Structure of Social Action* was called a "technology," the analysis of the patternings of action relative to such a single given goal. Technology always involves two aspects or sets of factors, those pertaining to the conditions of success, and those concerning the "cost," which is ultimately the sacrifice of alternative goals involved in the expenditure of resources for the one in question. "Efficiency" is the measure of the effectiveness of a technological process relative to its cost.

The second level of organization introduces considerations of "economy," which consists in the process of the allocation of resources relative to a plurality of alternative goals. Here cost is not a constant but a variable in that there is explicit consideration not merely of the minimization of expenditure compatible with effectiveness, but of allocation of resources between alternative goals. This is what the decision-making process does with the facilities of the social system.

The third level of organization of rational action is concerned not with economy but with the maximization of power in the political sense. Here the orientation is to the maximization of total command of facilities in the social system held by one actor, individual or collective, relative to others. There is hence, as we pointed out in Chapter IV, no inherent limitation of scope, but anything, especially in the sphere of relational possessions, which can have significance as a facility, may become involved in the political power system.

Technology and economy on the basis of the individual personality can be said to constitute psychological problem areas, whereas the relational character of political power makes it impossible to consider it wholly from a psychological point of view. On the social system level, on the other hand, technology can be the analysis of the goal-orientation of a collectivity as an organization, which involves its role structure, and hence involves problems of institutionalization, whereas economy involves the interrelations of a plurality of actors individual and/or collective. This perspective, however, involves a specific institutionalized limitation of scope.

Hence we may say that the implications of the postulate of rationality are within certain limits psychological, that is, they rest in the theory of personality, but that economics as a *social* science is concerned with the phenomena of rational decision-making and the consequences of these decisions within an institutionalized system of exchange relationships. This is, within the theory of action, such a highly distinctive complex that the claim of economic theory to autonomy with respect to it seems quite justified.

The case of political science is a wholly different one. Variant definitions of its scope are current within the profession itself. Here we are concerned only with the claim that it should be organized about an analytical theoretical scheme of a scope and character parallel to that of economic theory. The only current formula for this claim is that it should be treated as the theory of power. In this connection one fact will strike the reader immediately, namely, that in technical elaboration as a conceptual scheme, there is no such thing as a theory of power which is remotely comparable with economic theory. We believe that the above analysis (Chapter IV) has given the fundamental reason for this fact, namely, that power in the political sense is inherently diffuse as contrasted with the specificity of economic power. This means that a theory of political power must in the nature of the case take into account as *variables,* most of the variables of the social system.

In view of this fact it is in fact appropriate to treat political science as the discipline concerned with political power and its use and control, but because of the diffuseness of political power this makes it a synthetic science in the social system field, not one built about a distinctive *analytical* conceptual scheme, that is, a strictly limited set of variables. The common designation as the field of "government" comes relatively close to this conception.

In the light of these considerations we may come back to the question of the scope of sociological theory. Institutionalization of cultural patterns means, as we have often emphasized, in the integrated sense internalization of the same patterns in the personality. Psychologically an internalized pattern is no longer an object of the situation. It is not possible to treat it as an instrumental means or condition. There is a specific mode of cathectic integration of the actor's need-dispositions with an internalized pattern. This fact has a fundamental methodological significance. It means that the orientation of "instrumental rationality" *cannot* be the attitude defining the actor's orientation to internalized patterns.

We derive, then, a most significant complex of relationships. The value-integration of the social system is defined by the system of patterns of value-orientation which have become institutionalized to constitute the definitions of its constituent role-expectation patterns. The institutionalization of these patterns in turn means that typically they have become internalized in the personality systems of the actors in the social system and this fact in turn means that their relevance to the determination of behavior cannot be primarily through the "mechanisms" of instrumental rationality but *must* be through what are sometimes called the non- and irrational mechanisms of the functioning of personality.

This is the fundamental reason why the sociologist cannot follow the lead of economics or indeed of the whole of utilitarian theory in his fundamental account of the motivational forces in institutional behavior, and why the concepts of modern "dynamic psychology" have come to be of such critical importance to him. This again is why a sociological theory which can get beyond structural description and the classifications of "formal sociology" must be adequately integrated with the theory of personality precisely in the modern psychological sense.

Sociological theory, then, is for us *that aspect of the theory of social systems which is concerned with the phenomena of the institutionalization of patterns of value-orientation in the social system,* with the conditions of that institutionalization, and of changes in the patterns, with conditions of conformity with and deviance from a set of such patterns and with motivational processes in so far as they are involved in all of these. As motivational processes these cannot be the processes of rational action in the economic sense, but involve the processes of value-acquisition through identification and of deviance and social control as these have been analyzed above. Since we have only indicated where economics and political science fit in, the present volume can, in these terms, be regarded rather strictly as a contribution to sociological theory.

It is hoped that it will be entirely clear to the reader that this view does not constitute the "reduction" of sociological theory to psychological terms, but the extension of the structural aspect of that theory to an explicit statement of its concern with motivational process within the context of the functioning of the social system as a system. The processes are, as has been repeatedly stated, exactly the same concrete processes which are involved in the functioning of personalities as systems. But their context of theoretical relevance is that of the social system as a system and not of the personality as a system.

Now we are in a position to say something about social psychology as a discipline. We would interpret its place as that of an interstitial mediating field between sociology and psychology in a sense directly analogous to that of biochemistry or of psychobiology or physiological psychology. We could say, then, that the social psychologist is not directly concerned with the analysis of the structure of social systems, but with motivational processes and personalities in their specific relations to and interdependence with the structure of social systems, notably, that is, their bearing on the explanation of socially structured and "mass" phenomena.

It follows, however, that social psychology as a theoretical discipline should not have the same *order* of independent theoretical significance as does either psychological theory or sociological theory. Above all there can be no such thing as good social psychology without explicit and systematic reference to the sociological aspects of the theory of social systems. Without that it becomes merely a cover for a "psychological bias" in the interpretation of social phenomena. The only alternative to this view is to hold that since all action is "process of the mind" or "behavior" there is no place for a distinct theory of the social system at all. The unacceptability of such a position is, in the light of the whole above discussion, abundantly clear.

Finally, we may say a word about the implications of the relations between culture and social systems for the classification of the sciences of action. There is, in our opinion, an important place for a "theory of culture" as part of the theory of action, which is quite definitely not sociological theory in the sense in which this has just been defined. This is what, according to the present trend, anthropological theory is tending to become. According to this view culture, as an empirical phenomenon, is not more independent of personalities and social systems than are social systems of personalities. As part of the theory of action, then, the theory of culture must be the theory concerned not only with the properties of culture as such but with the interdependence of patterns of culture with the other components of systems of action. It is, of course, concerned with the structure of systems of culture patterns, with the different types of such systems and their classification. But it is also concerned with their involvement in social systems and personalities, and with the implications of this involvement for their maintenance as "living" cultures in action systems, and for their tendencies of change. The focus, however, is always on the culture pattern system as such, and neither on the social system in which it is involved, nor on the personalities as systems.

Only by some such definition of its scope can anthropology become an analytical empirical science which is independent both of sociology and of psychology. This view gives it a scope which partly justifies the breadth of the term Anthropology, because of the involvement of culture both in personalities and in social systems. The alternative is to take the name literally and make it the "science of man." As a theoretical science this is scarcely to be seriously considered, for surely physical anthropology as human biology is not theoretically a distinctive science. And surely the anthropologist is not going to try to absorb all of humanly significant biology, including all the medical sciences, all of psychology and all of sociology, to say nothing of history, economics and political science. It might be possible to make it a synthetic empirical science of man, drawing on these many theoretical sciences, but not itself an independent theoretical science. But as an alternative to this the above offers a definition of the possible theoretical scope of anthropology which is compatible with those of the other sciences of action which have been advanced here. Furthermore it is clear that such a theoretical science is needed in order to complete the roster of the theoretical sciences of the field of action. The place of culture is of such fundamental importance that we cannot afford to have it omitted.

One other point needs to be made. Anthropological theory defined in this way should be clearly distinguished from what in Germany have been called the *Geisteswissenschaften,* or are sometimes called the "formal" disciplines. These deal with analysis of the content of cultural pattern systems for its own sake without regard to their involvement in systems of action. Thus, logic or mathematics, the methodology of scientific theory, or the analysis of art forms fall in this category. Clearly the anthropological theorist must lean on these disciplines just as the psychologist must lean on the biologist. But anthropological theory as here conceived clearly belongs to the sciences of action, not to these formal disciplines.

The above has been a highly schematic classification of the theoretical sciences of action. Naturally it is not expected that the actual fields of empirical interest and research activity of persons belonging to the various disciplines will follow such a scheme with neat precision. Indeed this would be altogether incompatible with the nature of a vital growing scientific tradition. But this fact does not in the least diminish the importance of clarity about these fundamental points of reference around which the theoretical content of the sciences of action is organized. The disappearance of the relevance of the major distinctions of such a scheme will mean that theory itself has evolved to an altogether new level.

Also we have confined our attention to the sciences which are primarily organized about a distinctive theoretical scheme on an analytical level. This clearly precludes the inclusion of history as standing on the same level. In so far as history is a social science and not one of the humanities, it clearly is not organized about any one of these distinctive schemes unless it be that of the social system as a whole. It seems better to conceive history as a synthetic empirical science which is concerned with the mobilization of all the theoretical knowledge which is relevant in the explanation of processes in social systems and in cultural change in the past. There are, besides political science, according to the view of it as stated above, several others of these synthetic disciplines dealing mainly with contemporary phenomena such as population studies, "regional studies"—if it be a discipline at all—or "international relations."

We have now reached the end of our long analysis of the complexities of the social system. In conclusion, it may be appropriate to quote part of the closing paragraph of the *Structure of Social Action* written fourteen years ago in 1937.

"It is not, therefore, possible to concur in the prevailing pessimistic judgment of the social sciences, particularly sociology. . . . Notable progress on both empirical and theoretical levels has been made in the short space of a generation. We have sound theoretical foundations on which to build."

This statement seems to have been amply justified by the event. Further empirical progress has certainly been made in the intervening years with many students contributing to it. Similarly on the theoretical side, which has been our concern in the present book. *The Structure of Social Action* proved, as it was hoped that it would be, only a beginning. If the theory of the social system had not advanced notably since it was written, the present book would not have been possible. By the same token, the present effort is only a link in a much longer chain. We can have full confidence that many further links will be forged, and soon.